A Note on the Text

It is customary in Romantic scholarship to refer to the poet William Wordsworth by his surname. In this book, which is a personal exploration of the emotional power of the Lake District and its poets, I call him William throughout because I write about him in the context of his family, most of whom share the Wordsworth name. For the same reason I refer to Dorothy Wordsworth by her first name; to do so for both siblings also resists establishing a hierarchy of import-ance between them. After initial introductions, I also use first names when writing about the Wordsworths' friends who are also siblings: Charles and Mary Lamb; Mary, Sara, and Joanna Hutchinson; Edith, Sarah, and Mary Fricker. Conversely, I follow the Wordsworths' example of calling their close male friends and poetic collaborators by their last names: Samuel Taylor Coleridge is either Coleridge or 'S.T.C.'

In the Wordsworths' day the modern county of Cumbria did not exist. Grasmere was part of Westmorland, whereas the Wordsworths were born in the old county of Cumberland, situated directly to the north and containing the towns of Cockermouth, Penrith, Keswick, and Whitehaven. William's school in Hawkshead was in the northernmost part of Lancashire, and the east Cumbrian villages which William and Dorothy walked through in December 1799 were then in the West Riding of Yorkshire. In 1974 these areas were combined to form the administrative county of Cumbria. When talking about events of 2009 I refer to Cumbria, but I use Westmorland, Cumberland, Yorkshire, and Lancashire when describing events that took place before 1974. However, I use the adjective 'Cumbrian' throughout, as it has been in use since at least the 1740s in reference to the region.

At the centre of Cumbria is the Lake District National Park, founded in 1951. The term 'Lake District' long predates the park's creation, for the concept of this corner of England as a distinct geographic entity had become current by at least the 1770s. Thomas West's pithily titled *A Guide to the Lakes: dedicated to the lovers of landscape studies, and to all who have visited, or intend to visit, the Lakes in Cumberland, Westmorland, and Lancashire* (1778) was the first publication to refer to the region as 'the Lakes', though the earliest recorded use of the descriptor 'the District of the Lakes' was by cartographer Jonathan Otley in his 1818 map of the area. In 1810 William Wordsworth cemented the character and appeal of 'the District' in his (then anonymous) essay for *Select Views of Cumberland, Westmoreland, and Lancashire*, a collection of forty-eight sketches of Lake District landscapes by the Reverend Joseph Wilkinson. The essay was later revised, extended, and republished, first as a 'Topographical Description of the Country of the Lakes in the North of

ESTHER RUTTER's first book, *This Golden Fleece: A Journey Through Britain's Knitted History*, was published by Granta in 2019. She studied English at Oxford University's Magdalen College, where she held an academic scholarship, and has worked at the Wordsworth Trust and at the Robert Burns Birthplace Museum. She is now a Research Fellow specialising in landscapes and cultural identity at the University of St Andrews, and lives in Fife.

ALL BEFORE ME

A Search for Belonging in
Wordsworth's Lake District

ESTHER RUTTER

GRANTA

Granta Publications, 12 Addison Avenue, London W11 4QR

First published in Great Britain by Granta Books, 2024
This paperback edition published by Granta Books, 2025

A CIP catalogue record for this book
is available from the British Library.

1 3 5 7 9 10 8 6 4 2

ISBN 978 1 78378 797 5
eISBN 978 1 78378 796 8

Typeset by M Rules

Printed and bound by CPI Group (UK) Ltd, Croydon, CR0 4YY

www.granta.com

MIX
Paper | Supporting
responsible forestry
FSC® C171272
FSC
www.fsc.org

To everyone who has come to Town End
and found their lives changed: this is for you.

'Not in Utopia, subterraneous fields,
Or some secreted Island, Heaven knows where;
But in the very world which is the world
Of all of us, the place on which in the end
We find our happiness, or not at all.'

William Wordsworth, *The Prelude* (1805),
Book 10, ll. 723–7

CONTENTS

England' alongside his Duddon sonnets in 1820, then as *A Description of the Scenery of the Lakes in the North of England* in 1822 and 1823, and finally as *A Guide Through the District of the Lakes in the North of England* in 1835. I use 'the Lakes', 'Lake District', and 'Lakeland' interchangeably throughout this book.

The autobiographical events featured in this book mostly took place in 2009, and record my personal experience of living and working in the community of Town End in Grasmere at that time. It is not a comprehensive history of the Trust, but combines material from oral histories and interviews with printed ephemera to piece together a sense of the place during the late twentieth and early twenty-first centuries. In 2021 the Wordsworth Trust rebranded the Dove Cottage site and its activities as Wordsworth Grasmere, though its governance, structure, and status as a charitable trust did not change. I have referred to the organisation as the Wordsworth Trust throughout, as the arrangement of Trustees, staff, volunteers, and graduate trainees continues to operate much as it did in 2009. The Wordsworths' home is still known as Dove Cottage, and the Wordsworth Trust continues to care for the building and those that surround it, facilitate and support research into Romanticism and the Lake District, and deliver a programme of events and activities, though funding cuts have meant that, at the time of going to press, it no longer hosts annual year-long poetry residencies or a regular programme of in-person public poetry readings.

Prologue

'The earth is all before me: with a heart
Joyous, nor scar'd at its own liberty
I look about, and should the guide I chuse
Be nothing better than a wandering cloud,
I cannot miss my way.'

William Wordsworth, *The Prelude* (1805),
Book 1, ll. 14–18[1]

In January 2009 I moved from Suffolk, on the east coast of
England, to Cumbria, a county hundreds of miles away on
the border with Scotland. Dove Cottage was my final destin-
ation, the house in Grasmere where William and Dorothy
Wordsworth had lived two centuries earlier. Along with nine
other young people, I was going to spend a year working
at the cottage and the adjacent museum dedicated to the
Wordsworths' lives and writing. We would live together in
the houses surrounding their former home, and take part in

the activities run by the museum: poetry readings, writing workshops, exhibition events, and other celebrations of the written word.

Lying in the heart of the English Lake District, Grasmere is a centuries-old village with a small stone church, renowned gingerbread shop, and clusters of slate-faced cottages. Its peaceful lake and wooded hillsides stand in contrast to the dramatic beauty of the steeper mountains and valleys nearby, among which you can find both England's highest peak and its largest lake. The region is recognised across the world from the *Swallows and Amazons* books of Arthur Ransome, from the timeless animal tales of Beatrix Potter, and – of course – from the poetry of William Wordsworth and the journals of his sister Dorothy, much of which was written during their time living in Dove Cottage.

I was twenty-three when I moved to Grasmere, not long out of university. The previous year I had experienced a mental breakdown and, after months of distress and uncertainty, my life needed a new and different shape. A structure I could pour myself into whilst I worked out who I was, perhaps something that would halt the cycle of mental illness that had become a defining feature of the adult life I'd only just begun. I didn't know what Dove Cottage might hold, but I hoped that I might find a new way of living among the mountains and in the company of poets – however long dead.

Looking into the void that had become my life had made me sick and dizzy. I had no job and no partner, and the only entries in my calendar were for medical appointments. I knew I needed to do something that would take me out of myself – but what? And who might want me? I had lost not just my confidence, but also the belief that I would ever be happy again. I dreaded spending time alone, but knew that I made despondent company. Though my thoughts no longer bordered on psychotic, as they had done eight months earlier, I was very far from well. I had spent the best part of a year trying to get better, wanting to believe that one day I would feel like myself again.

My parents encouraged me to look for work or volunteer, to find something to occupy my body whilst my mind whirled. I scanned jobs pages online, but nothing offered a whit of what I wanted. In truth, I didn't know what that was. Since becoming ill, taking an interest in anything had become impossible. My mind felt stuck, looping, unable to fix on anything outside myself. Even reading – an escape and occupation I'd adored since I was four – was beyond me. When I picked up a book, each story seemed to twist so that it appeared to have been written expressly to expose the failures of my life. Sometimes I took a pen and scribbled in the margins, railing against the author's spite in reducing my situation to a string of unforgiving type.

Nevertheless, I tried to remember what else the old me had enjoyed. As well as loving books, I had always delighted in the sound and shape of words, keeping notebooks full of diary entries and unfinished plans for stories. The past also intrigued me, and I'd spent my university summer holidays volunteering in museums, where I'd catalogued Victorian police files and researched references to herbal medicine in the writings of Shakespeare – 'there's rosemary, that's for remembrance; pray, love, remember'. I liked old things: old books, old furniture, old pictures. The greenness of ancient lanes, overgrown cottage gardens, the dusky allure of dark, smoke-stained pubs. At least I had done. Now I needed to rehearse being myself. Could I summon ghosts to hold communion with who I used to be?

For a few weeks I thought I might learn how to become a reed thatcher on the Norfolk Broads, but my application for a training post was rejected, my experience too much in books and not enough in building. Then, as November blew itself out in a storm that raged for days, I stumbled across an advert that offered the chance of something better. An internship with the Wordsworth Trust in Grasmere, fully residential, with £47.95 a week to live on in exchange for spending my days giving tours of William and Dorothy Wordsworth's cottage. The money was no more than the benefits I was already claiming for being out of work, but it would guarantee me a reason to get up each morning. Attached to the cottage was a museum dedicated to the Romantic poets, their lives, and their writings. Until this point my literature degree had weighed heavily, bringing no sliver of advantage in a job market where practical experience was all. Now an interest in the Romantics was not just 'desirable' but fundamental.

Even then, I wasn't certain I should apply. Panic attacks still regularly left me breathless. I had never been to Cumbria and knew no one there. Moving would mean leaving home again, risking everything I'd unknowingly imperilled when I went away before. How would the small, fragile ship of myself fare on new and unfamiliar waters? My capacity to make decisions had been reduced by what

I'd been through, my confidence in my thoughts worn thin by the magnitude of their depressive strength. How could I trust myself again?

I tried to persuade someone else to make the decision, sending the advert to a friend from university who was also unemployed. She adored Romantic literature and had chosen to study William Wordsworth's poetry for her thesis. Surely the Wordsworth Trust would be a perfect fit? But no: having spent the last year living and working on a small Scottish island for hardly any money, she wasn't keen to hole up in the English countryside to continue living on beans again.

The day after the official deadline passed, I finally applied. Writing down the details of my education and experience felt like putting on an old school uniform. Familiar, but strange and unseemly, as if I was trying to squeeze into a dried carapace of myself. What else did I have? Thirteen years of study distilled into four brief lines of print, a few small boxes detailing my hobbies filled in and ticked. My life seemed so thin. I hesitated before sending off the form, convinced it was a waste of time – late, uninteresting, irrelevant. Finally, I decided to put my trust in someone else's judgement, and off went my application.

Then a small miracle happened. A tiny piece of ordinary magic that, like stones falling into a river, altered my course. I was invited to an interview in Grasmere. Two hundred years earlier, as the home of the celebrated Romantic poet William Wordsworth and his sister Dorothy, it had been the centre of a new cultural epoch that would forever shape the way we experience and respond to the world. At the heart of this new Romanticism was the need to feel kinship with nature and humanity, the desire to 'see into the life of things' through personal reflection, and the belief that the experiences of ordinary people are intrinsically important and worthwhile. William and Dorothy Wordsworth and their friend Samuel Taylor Coleridge changed not just the shape of literature, but also the way we understand ourselves and what surrounds us. This was what I needed: new ways to see myself and the world.

They say that you only need to make a handful of good decisions in your life. Applying to come to Grasmere was one of mine.

When William Wordsworth arrived in Grasmere in 1799 at the age of twenty-nine, he was not the titan of English literature we regard him as today. Though his *Lyrical Ballads* (1798), co-produced with Samuel Taylor Coleridge, are now heralded as the harbinger of the Romantic movement, much of his early work was viewed by contemporary critics as experimental, unsophisticated, even downright unappealing. Far from being able to support himself through writing, for much of his life William was dependent on money given to him by friends and family. Several of the latter did not share his conviction in his vocation as a poet, and throughout the 1790s William had struggled to make an independent living. He travelled through Europe, fathered a daughter with a Frenchwoman at the time of the Revolution, lived in grace-and-favour lodgings in London, Bristol, and Dorset, and attempted to establish himself as a writer and philosopher in Germany. Though he had been to school in Hawkshead, a village in the centre of the Lake District, William had spent no more than a few weeks in Lakeland since leaving for university at the age of seventeen.

The Lake District of the 1790s was not yet the fashionable playground for the leisured classes that it was to become. It was distant from London and difficult to reach, especially by the standards of the day, and its mountainous geography meant that few people from outside the area knew it intimately. Though artists and writers had portrayed its rugged landscape in books and paintings since at least the 1720s, the region was widely viewed by outsiders – or 'offcomers', as they are still termed locally – with suspicion, even fear: an early guidebook saw its author experiencing 'terror at the wild craggy landscape of Borrowdale'.[2] Lakeland was culturally distinct too, with a low population density, few libraries, and little 'society' of the type William had enjoyed (and alternately reviled) in London and Bristol. Deciding to move to Grasmere was not the obvious next step for a young man burning with the desire to write and establish a literary career for himself, but it was to prove to be a critical moment both in his own creative development and in the story of English literature.

Whilst living in Germany in the winter of 1798–9, William had begun work on a poem which attempted to explore how his childhood experiences in the Lake District had shaped who he was as an adult. This poem was envisaged as the introduction to a much longer work titled *The Recluse*, which aimed to examine the entirety of the human condition within the context of history, faith, and society. *The Recluse* had its genesis in the fantastically creative friendship which developed between William, Dorothy, and Samuel Taylor

Coleridge in 1797, and all three hoped that it would establish beyond doubt William's literary talent. Unfortunately, William found the poem almost impossible to write. Instead, he spent over forty years working on that introductory exploration of his experiences and psychological development. The poem grew to over 8,000 lines in length and was finally posthumously titled *The Prelude: Or, The Growth of a Poet's Mind* in 1850.

Despite its publication after William's death, *The Prelude* became a defining work of the Romantic era: the first epic poem in English with the writer's own life as its central subject. This daring novelty did not meet with immediate approbation; one of its early readers, Stopford Augustus Brooke, Wordsworth scholar and co-founder of the Wordsworth Trust, rechristened it an 'autolalestical'[3] (self-praising) poem' for its self-centredness. Nevertheless, its publication signalled the beginning of a fundamental shift in how we think and write about ourselves. *The Prelude*, with its detailed exploration of how place and experience contribute to the development of the psyche, unintentionally created a new approach to how we make sense of our own experiences. It ushered in a new style of literature within the English language: poetic autobiography that not only records the otherwise 'little, nameless, unremembered acts'[4] of an individual's life, but also explores the impact they have on who that person becomes.

Nostalgia and narrative-building, introspection and retrospection: all played a critical role in the eventual completion of *The Prelude* and were shaping forces for the Wordsworths and their writing. This book is concerned primarily with attempting to understand the Wordsworths' experience as young people, looking at their lives in their teens, twenties, and thirties. It uses letters, notebooks, journals, and poems written before the Wordsworths moved away from Dove Cottage in 1808 to examine how and why William and Dorothy came to live in Grasmere, and what that experience felt like at the time. Rather than referencing the final 1850 text of *The Prelude*, usually regarded as the definitive text of the poem, it uses the two-book 1798–9 and thirteen-book 1805 versions to analyse not only how the younger Wordsworths felt about their childhood experiences, but also what their impact was on their creativity during their so-called golden decade of 1798–1808. In so doing, this book aims to preserve the youthful hopes, dreams, difficulties, and contradictions of the Wordsworths as they strove to build their lives, hoping to better understand the siblings' process of creativity and personal development.

In this book I also examine two texts with the individual experience of the Wordsworths in Grasmere at their centre: 'Home at Grasmere', William's only significant poem not to be published either during his lifetime or just after, and Dorothy's Grasmere journal. Both were written – or, in the case of 'Home at Grasmere', first drafted – during the Wordsworths' early years at Dove Cottage and vividly capture the sensations and experiences of coming to terms with yourself as a young yet independent adult. William's writings conveyed 'the character of blissful effusion of one joyous spring season, a spontaneous paean celebrating the time when the glory and the dream were realities for Wordsworth in Grasmere',[5] combining them with observations about the domestic situation of others living in the valley. Dorothy's journal further demonstrated the complexities of living here, for she recorded instances of death and illness, poverty and instability, and loneliness and suffering in the valley, as well as her own deep joy of sibling companionship and delight in the surrounding landscape.

This book aims to explore the Wordsworths' experiences of childhood, adolescence, and young adulthood, assessing their impact not only on William and Dorothy's writings, but also on those of later writers who, as William prophesied, 'among these hills / Will be my second self when I am gone'.[6] By placing the siblings' experiences in the context of subsequent generations of young people who have come to live, work, and write in Grasmere, *All Before Me* offers a modern context for the Wordsworths, shortening the chain between the reader and literary figures, who can feel remote from life in the twenty-first century. Yet love, friendship, purpose, and above all the quest to understand oneself: these were critical concerns for William and Dorothy, just as they continue to be for all of us as we work out how to become our adult selves.

When I moved to the Lake District to work at Dove Cottage, my experience of and recovery from mental illness became intimately intertwined with learning about the lives, writings, and creative homecoming of William and Dorothy Wordsworth. In their work and experience I found a language and approach to understanding trauma, identity, and the self which were just as sophisticated as the psychoanalysis of Freud that followed a century later. Romanticism contains many of the roots of later psychological tenets, but with an added sensitivity to our internal creative forces and the power of the external environment. It was at Dove Cottage that my recovery became possible, where place, history, literature, and community merged to create a new home for me, with all its possibilities. Though I didn't know it when I arrived in Grasmere, I was searching for the chance to belong, looking for what had once been known as 'kith': a place to feel at home and most like myself. And not just kith, but kin too, for loneliness had been a factor in my illness. As William, Dorothy, and Coleridge discovered, we all need connection, companionship, to love, and to be loved, and those were to become Grasmere's lasting gifts not just to me, but to generations of young people who have come, intentionally or otherwise, to find or better understand themselves whilst living in the community around Dove Cottage.

I

Calls Home the Heart

'Grasmere was very solemn in the last
glimpse of twilight; it calls home the heart
to quietness. I had been very melancholy in
my walk back. I had many of my saddest
thoughts, and I could not keep the tears
within me. But when I came to Grasmere I
felt that it did me good.'

Dorothy Wordsworth, *Grasmere Journal*,
16 May 1800[1]

It is the beginning of December 2008 when I travel to Cumbria for an interview at the Wordsworth Trust. In my rucksack are pyjamas, wash things, a sleeping bag, and a towel, squashed underneath a neatly folded dress that I hope will still look smart tomorrow. Though the interview will last only an hour, I need to stay overnight: Suffolk to Grasmere is a journey that takes a day each way by public transport. My mum waves me off at the station, and as the train pulls away I feel my stomach lurch. The giddy nausea that has been a hallmark of my illness is still with me, and I feel shaky in the hope that ahead lies a future preferable to the mess I've made at home. As the train rattles across the fens I start to panic at the thought of the coming interview. My mind is wandering, and I try to yoke it to the task. 'Tell us about yourself,' they will say. 'What have you done before coming here?'

In the closing months of university over a year before, I had been looking for an adventure much further away from home than the Lakes I was heading to now. I had applied to the British Council to take part in the JET Programme, a scheme run by the Japanese government which places recent university graduates from other countries in schools across Japan. Founded in 1987, JET has brought over 70,000 young people from around the world to live and work in Japan. I was there to stay, for a year or possibly longer, with the aim of increasing students' linguistic ability and fostering meaningful cross-cultural exchange. After an interview and language test, I was appointed as an Assistant Language Teacher (ALT) for Kikugawa and the surrounding villages in Yamaguchi Prefecture. Between 9 a.m. and 4 p.m. every weekday, it would be my job to help teach students English.

Aged twenty-one and just out of university, I rented a small apartment close to the Tabe River on the southern tip of Honshu, in a village whose name means 'Chrysanthemum River'. Kikugawa was a tangle of houses, shops, and shrines, edged with farms and fields that stretched into the Chūgoku mountains. From my window I watched rice ripening in the late-summer sun, and as I cycled to work white egrets flapped overhead, trailing thin black legs like afterthoughts. After three years of living in the congested bustle of an English university city, arriving in rural Japan felt like a chance to draw breath, to recalibrate myself as an adult as I explored life on the other side of the world.

When I arrived in Japan I thought the wall of heat that hit me as I stepped on to the airport tarmac was coming from the plane's huge engines. Summer is Japan is hot and humid; apprehensive excitement slid off me as my hair frizzled in the heat and sweat puddled in my armpits. Two of my new colleagues from the Board of Education were waiting at the terminal to drive me to the western edge of Yamaguchi Prefecture.

In Kikugawa I greeted the rest of my colleagues, noting the little cloths they carried to delicately dab away their perspiration. We exchanged small gifts: mine were chosen to be light enough to stay within the airline's baggage allowance alongside a year's worth of belongings, and consisted of paper boxes of tea – English Afternoon, Earl Grey. After taking me to my four-room flat and making sure I knew how the air-conditioning unit and rice cooker worked, they left me to settle in. Once I'd unpacked my bags and bought a few essentials at the shops, I made my way to the Board of Education office, where for a month I conscientiously planned lessons about me and where I came from. When I'd finished preparing for the new term, I spent hours studying Japanese and playing memory games with myself as I tried to learn the pictograms for staffroom, library, and gym hall.

This wasn't my first trip to Japan. As a teenager I had taken part in a school exchange programme where I spent a month living with Japanese families, staying in cities, towns, and villages across the country. My friends and I went to school with kindergarteners in Hiroshima and high school students in Oita, fell asleep to costumed *Noh* plays near Osaka, and bathed naked in *onsen*, outdoor geothermal hot springs, in the mountains near Fukushima. In the heat of a July night, we walked through downtown Tokyo, eating green tea flavoured ice cream and marvelling at the neon life of Harajuku. I had loved the exotic glamour, of feeling myself translated, and promised myself that one day I would return.

Four years later, in Kikugawa as an ALT, I was alone and the only non-Japanese person in the village. One night someone pushed an anonymous note under my door, suggesting that I should make sure the curtains in my kitchen were properly closed. After that, I half-expected to find someone outside my window when I drew my curtains every morning. This didn't feel like paranoia: I already knew that I was being watched. Everyone in the village knew who I was on sight. In the supermarket children cheerfully rooted through my shopping basket to see what I was buying, and older people would occasionally reach out to see if the roundness of my hips was real.

This was the first time I'd lived entirely by myself. Before leaving England, my homeland had been a safety net from which I'd been desperate to escape. After the relative cosiness of university and the familiarity of the small town where I'd grown up, I was eager for adventure, wanting to shape myself in a new image. When I told people that I'd be living alone in Japan several had asked 'Aren't you scared?', but the truthful answer was no: I was excited. After a lifetime of living in England, in tied cottages, council houses, and student accommodation, the dream of having my own flat in this different country was exhilarating. I couldn't wait to go, to return to a place that had lived vividly in my memory since I was seventeen and which I always hoped might call me back.

My ALT predecessor had left me her red sit-up-and-beg bicycle, adorned with a wicker basket and cheerful metal bell. In the evenings, when Kikugawa dimmed in the late-summer light, I rode it along the village lanes, wheeling past sunken rice fields and farmhouses roofed in thick brown tiles. One evening, a little way up the hillside I came across a small shrine guarded by two stone lion-dogs. One of them had its muzzle pursed; the other bared its teeth in warning. The gate was locked, so I peeped through the wooden shutters that flanked the door. The only thing I could make out was a painted board, hung close to the ceiling, showing two men in loose robes fighting with curved swords. In the final image, one lay prone and bloody on the floor, the other standing triumphant above him. I shivered in the still-warm air, and turned back down the hill.

With September came the start of term, and I stood in front of class after class explaining that the UK is made up of four different countries and that many languages are spoken there. My predecessor came from Iowa, so the youngest children – aged four and five – spoke their few words of English with perfect Midwest American accents. Older students either were silent or mumbled as they spoke, as embarrassed as I was by our shared lack of fluency. When I was with them I found myself not speaking as I did at home, but mirroring their intonation in an effort to fit in. To help them understand me, I shortened phrases, switched complex words for simpler ones, and used grammar that mimicked Japanese constructions: 'let's enjoying', 'let's having fun'. We jokingly called this strange hybrid 'Janglish', the necessary love child of two languages which do not share alphabets, grammar, idioms, or syntax.

In Kikugawa no one shared my mother tongue, and most people, though friendly, were too nervous about their ability in English to speak it with me. My halting, imperfect Japanese had to suffice, though occasionally my colleagues shyly approached me with a well-rehearsed English phrase that they were keen to try out. Sometimes I would be extravagantly praised for my attempts in Japanese – *nihongo jōzu desu ne!* – but sometimes such adulation felt insincere, like when the taxi driver seemed delighted that I could pronounce the name of my neighbourhood. It was only Ta-be, two simple syllables.

Though I was the only non-Japanese person in my village, there were several other ALTs scattered across the prefecture. Yamaguchi Prefecture is split into thirteen administrative regions centred around its cities, and Kikugawa was part of Shimonoseki, the historic port that makes up the southernmost tip of Japan's main island. As well as the four ALTs who lived and worked in the city itself – Katy from Oregon, Darryl from Ontario, Monica from North Carolina, and Louise from England – there were three further ALTs based in Shimonoseki's rural education boards. Scottish Marc, Australian Markus, and Texan Jonathan all lived as I did, in small villages spread between the Sea of Japan and the western Chūgoku mountains. Although we were separated by less than twenty miles, a lack of bus or train routes made meeting up during the week almost impossible.

Weekends were a different matter. After school on Friday ALTs across the prefecture headed to the bus and train stations, eager to let their hair down. Parties, meals out, notorious *nomihōdai* ('all you can drink') karaoke sessions – long and sometimes lonely weeks exploded into a fiesta of eating, drinking, speaking English, and lots of hugging, for we missed the casual physical communication of North American, British, and Australasian culture. It was a double life: weeks of linguistic solitude interspersed with weekends of conviviality, excess – and also performance, as these meet-ups often coincided with *matsuri*, local festivals that celebrate every conceivable aspect of daily life. Japan is a country of 'eight million gods', as the saying goes, meaning that every part of life has its own deity, each requiring veneration at the appropriate *matsuri*. Following these festivals, we half-drowned ourselves in *sake* in Hiroshima, raced to catch giant prawns in the warm waters around Himeshima, and watched *yabusame*, ancient horseback archery, from yurts in the mountains near Tsuwano.

As the autumn term wore on, I had to decide: should I go back to Britain for Christmas, or see in the new year in Japan or another country now on my doorstep? Tickets home were expensive, and it was a long way to go for less than a fortnight, so I tamped down the flicker of yearning I felt when I called my family and threw myself into planning a trip to Vietnam with some ALT friends. In place of the usual round of relatives, presents, and too much food, we would climb Mount Fansipan, the highest peak on the Indochinese peninsula, swim in the South China Sea, and zoom through Hanoi's crowded streets on motorbikes. Not going home would mean missing my dad's sixtieth birthday, but I'd already thought of a present for him: return tickets to Japan. Dad had not left Britain for almost twenty years, so my brothers arranged for him to get a new passport and we clubbed together to get him tickets to fly to Japan in April.

Returning to work in January coincided with me getting sick – physically sick, vomiting on and off for days. At night, I began to find it hard to fall asleep. I started to wake earlier, lying alone in the February dark to wait anxiously for the dawn. My thoughts, which had been full of plans and pleasant daydreams about things I wanted to experience in Japan, became edged by intimations of disaster. Odd ideas appeared in my head like revelations, and panic welled in my chest whenever I was on my own. I was becoming psychically ill, though it did not occur to me that my thoughts were becoming increasingly bizarre. By the time winter became spring, I had come to believe that the only reason I could feel so bad was that I was simply a terrible person.

In February I went to the famous *yuki matsuri* (snow festival) at the other end of Japan, taking the *shinkansen* (bullet train) to the northern tip of the mainland, then the overnight ferry to Hokkaido. By this time my mind was racing like the *shinkansen* itself. A friend I met up with at the festival noticed that something seemed amiss, but I brushed off her concern. We picked flesh from the spiky limbs of spider crabs, drank beer, and gazed at castles made of ice. I didn't sleep. As we prepared to head back to work, I became upset about saying goodbye and almost missed my plane. Once on board, I spent the flight curled up in my seat and shaking with the effort not to sob.

April arrived, and when I went to meet my dad at the airport I started to cry. This surprised us both: ours is not a family given to outbursts of emotion. After introducing Dad to my neighbours, who enjoyed showing him round Kikugawa and Shimonoseki, we all went to see the famous gardens at Adachi. There we marvelled at the way the plants and stones were shaped to make perfectly framed views, flawless as pictures. They also took my dad shopping for seeds and *gunshoku*, traditional two-toed workman's socks. We caught the *shinkansen* to see Himeji's ancient castle, though I felt crushed with disappointment when the cherry trees weren't in bloom for our visit. I was hardly sleeping, but I wanted everything about Dad's trip to be perfect.

After Dad went home, I invited an ALT friend to stay with me for the weekend, in the hope that her company would stop me dwelling on his departure, or on what I felt were the failures of his visit. Sitting with a bottle of wine, half-watching a film set in the city where I'd studied for three years, I suddenly felt a rip by my breastbone. A hole seemed to have opened in my chest, right where my heart had been. In that moment it seemed the beating centre of my self was gone, and with the realisation of its absence came an unshakeable conviction. I knew, more certainly than anything I had ever felt before, that I could never be happy again.

This was the first time I had empirically known something with my body. Usually knowledge, the quicksilver cerebral certainty of fact or comprehension, appeared in my head, like jigsaw pieces clicking into place. I trusted the revelations that came to me this way – that synapse snap, that comprehending 'oh!' – what splendour when it all coheres! University had honed my skills at argument and research, encouraging me to find that 'aha!' moment of intellectual satisfaction. But in a second, I realised I had never *known* anything before. Suddenly my whole self was a sham, and I was possessed of the knowledge that happiness would forever pass me by. I knew it. It was a fact of myself, as surely as I knew my foot, my hand, my own reflection. This 'revelation' was nothing more than another of my increasingly peculiar thoughts, but it felt truer than anything I had ever known.

After that I lay awake in bed every night. For a fortnight I did not sleep at all; my stomach churned and my temples pounded day and night. I called my boss to say I couldn't come to work and, after a few days' absence, he took me to the doctor, who prescribed pills. I felt relieved that someone wanted to help me, but the next morning everything was worse. I felt so nauseous that standing up made me dizzy, and when I tried to walk, stomach pains bent me double. My boss called another ALT, an Australian who oversaw the welfare of new arrivals, who came to see me. I told her I felt dreadful, that I needed to escape, so she drove me to her house. Once we were at hers, she advised me to buy a plane ticket home and passed me her laptop.

With one press of the return key my world slid out of control. As I bought the ticket, someone in my head started shouting at me that this was the wrong thing to do. I was letting everyone down by coming home. It was a waste of money, time, and effort – and no one wanted to see me. A strange feeling I misidentified as conviction started my heart racing, and I rushed to the kitchen to ask the ALT if the ticket could be cancelled. In the doorway I stopped short: every surface of the room was covered with empty bottles. Tangled in the drama of my own anxiety, compassion left me and I was consumed with anger – how could I have trusted this person, with their wild drinking, to help me? As furious panic rose in my chest, I screamed and reached for a bottle to smash, but it was taken out of my hands. My head whirled and I thought that I would vomit. 'What am I doing?' I screamed. 'I feel so awful I want to die.'

Everything slipped out of focus. The Australian ALT called the JET helpline provided for emergencies, and soon a teacher from a nearby school picked me up in her car to take me to hospital. There, a Japanese doctor came to talk to me, and the teacher translated his questions and my answers. Here came the killer: had I been thinking about ending my life? I hated it that this kind and friendly woman, with tears streaming down her cheeks, had to answer 'yes' on my behalf.

After being admitted, I was taken upstairs into the men's wing of the hospital because there was no space in the women's wing. No one could tell me how long I would be there. I would miss the plane I'd booked if I didn't leave the next day, but two nights passed and I was still there. At night I could hear people crying and I hid from them in my bed, getting up only to go to the toilet in the corner of my room.

The toilet was at the edge of the room bordering the corridor, but instead of being separated by a wall, thick metal bars were the only division between myself and passing staff. I hated using it because it meant that anyone might see me, but of course that was the point: I was not trusted to be alone.

Days turned into weeks, and no one could tell me when I might go home. I ate meals from plastic trays – rice, soup, pickled vegetables, fried fish – and swallowed handfuls of mysterious pills. During the day I was allowed to enter the women's wing, and there a young woman helped me write an apologetic letter to my workplace to explain my absence. She instructed me on how to use the most intricately formal register of Japanese, which even native Japanese speakers sometimes find difficult. I had nothing to offer in return for her time and patience, but this did not matter. Once I had finished writing she handed me a bracelet made of seven purple beads strung on a piece of leather, taking it from her own wrist, where it nestled among scars as thick as armour. The beads were a bond of psychiatric sisterhood, an acknowledgement of our shared distress.

More days passed. I couldn't leave the ward: the doors required codes or cards that I did not possess. The windows were either barred or set well out of reach. My phone had been taken away from me when I was admitted, so I couldn't call anyone to come to my rescue. Computers were not permitted, so there was no way of sending an electronic SOS to my family. I was not sure if they even knew that I was here. As the weeks threatened to become a month, I started to think I'd never be allowed to leave.

Phrases chased themselves endlessly around my head, like adverts repeated on the telly. 'Fucking benzos' was one, in the unmistakable Australian twang of the person who had helped me buy the plane ticket and whose kitchen was full of bottles. Another was *dō iu imi desu ka*', a Japanese phrase I had used every day since coming here: 'what does it mean?' Every third thought was 'I want to die.' This didn't strike me as worrying or unusual. To my mind, it was the logical way out of feeling awful. I had wanted out before I came here. I didn't want 'in' more now that my life was confined to a hospital cell.

One morning a doctor told me to pack the little that I had into a bag and follow him out of the ward. Before I could process what was happening, I was given an envelope stuffed with documents and was escorted to a car. After an hour's drive, I was walked through an airport to the waiting doors of a plane. Here I was told that I was going home, but that I must have the constant accompaniment of a doctor. I had been assigned to a man I did not recognise, but who apparently worked in the hospital where I had been held. After bowing our heads in greeting, we made the immediate, tacit agreement to ignore each other. I felt a surge of anger at his presence: why was I not trusted to travel by myself?

The journey was long, and I tried to lose myself in one of the onboard films. I chose *Gandhi, My Father*, a biopic of Mahatma Gandhi's son which details his childhood, difficult relationship with his father, and descent into alcoholism. It was the worst possible choice: the central narrative details the failure of an adult child to live up to their parents' – and their own – expectations. Every piece of dialogue felt full of coded messages that mocked me. I watched it through a storm of tears, red-faced with the effort of subduing my sobs. After the film ended, I sat and thumbed through the pieces of paper I had been given by the hospital. Most of them were in Japanese, but written across the top of one, in unforgiving English, was 'PSYCHIATRIC SECTION'. It felt as final as a death certificate – going mad had always been my greatest fear.

Twelve hours after leaving Japan we were back at Heathrow. I could see my family gathered by the gate, crying as I walked towards them through Arrivals.

'It wasn't the way I thought I'd come home,' I practised saying to myself.

After an hour on the train from Bury St Edmunds I arrive at Peterborough, where I switch to the fast train for Leeds. Two hours later I change again, bound for Lancaster, where I finally get on the direct train to Windermere. Clouds hang ominously above as I pass through Staveley and Burneside, single-platform stations where nobody gets on or off. By the time we arrive at Windermere the rain has started, and in the ten minutes I have to wait for the bus it rains so hard my hair gets plastered to my head. Welcome to the Lake District.

Though I lived in England all my life until moving to Japan, I have never been to the Lakes before. I grew up in East Anglia, the eldest of three children. Dad worked as a gardener, and from the time I was five we lived next to a farm on the estate where he worked. Our house, a cold, narrow cottage which had once been a dairy, was edged by low fields where sheep grazed and turnips fattened in the clay. Beyond the farm and fields were the gardens where Dad worked: a walled Victorian potager, an orchard, a pond, and a wide, soft croquet lawn, all surrounded by woodland. Dad's work wasn't well paid, but it gave our family a kind of feudal safety, a place to belong – something that was particularly important since we'd lost our own house to bankruptcy the year before we moved there. We could stay in this tied cottage for as long as Dad was working, and at Christmas there'd be a brace of pheasants, glossy in their plumage, a crate of beer, and chocolates for the children.

Ours was a stay-put childhood, for a gardener's pay is usually low and the work doesn't make for easy travel. Gardens need tending all year round, and the heat and light of spring and summer are particularly precious, too valuable to waste in leisure. Our annual holiday was the same every year: a week at Wells-next-the-Sea on the Norfolk coast, carefully timed to fall between the village flower show, the apex of Dad's gardening year, and the new school term. We always stayed in the same one-room wooden chalet costing £5 a night, which did not include an inside toilet or bathroom. A commode, with a handsomely embroidered seat cover, contained a removable plastic bucket, which we emptied out each morning in the washroom across the garden. The washroom also had an ancient pay-as-you-go shower, which we had to feed with coins from a carefully hoarded supply of out-of-circulation ten pence pieces. In exchange, we were rewarded with intermittent drizzles of warmish water.

Nor did the £5 cover the cost of beds. Instead, mattresses were heaped in a corner and we had the freedom

to drag them to exactly where we wanted to sleep. There
were perhaps twenty to choose from, all in differing states
of disrepair, and we delighted in being able to pile them
two or even three high to make a sleeping platform suitable, in our imaginations, for even the choosiest princess.
Across the yard was a kitchen, a tiny room tacked on to the
adjacent Quaker meeting house, where a polite handwritten notice asked visitors to refrain from cooking kippers
on Sunday mornings lest the odour put the faithful off
their silent contemplation. 'Better than camping' was my
parents' assessment of the accommodation. We children
adored it.

Part of the chalet's appeal was that it lay a scant twenty-
minute walk from the sea. The quay at Wells is a curving
concrete wall that rises high above the low-tide mud, and
beyond it lies a salt marsh wilderness. Sand bars rise from
the sea as the tide flees, and shallow creeks snake between
the hummocks of mud and sand. Fishing boats come and go
through The Run, the deepest channel that leads to open
water. Sailing boats tack lazily between the town and the
sea, and come low tide the skeletal hulls of long-abandoned
hulks appear, lolling on the mud like seals. Above them the
sky stretches out forever. In Norfolk we exchanged the fields
of home for sand and sea, but in both places the landscape
was a footnote to the high drama of the sky.

I can count on one hand the times we left East Anglia
as a family. Most of these sorties happened before Dad
took up gardening, when he was running his own business
designing, making, and racing motorcycles. There had been
a weekend in the Yorkshire Dales that I was too young to

remember, and a rare boat ride from Holyhead to the Isle of Man for the Manx TT when the elder of my brothers was still in nappies. Once we took an overnight train to visit my maternal grandparents near Aberdeen, and then there was a long drive to Cornwall to see some cousins just before I reached double figures. A week in Holland when I was five, this time to see Dad's bike race in the Dutch TT, was our family's sole taste of another country. Later, school trips took me as far north as the Peak District, and university introduced me to the Wolds, but otherwise England was, to me, a low flat land, edged with open skies.

Now I'm in Cumbria, on my way to the place most intimately associated with the Wordsworths, and it feels like I am looking at another country. Through the fogged-up windows of the bus I can see a landscape that is high, wild, and full of water. Mountains glower down at us, streaming mist and wind-whipped clouds, whilst rivers rumble under bridges in their rush for open water. This landscape is a living thing that roars and weeps, pitting rain against rocks. We follow the eastern curve of Windermere as the wind lashes its surface into so many waves I think I might be looking at the sea. The double-decker bus sways and groans like a tall ship under sail. As we drive, puddles breach the low step of its doorway; at one point I have to drag my rucksack on to an empty seat to keep it dry. My feet sway in the air as a strange grey tide rolls in beneath them, bringing the outside world close enough to touch.

The rain blurs everything, softening my focus, but even in the half-light I can see hills towering above me. Darkness has begun to gather by the time we reach Ambleside, the small town at the northern tip of Windermere, and we drive on towards night. As we round the curve of Rydal Water, a cluster of stone buildings puffs out smoke, lights glittering from little leaded windows. Soon we pass a sign announcing 'Grasmere', and I quickly press the bell. The driver doesn't seem to hear and I begin to fear I've missed my stop, but suddenly the brakes slam, and I climb out beside a car park marked with a sign proclaiming 'Dove Cottage and the Wordsworth Museum'.

Two hundred and nine years earlier, on a similarly wintery afternoon in December 1799, siblings William and Dorothy Wordsworth arrived in Grasmere to begin a new chapter in their lives. The sun had already set by the time they stepped down from the Kendal post-chaise on the eve of the year's shortest day, and the cottage they had agreed to rent stood before them dark, empty, and cold. Only a flicker of fire, lit by a thoughtful neighbour, smouldered in the grate. Brother and sister, aged twenty-nine and almost twenty-eight respectively, had travelled more than eighty miles on frozen roads from the welcoming house of friends at Sockburn near Darlington to move to a little village where they knew no one. Nevertheless, as Dorothy recalled sixteen years later, 'we were young and healthy and had attained an object long desired, we had returned to our native mountains, there to live'.[2]

Though Dorothy came to view their arrival as a kind of homecoming, she had visited Grasmere only once before 1799, staying just a single night. Dorothy was born on Christmas Day 1771, and she and her four brothers – Richard (born in 1768), William (1770), John (1772), and Christopher (1774) – spent their early years in the town of Cockermouth, thirty miles from Grasmere in the old county of Cumberland. Their father, John, was a lawyer, working as an agent for the Earl of Lonsdale as well as serving as Bailiff and Recorder of Cockermouth and Coroner for nearby Millom. Their mother, Ann, was the only daughter of comfortably middle-class linen-drapers William and Dorothy Cookson, from the market town of Penrith. Ann and John frequently sent their older children to stay at Ann's parents' house, often for months at a time whilst Ann birthed and nursed each new arrival. At Christmas and in the summer the Wordsworths visited their father's brother Richard and his family at the port town of Whitehaven, but there is no record of the family coming to Westmorland, the old county to the south of Cumberland with Grasmere at its north-western edge, until after Dorothy went to live in Yorkshire at the age of six.

That move signalled the abrupt end of the Wordsworth children's shared infancy, for it followed the death of Ann Wordsworth in March 1778. She was only thirty, with the youngest of her children not yet four years old. Widowed John, busy with his work, felt unable to care for his five young children, so it was decided that the siblings would be split up and raised by an assortment of relations. Richard and William, aged ten and eight, continued to live with their father in Cockermouth, whilst young John and Christopher were looked after by the Cooksons in Penrith. As the only girl, Dorothy was sent to live with her mother's cousin Elizabeth Threlkeld in Halifax, over one hundred miles away. She would never see her father again, nor her brothers for almost a decade.

Though it seems cruel to separate one child from her siblings following their mother's death, the choice of 'Aunt' Threlkeld as Dorothy's mother-substitute proved to be a good one. Remembered as 'a Woman of high natural Talent, and great energy',[3] Elizabeth ran a draper's shop whilst also looking after her sister's five orphaned children, Martha, Edward, Ann, Samuel, and Betty Ferguson. She was loving and diligent in the care she provided to them and her young second cousin; Dorothy later wrote that 'the loss of a Mother can only be made up by such a friend as my Dear Aunt'. Dorothy would remain with 'Aunt' Threlkeld for the rest of her childhood, becoming part of a large social circle which included the welcoming and wealthy Pollard family. Jane, the sixth of seven Pollard daughters, was a year older than Dorothy, and the two became close friends.

Dorothy also received a good education under the aegis of Elizabeth Threlkeld. In 1782, aged eleven, she was sent to school at Hipperholme, five miles from Halifax. This school provided education to both girls and boys, and Dorothy was taught by Mrs Wilkinson, a teacher she described as 'most excellent-tempered motherly and sensible'. Though for nine years she did not see her brothers or return to Cockermouth, Dorothy's life was full and varied, and she later described Halifax as 'that dear place which I shall ever consider as my home'. In contrast, in letters she frequently referred to the house where she was born and spent her infancy as 'my father's house', a phrase heavy with biblical rather than familial resonance.

Dorothy's brothers developed a very different sense of home and belonging. In May 1779, Richard and William (aged eleven and nine) started school at Hawkshead, a village thirty miles south-east of Cockermouth. It was too far to make the journey daily, and so for much of the year they lodged near the school. Most boys boarded with the master in the Hawkshead schoolhouse, but John Wordsworth arranged for his sons to live with Hugh and Ann Tyson, a couple in their sixties who lived in a cottage close to the school. Richard and William were their first lodgers, but over the following decade all four Wordsworth boys came to live with the Tysons.

The young Wordsworths may have lost their mother and been separated from each other, but their father's decision to lodge his children with Elizabeth Threlkeld and the Tysons indicates his concern that they should have good substitute homes – and mothers. His notebooks demonstrate both his affection for them and his involvement in their lives. He often refers to them by nicknames – Dickie for Richard, Dolly for Dorothy, Kit for Christopher – and in giving John the epithet 'Ibex', the shyest of beasts, we can see that he was well acquainted with their individual characters. Ensuring that Dorothy was educated at the comparatively expensive Hipperholme school despite not being a wealthy man shows the value John placed on education and his appreciation of the potential of his clever daughter. Arranging private lodgings was more costly than having the boys board with their schoolmaster – it was the Cooksons who paid the school entrance fees for their grandsons, indicating that John was not in a strong financial position himself – but the decision to have his sons live with the Tysons would prove to be to the boys' lasting benefit.

The Tyson cottage in Hawkshead was rather cramped and ordinary compared with the grand townhouses of Cockermouth and Penrith, but it provided the Wordsworths with a welcoming and steadfast home. Though the children had lived with their Cookson grandparents for months at a time throughout their infancy, theirs was not a close relationship. The Wordsworth boys were regarded as wild and ill-mannered by the Cooksons, and William was thought to be particularly difficult and headstrong; he once slashed a painting at his grandparents' house with a whip from a spinning top. In turn, the boys remembered their grandparents as people of narrow experience and rigid conscience, their lives governed by a 'feverish dread of error or mishap',[4] which they later recalled as markedly absent from their mother's demeanour: she was fondly, if hazily, remembered as the 'hinge of all our learnings and our loves'.[5]

As Ann Wordsworth had been, Ann Tyson was a warm, welcoming presence. She had worked as a domestic servant in Westmorland and Scotland as a young woman, and since her marriage to Hugh, she and her husband had combined his carpentry work with running a small shop in Hawkshead. Ann was a great storyteller and many of the boys in her care later fondly recalled her tales, which memorably inter-mingled folklore with local history. In the winter Ann and her charges played games and cards in the living room, and her small cottage with its 'plain comforts [and] home amusements by the warm peat fire' became for William and his brothers 'A sanctity, a safeguard, and a love'[6] until they finished school.

Schooldays were long, beginning at half past six in the morning and not finishing until five on summer evenings, but at weekends the boys' time was their own. They fished, caught birds, climbed trees to search for eggs, and when the weather grew colder scoured the woods for nuts. When winter had the valley in its grip, the frozen lake became their playground, and the valley rang with the hiss and clatter of their skates. Their 'steels' glinted in the moonlight, and on cloudless nights they would race to 'cut across the image of a star / That gleam'd upon the ice'.[7]

Delight was often mixed with near disaster. One wet day William went fishing in the river Duddon with a neighbour. Rain set in not long after they left Hawkshead and continued all day. On the way home, William became so cold and exhausted that the neighbour had to carry him bodily back to Hawkshead. There was also an abortive attempt at rock climbing with his friends near Coniston in pursuit of a raven's nest, where one of the boys became 'crag-fast' with fear and had to be rescued by some drystone wallers working nearby. One summer morning William witnessed the gruesome raising of a body from Esthwaite Water. James Jackson, a teacher at nearby Sawrey, had drowned and his corpse was brought to the surface by sombre men who raked the waters with long poles. A gaggle of Hawkshead schoolboys watched, agog.

Death was a part of life, and the Wordsworths knew it. In December 1783 the children were bereaved again after their father got lost on the Cumberland moors and spent a night out in the cold and wet. Pneumonia set in, and on 30 December John Wordsworth died, aged only forty-two. Richard, William, John, and Christopher attended his funeral in Penrith, but Dorothy remained in Halifax. When the boys returned to Hawkshead they found Hugh Tyson very ill and Ann too busy caring for him to look after her charges, who had to spend a few weeks at a neighbour's. Hugh died in early spring, and after that the Wordsworth boys moved back in with Ann, where they stayed for the rest of their schooldays. It was not until the summer of 1787, after Richard and William had finished their schooling, that the Wordsworth brothers would finally meet their sister – now aged fifteen – in person again.

The sun's last light has just left the sky when I step inside Dove Cottage for the first time. Entering the houseplace, the main living room into which the front door opens, I have to pause to let my eyes adjust to the darkness. There are no electric lights here and the fire in the grate is nearly out, the dark panelled walls deadening what little light it gives. A tall young man, long hair tied back in a ponytail, introduces himself as John and tells me to wait until the quarter hour, when the next tour, the last of this short winter day, begins. He suggests that whilst I wait, I sign my name in the guestbook open on a small table in the corner. Next to the guestbook is a page copied from Dorothy's journal, the diary she kept during her first three years of living here. Two hundred and seven years ago she had risen by candlelight, the world dim and gloomy on a 'showery unpleasant morning, after a downright rainy night'.[8] This afternoon has the same cold, wet feel and the whole valley is shrouded in low cloud.

When the clock on the staircase strikes the quarter and no one else has come to join us, John and I explore the house alone. Not much has changed, he tells me, since the Wordsworths' day. Before William and Dorothy moved in, the building had been a pub, and so is a little different from most traditional cottages in the village. Comparatively tall, the house has two full storeys, and instead of a front door facing the road, the entrance is to the side, under a small porch. In place of the usual brushed earth floor, the down-stairs rooms are covered in slate, better to bear the tread of boots and spills of beer. As well as a larder, it also has a buttery, a low room half-sunk into the hillside, where kegs of ale were kept cool by a stream that flows underneath the floor. There are also four good-size bed- and living rooms, plus a smaller bedroom in an outjutting that leans against the house's northern side.

Once my eyes have adjusted to the gloom, I begin to feel at ease. Though the rooms are, by modern standards, sparsely furnished, they contain familiar, homely items. A wooden washstand holds a ceramic basin, and there are tallow candles held in brass candlesticks for light. A small sofa is draped with a hand-knitted blanket, and a canopied bed is hung with patched and faded drapes. The walls of the outjutting are covered with sheets of newspapers, pasted on by Dorothy in defence against the damp. The feet-polished stairs gleam in the lamplight as John shows me out through a little door beside the staircase, and turning left I find my own way to the museum through the garden.

As I approach the door, I hear a clock chime five. The site is closing, and it is time for the first part of my interview to start. John is waiting for me at the museum desk, and from there we go through a long, low tunnel to the archive. In a bright room lined with books and pictures, a group of people are gathered around wide wooden tables. There are two other applicants about my age, introduced as Catherine and Helen, alongside Carrie, an older woman from the Trust, and two men – John and the curator, Jeff. Nervousness ripples through my stomach. I've not had an interview since I applied to go to Japan two years earlier, and my grasp on myself feels very shaky.

We are asked to introduce ourselves and the places we come from, so I try to think of something interesting to say about Bury St Edmunds whilst Catherine and Helen tell us they grew up, respectively, in Middlesbrough and Leeds. Then Jeff introduces the place to us. We are in the Jerwood Centre, a huge climate-controlled treasure trove and research room which opened just five years before. Ninety-five per cent of the Wordsworths' extant writings – manuscripts, letters, and diaries – are within a few metres of where we sit, along with their personal library. Before us is a first edition of William and Coleridge's *Lyrical Ballads*, regarded as the first, defining text of the Romantic era. This little volume began a revolution, championing the power of imagination and personal experience and endeavouring to renew humanity's relationship with nature.

We are in the nerve centre of Romanticism, the pan-European cultural movement of the late eighteenth and early nineteenth centuries. As we carefully turn the pages of the *Ballads*, Jeff slides open the doors to glassy cases that line the walls to pick out more treasures. Each has almost incalculable value, cultural gems recognised and lauded across the world: *Paradise Lost*, its pages marked with William's annotations; a first edition of Mary Shelley's *Frankenstein*, printed in three volumes. We are allowed to carefully prise open their soft spines and place them into cradles, keeping their pages open using curtain weights before gorging on the wonders inside.

The care required to turn these two-hundred-year-old pages without leaving crease or tear absorbs me, focusing my mind beyond myself for the first time in months. An hour races by before someone suggests that it might be time for dinner, so we head across the lane to the Trust's little cafe. Talking over pizza and glasses of wine, I find stories bubbling up despite myself. As the drink giddies through my blood, I hear my voice retell an exchange between De Quincey and Wordsworth that I remember reading about at university, where William called the younger man 'a nasty little opium-chewer'. People are not just listening, but laughing too. It feels like a long time since my words made anybody giggle, and the sound brings a gladness to me that I haven't felt in months.

After we've finished eating, someone proposes a trip to the pub. I hesitate, unsure of the wisdom of another drink, but everyone else is already putting on their coats and I do not want to be left out. 'Yes,' I say, 'that would be nice', and off into the dark we go. The stars are bright above us, the Milky Way a pale smudge across the inky sky. On this cold

December evening few people are out, and aside from one car passing us too fast, the village is still and quiet.

As we wind our way along the lane, John tells us about Tweedies. This pub is the locals' mainstay, a necessary oasis that buoys them through the winter and provides a place to share the joys of summer. After passing a low-steepled church, we come to the side door of a big hotel. Strings of coloured bulbs glimmer in the darkness, and the windows are opaque with condensation. Behind the grand frontage is a smaller door, through which we duck before stepping into the light. There's a row of handpumps on the bar, and the room is busy, noisy, warm. Someone gets a round in, and someone else ushers us into a back room for a game of pool. I don't have time to worry that I can't really play, and before I can object I'm pointing a cue across the baize. The room hums with companionable chatter. Though the wine has made me a little jittery, I also realise that, for the last two hours, I've barely thought about myself. Being here is interesting, and I am feeling well enough to notice.

A couple of hours later, Helen and I excuse ourselves, pleading interviews early the next morning. As we walk back in the dark, snow begins to fall. A white blanket settles on us and the road, covering the long stone walls that edge the pavements. It feels like another world. Outside Dove Cottage an iron streetlamp glows like a beacon, lighting up the doorways of the houses where we are to sleep. We say goodnight and, after clicking open iron latches, make our way through a pair of green-grey doors set into thick slate walls. I hear Helen shut another door behind her, and I make my way into the silence of this house.

I have been allotted a little bedroom in the first of three Victorian terraced houses which accommodate the Wordsworth Trust's employees. As I climb the stairs, all is dark and quiet; six heavy fire doors lie shut against me, one for every bedroom. Mine is on the top floor, and after negotiating two steep flights of stairs I brush my teeth in a little sink at the corner of my room, before laying out my sleeping bag on a bare mattress. A towel stuffed into a jumper will do for a pillow, though I find that once I lie down I cannot sleep. As the last of the evening's alcohol courses through my system, I feel a glow of something like excitement. The prospect of a future has been kindled in my chest.

As I wait for my brain to consider sleeping, I think back to another winter day when I felt enchanted by Wordsworthian possibility. I was seventeen when, one December morning, I'd woken early in a small, unfamiliar room at the college where I hoped to study. It was the day of my interview for a place at university, a place I really wanted, and my nerves were jangling too much to stay asleep. The sun had not yet risen, so I snuck out in the half-light, passing frosty lawns on my way to the river that snaked beside the college. The banks were shrouded in mist but, beyond the bridge, I could see the tops of grander buildings reaching for the first light of the day. Feeling like the only person in the world, I walked along the riverside, spellbound with the beauty of that morning.

Two hours later I was handed a sheet of poems. One was 'Composed Upon Westminster Bridge', with its 'domes, towers and cathedrals' at sunrise: 'a sight so touching in its majesty!' It could have been a description of my daybreak exploration and I understood at once the poem's vivid ecstasy. After discussing Wordsworth we talked about Donne, Shakespeare, and Defoe, and I knew before the interview was over that I had a place. Wordsworth's words felt like a portent, a guarantee of goodness. As I lie in the dark in Grasmere, the memory makes me smile, and I replay the poem's last lines in my head: 'Dear God! the very houses seem asleep; / And all that mighty heart is lying still!'[9]

The snow is still falling when I take myself across the freezing landing to the bathroom sometime after midnight. From the little high-up window, I can see the streetlamp outside Dove Cottage throwing light across the lane, illuminating whirling snowflakes and a trail of footprints that make their way into the darkness further up the hill. I crawl back into my sleeping bag and feel the beginnings of a smile at the corners of my mouth. I know that I want to come and live here if I can.

Early the next morning I stuff my sleeping bag and pyjamas back into my suitcase and put on my slightly crumpled dress. I eat breakfast in the kitchen on my own, rinsing my bowl and mug before pulling on my boots and coat. At nine o'clock, I knock on the museum's just-opened door and leave my suitcase behind the desk. I need to make a quick getaway; if I miss the ten-twenty bus I might not make it back home today.

Carrie takes me up into a little circular room above the museum, an eyrie with a view across the valley. Two men sit on the opposite side of a round wooden table that belonged to the Wordsworths, and they shake my hand as I take my seat. Beside Jeff sits the Trust's financial director, a small grey-haired man wearing a smart suit and a sombre tie. Jeff's face already feels familiar and friendly, his sandy hair standing up like grass and his eyes twinkling. He asks me if I've been comfortable in the terraced house, if I think I'd be OK living there. I say I think I would, that I like the quietness. 'It isn't always this quiet,' he remarks, and I hope I haven't made a misstep.

My stomach clenches and worries itself with nerves. But as I talk, I feel the old fluency come back. I describe my college days with something like excitement, and keep up a cheery brio when talking about living in Japan. Then Jeff fixes me with a knowing look, and asks an unexpected question:

'What is the hardest thing you've ever had to do?'

I take a deep breath, and stake my future on the answer.

I tell him about falling ill, about losing my mind in Japan. I tell him how I came back home, and describe something of the misery of the breakdown and the year that followed. I cry as I tell him about how I have been trying to find something to do with myself for months. Jeff hands me a tissue, and I wipe my face, which is hot with tears and embarrassment. I've never cried at an interview before, but now I cannot help it. At least I know that if they want to take me on, they know who I am and what has happened.

The next day, I get a phone call. One of the ten places on the internship is mine, if I want it.

I am in.

2

This Little
Unsuspected Paradise

*'the repose of this little unsuspected
paradise ... is peace, rusticity, &
happy poverty in its neatest and most
becoming attire'*

Thomas Gray, *The Poems of Mr Gray,
to which are Prefixed Memoirs of his
Life and Writings* (1775)[1]

January is halfway through when I finish packing up my old
life and get on the northbound train. Beside me is my bicycle, a three-speed BSA that my grandfather coaxed back
into working order after rescuing it from the tip. I've stuffed
my duvet and pillow into thick plastic bags and tied them
to the crossbar, strapping a holdall full of clothes across the
rear carrier. From the handlebars hang more bags, one with
a pair of wellies, the other a jumble of old waterproofs. The

rucksack on my back is stuffed with books and clothes. By the front door is a taped-up cardboard box containing everything else I think I might need in the next twelve months, with instructions for Mum to post it to me when – or if – I settle in.

I have committed to living in Town End for a year as an intern for the Wordsworth Trust. A cluster of buildings at the southern edge of Grasmere village, Town End is a traditional Lakeland hamlet, which has Dove Cottage at its centre. The cottage sits beside the old road that runs over the hill from Grasmere to Rydal, winding past a small pond and farmstead before turning into a broad, stony track on the terrace above Rydal Water. Today the A591 cuts across Town End to the west, the swish of its vehicles audible from Dove Cottage, but when the Wordsworths lived here that road did not exist. Instead, all traffic passed along the lane beside their door. For over a hundred years, the Wordsworth Trust has looked after the cottage and its sur-roundings, ensuring that the physical world of William and Dorothy Wordsworth remains as intact as possible from the passage of time.

Founded in 1890, the Trust's primary aim has been to pre-serve Dove Cottage 'for the eternal possession of those who love English poetry all over the world'.[2] Initially, this meant buying the Wordsworths' Grasmere home from its previous owner, Edmund Lee, a Bradford businessman and author who wrote the first biography of Dorothy Wordsworth.[3] More than three hundred people made donations to enable the purchase; John Ruskin, Alfred Tennyson, and Edward Burne-Jones all gave money, as did many ordinary people, like the anonymous 'working woman' who donated a single shilling to the cause. The cottage was bought for £750 and, following repairs and some set dressing, was opened to the public in 1891. By this point the house was known as 'Dove Cottage', an epithet inspired by its previous incarnation as the Dove and Olive Bough Inn, although in the Wordsworths' day it had no name.

Though it had been more than eighty years since any Wordsworth had lived in the house, the Trust was able to furnish the property with items that had belonged to the family. This included a bed 'said on good authority to have been used by Wordsworth himself'[4] and sitting-room chairs with covers embroidered in woollen threads and initialled 'D.W.'[5] The Trust also appointed a custodian, Mary Dixon, whose house was directly opposite Dove Cottage. Mrs Dixon had lived in the village since 1846, working as a baker and shopkeeper. She remembered meeting William Wordsworth in his old age, and had witnessed his funeral at Grasmere church in 1850. It was arranged that visitors would knock at her door and pay sixpence in exchange for a tour of Dove Cottage. Mrs Dixon was remembered as 'a woman of fine features & good manners', who 'year after year by her courtesy and kindness and racy stories added greatly to the attractions of Dove Cottage'.[6]

What the 'racy stories' of Mrs Dixon were has been lost to time, but it was the Dixon family's personal connection to the Wordsworths which made the Trustees anxious to maintain the living link between them. When Mrs Dixon eventually retired at the age of ninety-four, her daughter Elizabeth Philipson took over duties; after her death,

Elizabeth's daughter Emily Kirkbride inherited the custodianship. Emily's death in 1961 brought seventy years of the family's association with Dove Cottage to an end.

As well as preserving the physical legacy of the Wordsworths' life in the cottage, the Trustees also sought to build a collection of material relating to their writings. In 1898 Professor William Knight, a Trustee who had written several books about the Romantics, donated his library, which included many Wordsworth first editions, to the Trust. An academic at the University of St Andrews, Knight had been instrumental in establishing public interest in the relationship between William's poetry and the places which inspired it in his 1878 *The English Lake District: As Interpreted in the Poems of Wordsworth*. Knight's library now formed the core of the Trust's printed collection.

In 1904 the library was augmented by a substantial and important legacy from the Wordsworth family when Gordon Graham Wordsworth, William's grandson by his youngest son, became involved with the Trust. It was his wish that the family papers remain in Grasmere, and after his death in 1935, the bequest was made, forever tying the Wordsworths' written legacy to Town End. By then the Trustees had acquired another building, an old barn opposite Dove Cottage, in which manuscripts and Wordsworthian ephemera could be stored and displayed. The little hamlet was now one of the only places in the western world where the manuscripts of great poems could be viewed in the very spot where they were written. As founding Trustee Stopford Augustus Brooke observed, 'There is no place ... which has so many thoughts and memories as this belonging to our poetry; none at least in which they are so closely bound up with the poet and the poems.'[7]

Chief among the bequests were manuscripts of William's autobiographical poem *The Prelude* and four volumes of Dorothy's Grasmere journal. Slowly new and more complete editions of their writings – letters, poetry, and journals – were published from these manuscripts, and Dove Cottage became not just a place of poetic pilgrimage, but the centre of an international community of scholarship. In the 1950s, a former smithy adjacent to the cottage was purchased and turned into a library for visiting researchers. Though at first its upstairs was still used for storage by a local farmer, the downstairs space was converted for the use of scholars, including young Wordsworth academics Robert Woof, Stephen Gill, and the poet's great-great-great nephew Jonathan Wordsworth. By the light of an open coke fire and a single battered lamp, they and many others spent long hours with the Wordsworths' papers, delving into disintegrating cardboard boxes to explore the mysteries of living and writing in this place.

Now that the Wordsworth manuscripts were forever linked to Town End, the Trust decided to increase its physical perimeter, buying nearby barns, cottages, outbuildings, and even a boathouse to form a protective cordon around Dove Cottage. Its staff grew from four to fifty people, most of whom were able to be accommodated in these buildings. In the 1970s, the Trust began offering regular work placements to recent graduates, giving them the opportunity to turn academic interest into useful skills by supporting research into the Wordsworths' lives and works.

It also ensured that, in the spirit of the twenty-somethings that William and Dorothy were when they first came here, young people continued to be able to live in Grasmere. This vision of an idyll was no pipe dream: it cost money, and between 1970 and 2005, the Trust's annual budget soared from £19,000 to over £1 million. Raising this type of money required the constant application of charm, ingenuity, and persuasion, and Robert Woof, its dynamic first director, led a relentless decades-long quest to maintain not only the fabric of the buildings, but also the intangible spirit of this place.

Ten hours after leaving home, I arrive at Windermere. Sleet is falling as I walk along the platform, and the road is edged in slush. Although I planned to cycle the last few miles to Grasmere, the thought of riding my bike along unfamiliar roads slick with ice does not appeal. Instead, I get a lift from Helen – she and Catherine had also been offered internships – who has brought her car with her to the Lakes. And there she is, waving from the door of an elderly black Renault Clio. We pile my baggage into the boot, strap the bike to the roof rack, and head into the night.

Grasmere greets us with snowfall as we bundle my belongings out of the car and push our way through the first door in the narrow terrace of houses. These tall slate buildings did not exist in the Wordsworths' day and would probably have been hated by them, as they block the line of sight between Dove Cottage and the lake. Nevertheless, the houses, known as Lake Terrace, have provided handy accommodation for generations of staff, and each house has its own kitchen, sitting room, and bathroom, along with several bedrooms spread across three floors.

As I unpack my bags, I can hear a clatter of cutlery and plates that can only signal one thing: dinner. My stomach rumbles. Tomorrow I will need to visit the shops, but tonight I hope someone will take pity on me after my long journey and late arrival. I come downstairs to find my housemates leaving with plates, forks, and glasses in their hands. They tell me to grab some for myself: for this first meal in Grasmere, we interns will all eat together. Dinner is being served next door, and we slip through the sleet, eager to fill our bellies and meet the rest of the group.

We step into a house that steams with warmth. Mark, the Trust's handyman and long-term resident of House Two, has been stoking the kitchen fire all afternoon, and its roaring heat makes clouds of welcome promise in the air. Mugs of tea are passed round, and someone unearths a packet of biscuits from the back of a cupboard. Lake Terrace has been home for volunteers and staff for more than forty years and their legacy is everywhere. Hand-printed exhibition posters flutter on one wall, and heaped in a corner is a mountain of VHS tapes. A skull lies on the mantlepiece, and beside it a plastic pint glass full of tiny broken light bulbs. From a cupboard in the wall spill broken boxes of board games, interleaved with orphan playing cards, relics of friendships forged here.

Others have left their mark more permanently here. Across the window of one cottage is written in looping golden letters '*My dreams become your vision.*' Another window answers: '*My vision becomes your dreams*.' These are the words of an artist who lived in Town End a few years earlier and made the place her muse. Smiling, Mark tells us she asked him to paint the inside of the Trust's boathouse gold. Sitting on the lip of the lake that lies across the road, the building is an ornate Victorian edifice with a huge fireplace and curving beams holding up a roof of stone. The artist insisted that its insides must be gold so that they would glow in the firelight, and when sunshine lit up the lake its reflection would dance and glimmer on the water. She also asked a company in London to make her a boat from steel and silver, one that she might sail herself. The proposed boat was never made, so she had to be content with dreaming, sending ripples through the water in her mind.

The rain pours down as we listen to this story, imagining the jewel-box boathouse, which stands a hundred metres from where we sit, hidden by the mist. Leaning on the door jamb, Mark puffs cigarette smoke out into the yard and cool, damp air seeps in. We pull our chairs closer to the fire and talk about our homes, our studies, about the new and funny strangeness of this place. Of the ten new interns, everyone except me had visited Grasmere before they applied for the internship. Most are familiar with it from holidays and school trips from Leeds, Middlesbrough, Blackpool, and Preston. Only Emily and I come from the south of England. Then someone asks me: what drew you here?

Anxiety flutters in my chest, and I contemplate keeping my counsel. I want these people to like me, to be my friends, to not be put off by the madness which I have so far hidden from them. Buying time, I tell them about how I like the countryside, and how I felt uneasy in the city when I lived there for university. I tell them how, on mornings when the pressure of study felt unbearable, I would walk on to the high street and get the first bus out. It didn't matter where it was going; I just had to escape the city. Sometimes friends came too, and once three of us set out to find a ring of ancient standing stones. We had a map that showed these megaliths in the middle of a field, but unfortunately the bus route and our map never quite converged. Instead, we found ourselves standing by a busy A-road in a rainstorm, watching the bus drive away as we tried to work out how we might walk onto the map. Soon a small red car screeched to a stop beside us, and an old man flung open the door. 'Get in, you maniacs!' commanded the driver. We had little choice but to obey.

Once we were squeezed on to the back seat, our rescuer demanded to know what we were doing. We sheepishly explained our plan, which now seemed embarrassingly silly. Dr Harker – as he had introduced himself – roared with laughter and, as he drove towards the nearest town, regaled his soggy passengers with tales of his own student days. There had not been much study ('I drank and I rowed') and he laughingly approved of our attempt at adventure. Waving goodbye to this unlikely rescuer at Chipping Norton, we stood in the doorway of a pub wringing out our clothes before going in to sink some welcome pints and giggle at the daftness of it all.

Everyone laughs as I tell the story, and as I sit and listen to the others chat about home, I remember the escapes I made in last year's wild, unhappy summer. How I tried to run away, searching for a version of myself that had once seemed happy. One bright autumn day, I took a ferry to the Isle of Wight, where an old boyfriend and I had often gone on holiday. Catching the train to Lymington, I felt haunted: my once-glad self seemed everywhere. Just out of sight, I could feel her slide into the old-fashioned train compartments, squeezing on to a bench beside the window. On the ferry she was at the corner of my eye where the wind whipped my hair. Once on the island I walked along a lane where I'd seen fireflies years before, and she felt so close that I could almost touch her. Yet every time I thought I'd seen her she vanished, leaving me to wonder if I would ever find her again.

I became frantic with the idea that being at ease with myself would eternally elude me. There was a chance that this new, mad me would always be gripped by a mania that offered little respite, or that my adult life would be a seesaw ride between ecstatic highs and devastating lows. A university friend – one of the escapees on the search for those standing stones – invited me to stay with her soon after I got back from Japan. Sally was living in Kingussie in the Scottish Highlands, and told me I was welcome to come and listen to the whirl of the curlew and smell the coconut perfume of the gorse for as long as I needed. I hoped that doing so would return me to myself.

The journey there – ten hours by train – felt like it might be my last. At Perth, waiting to change on to the Inverness train, I'd had to fight myself away from the edge of the platform, away from the soul-sickening draw of passing trains. My body felt their lure so keenly that it took all my self-control to contain a rebellion that was being fought within me. As I stood by the railings at the end of the platform I felt sick to my fingertips and began to retch, doubled forward in an agony that I had to purge from myself. Dry heave after dry heave rolled through my throat as I retched and retched with this self-sickness.

But coming into the cottage at Kingussie gave me a sliver of that old familiar feeling, and I dared to think that what had happened in Japan might just pass like a dream. Though I had never been there before, I recognised Sally's cushions, cups, and blankets from our student days. The books on the shelves felt like old friends, and after dinner Sally put on a film, one we had watched as students. It finished just as the stars began to twinkle in the creamy blue evening sky above the Cairngorms. As I drained the glass of whisky Sally gave to me as medicine, I felt the glow of being myself, the flicker of normality fed by being there, go out.

Any feelings of being less than awful vanished. A tide had turned, sweeping my old self away. From the outside, Sally told me it looked like someone had switched off a light, or drawn a curtain behind my eyes. One moment I had been there, smiling and reminiscing, and the next I was gone. All I could do was hope that one day the tide would turn and I might be myself again. There seemed to be no shortcut to the life I sought. I felt like an impossible guest, listless and desperate, quite unable to be comfortable company for anyone. The following day I took the train back south, knowing I had to find another way of living.

As my illness seemed to have come from nowhere, when I first came back to the UK I put it down to the isolation I'd experienced in Japan. But living at home had not returned me to health. Even among friends and familiar things, my head was full of thoughts I didn't want. I jarred and jangled, chafing at myself. The problem wasn't just Japan: something inside me seemed to have been eroded. I had lost myself and was paralysed by fear. Why did I feel this way, and could I ever find myself again?

I was desperate to get away from how I felt, to escape what felt like the burning miseries of being me. My internal dynamo, driven by willpower as often as by desire, had always pushed me on – but no longer. Now it lay broken, an angular wreck of snapped metal. One part lodged at my neck, one under my stomach. On its way up or down, one of them had gouged a hole in my chest. Where my heart once had been was a jagged vent. My very self seemed spent.

I tried to plug the gap by forcing opportunities upon myself, but every time I pushed towards a new life my body rebelled. A few months after coming home, I began a part-time journalism course at a London college. I'd always wanted to write and at university thought nothing of sitting through two-hour classes, but my concentration was now so bad that I couldn't follow the lecturer for more than a few opening remarks on learning shorthand. I made it to two classes before quitting, and spent the rest of the summer hiding in a friend's childhood bedroom whilst her parents pretended not to notice that I wasn't studying.

Early in the morning when I should have been at college, I headed to Victoria station and walked through a pair of open gates without a plan or ticket. I took the train south until it stopped at Arundel, then I walked and walked, out into the Weald, across a land I did not know. After a few hours I stopped at a village pub, where a man bought me

pints of cider and kept me chatting at the bar. He offered me
a lift to the nearest town in his car, and I took it. My feelings
were mired in a despair so deep that any consideration of
danger could not touch them. He dropped me by the station
and, after waiting for his car to go, I walked in the opposite
direction.

By the evening I had to try to find somewhere to stay, but
the hotels were full, closed, or expensive, so I spent the night
walking across the Downs. As I plodded through the gloom,
the footpath seemed to shimmer beneath my feet, its chalky
dust ghosting my shoes and socks. At one point I passed a
military base, skirting its chain-link fence as my heart thud-
ded in guilty panic against my ribs and dogs barked at the
darkness. Eventually dawn stained the sky. Not long after, I
came across a station and took the first train back to London.
At home, my friends – and parents – were wild with anxiety at
this disappearance. It hadn't occurred to me to consider this:
my own feelings were so overwhelming that thinking about
how my actions might affect other people was beyond me.

Another day I took a train to Manningtree and left three
hours later with a tweed coat, a leather bag, and a bottle of
Calvados, none of which I could afford. Before the days of
chip and pin, you could get away with signing for things if
you were on the black edge of your overdraft at the beginning of the day, even if you'd teetered into red by the time
you stood at the shop till. Wrapped in the coat, with my
old bag stuffed into the new one, I drank that bitter apple
brandy as I cried my way home on the train.

I made several of these quests, always hoping to find
a happy version of myself, or at least trick myself into

feeling normal. One night I walked into a grubby hotel near Chichester and spent a night lying in a bath, promising to send a cheque when my card was declined at the desk. My mother eventually paid that bill for me. Another time I took myself out to lunch, gambling on my overdraft holding out until after I'd left. The bank soon caught up with me, and I was still slowly paying back the money and clearing the giddying charges for going overdrawn as I tried to buy my way back to myself. For a long time after that lonely summer, the empty Calvados bottle sat at the corner of the kitchen, a reminder of just how mad – and sad – I'd been.

I've been sitting quietly, lost in thought, and suddenly realise that Helen is asking me if I'm OK. I take a deep breath: this is the time to tell them. Trying to control the shake in my voice, I outline what happened to me in Japan. Nervous breakdown, psychiatric section, wanting to die: these aren't comfortable things to say, or hear. I keep my eyes on the fire as I talk, fiddling with the mug in my hand. When I finish I look up, and see that everyone is staring at me, unsure of what to say. Mark breaks the impasse by handing me a cigarette and, though I don't usually smoke, I am grateful for this gesture of acceptance. Helen leans forward to refill my mug with wine, and Jane, one of the other interns, stands up to hug me. In the embrace I spill my drink, and soon the moment dissolves into a flurry of laughter and dabbing cloths. As I walk back to my room an hour later, I realise a weight has fallen from my heart. Here is a place where, in one short winter evening, I already feel at home.

*

Three days after arriving, it's time to begin work. Some of us have volunteered in museums before, but being here is a far more intimate and immersive experience than spending a few days cataloguing documents. Dove Cottage is the first thing most of us see from our bedroom windows each morning and the last thing we glimpse as we draw the curtains at night. Every time we go to work we are greeted by William's image: his silhouette is the Trust's logo, appearing at the top of every letter the Trust sends, on our email footers, as well as on the signs outside the car park and the archive. Every time we come into the cottage we read that day's extract from Dorothy's journal, quotations from which also adorn fridge magnets, tea towels, and mugs in the shop. The Wordsworths are everywhere, becoming the lens through which we see this world.

As interns, we will be doing two types of jobs. First, we will help with the day-to-day running of the place: staffing the museum desk, selling tickets and gifts in the shop, and giving guided tours. Second, we will be working behind the scenes, supporting staff and visiting researchers with creating exhibitions, planning events, and preparing items for display or storage. We can choose what interests us – literature, history, contemporary poetry, art – and Jeff will arrange for us to get experience in that area. Jeff came to the Trust in the early 1980s, and over the intervening decades worked his way from trainee to curator, doing everything necessary to keep things working. Now, as the Trust's most senior employee, he has oversight of the preservation of almost the entire hamlet.

In Town End the new year begins with cleaning. Every January the Trust closes its doors to the public so that the buildings and their contents can be carefully inspected, washed if required, and repaired. We are divided into small teams, and are shown how to methodically check the treasures of the cottage and museum. Mark knows the best way to lift the Wordsworths' chests and tables in Dove Cottage so that the floors and walls beneath them can be cleaned, and he shows Catherine how to polish their pitted tops with beeswax. In the museum, Wendy and I lift letters from plastic cradles and lay them out on beanbags so that the assistant curator can examine them for evidence of damp or insects. Helen is shown how to cover the nozzle of a tiny vacuum cleaner with a stocking so that she can gently remove dust from fragile objects: a knitted pillowcase of Dorothy's, William's long grey stockings, a baby bonnet edged with lace as fine as feathers.

Once the letters have been checked, Wendy and I place them back on the plastic cradles and secure their open pages with slivers of transparent film. Dorothy and William were prolific correspondents, and the museum has hundreds of pages of their letters, both sent and received. These are some of the most fragile relics of their history, and most are not kept on permanent display. Often the handwriting on them is faded and hard to read, but I am astonished at the intimacy of having these papers in my hands, a person-to-person connection that extends beyond the author and recipient to me.

The museum is home to other treasures, including the Wordsworth family Bible. A huge leather-bound volume, its pages are laid open to show the first verses of Genesis, opposite which the names of the Wordsworth family have been written in an unacknowledged hand. The use of the Bible as a witness and necessary record of family history was widespread before systematic state record-keeping was developed in the nineteenth century, as a Bible was often the only book in a family's personal library. Beside the name of each member is their birthday and their date of death. Short lives reduced to two lines of hand-looped letters: Ann was thirty when she died; John forty-two.[8] Five children orphaned. Succinct tragedies in ink.

At the time of his death in 1783, John Wordsworth was living in the large house on Cockermouth's main street where his children had been born. The building was provided by his employer; as law-agent for Sir James Lowther, First Earl of Lonsdale, part of John's role was to entertain those upon whom Lowther wished to exert political influence. At the time, 'Wicked Jimmy' had several boroughs in his pocket, including Cockermouth. Nine MPs in the House of Commons were under his control, and John Wordsworth's account includes the settling of bills for £24,000 (over £2 million in today's money) under the murky heading 'election expenses'. The Wordsworths' home, with its high-ceiled entertaining rooms and fine carpets, was designed to impress, and Lowther recalled the property immediately upon hearing of his agent's death.

John Wordsworth's death not only made orphans of his children, it made homeless indigents of them too. Unusually for a lawyer, he died intestate. John's brother Richard Wordsworth and his brother-in-law Christopher Cookson had to apply to the courts for letters of administration to sort out his estate on behalf of his children. As well as managing his employer's affairs, John had been politic in acquiring land and property in his own name – resulting in him being owed a lot of money by both tenants and the Earl. At the time of John's death, 'Wicked Jimmy' was indebted to his agent for £4,625 (the equivalent of £400,000 today[9]) from both unpaid bills for work completed and cash spent on his behalf. Chasing these debts would occupy John's surviving relatives for much of the following two decades.

Though her mother's death in 1778 removed her from her immediate family, the moment of true 'homelessness' came for Dorothy nine years later. In May 1787, her Cookson grandparents decided that the time had come for their teen-age granddaughter to finish her formal education, so they summoned her from Halifax to live with them in Penrith. Despite having hardly seen Dorothy since Ann's death, they decided it was time for her to earn her keep by joining their household and assisting in its upkeep. It could have been a kind of homecoming – Dorothy was after all the only daughter of their only daughter, and had spent many months living in Penrith at her grandparents' house when Ann was alive – but instead this would-be repatriation only showed Dorothy the extent of her division from her family.

Dorothy remembered her grandparents as critical, petty, and dismissive of their grandchildren's needs. Not only was Dorothy not allowed to light a fire for her own sake in their house, but she found that there was 'so little of ten-derness ... or anything affectionate' in her grandmother's manner that she wrote 'whilst I am in her house I cannot

at all consider myself as at home'. It is a cruel paradox
that Dorothy's reconnection with her blood relations was
the thing that made her feel most homeless, most like an
orphan. In a letter to Jane Pollard, Dorothy states the impact
of such cool indifference: 'Never, till I came to Penrith, did
I feel the loss I sustained when I was deprived of a Father.'
She found '[t]he cold insensibility of my Grandmother
and the ill-nature of my Grandfather'[10] very hard to bear;
little about this return to her natal county felt like a
homecoming.

Her uncles Christopher and William also shared the
house, and whilst William encouraged his niece in her education, spending time teaching her French and providing
her with books, 'Uncle Kit' was a figure feared and hated.
Christopher had been appointed one of the guardians of
the Wordsworth children upon John's death, but he was
a greedy tyrant who took a stern and controlling attitude
towards his orphaned niece and nephews. He kept precise
notes of everything spent on them, whilst at the same time
using their estate as a petty cash box, eventually owing it
around £4,000.[11] In the summer of 1787, he 'forgot' to send
horses and a carriage to Hawkshead to collect his nephews
at the end of term – something for which neither Dorothy
nor William ever forgave him.

Yet that summer did provide Dorothy with the possibility
of homely belonging. Returning to Penrith brought renewed
friendship in the form of the neighbours Mary and Margaret
Hutchinson. The eldest daughters of a family of ten children,[12] the Hutchinsons had been, like the Wordsworths,
orphaned young and brought up by relations. They had been

contemporaries at Ann Birkett's dame school in Penrith, attended by the Wordsworths when staying with their grandparents, and when Dorothy returned from Halifax, they renewed their schoolroom friendship ('the only *agreeable* Variety which Penrith could afford'[13]). It was a close, confiding relationship, where they 'compared grievances and lamented the misfortune of losing [their] parents at an early age and being thrown upon the mercy of ill-natured and illiberal relations'.[14] In the evenings the three girls 'used to steal out to each other's houses' to have 'our talk over the kitchen fire', and Dorothy noted that these meetings ended with reluctance as the girls would 'delay the moment of parting [as they] paced up one street and down another by moon or starlight'.

In June 1787 William, John, and Christopher arrived at Penrith, and the siblings were reunited at last. Dorothy wrote to Jane a short while after her brothers' arrival to declare them 'just the boys I could wish them, they are so affectionate and so kind to me as to make me love them more and more every day'.[15] The Wordsworths spent long hours exploring the area around Penrith, often in the company of the Hutchinsons. They climbed Penrith Beacon, with its views towards Scotland in one direction and of the Lakeland fells in another, and explored the banks of the river Eamont and the grounds of Brougham Castle. The siblings also discussed their financial situation, family, and plans for their future. Dorothy wrote that '[m]any a time have William, John, Christopher, and myself shed tears together, tears of the bitterest sorrow, we all of us, each day, feel more sensibly the loss we sustained'. Yet the

Wordsworth brothers had remained together – the greater loss was Dorothy's.

Working in the museum brings us hand to hand with the manuscripts of William's poetry, the earliest surviving of which dates from around the time of the Wordsworths' Penrith reunion. Encouraged by his teachers (and having had some success with his 'Sonnet on Seeing Miss Helen Maria Williams Weep at a Tale of Distress', which had been published in *European Magazine*[16]), in the spring of 1787 William began a poem about his Hawkshead childhood. Though it was never finished, and was published for the first time only in 1940, 'The Vale of Esthwaite' is important because it shows us what the adolescent William felt about this place – without the distorting lens of adult memory.

'The Vale' was written in two sections, the first before June 1787 and the second that summer. The poem opens with an image of a lark singing by the lake as morning mist hangs across the valley. The top of a nearby hill appears like 'an island in the air', and into this pastoral scene comes a shepherd boy, whose heart gladdens at seeing smoke rising from his cottage chimney. After twenty lines the poem darkens: gone 'is the lark and the dewy dawn', replaced by 'gloomy glades, Religious woods and midnight shades'. Though it appears a paradise, for William, Esthwaite valley is plagued with spectres.

Woodsmoke hangs 'like a Spirit on its way', owls moan and scream in the darkness, and the chain of a 'Fisher's skiff' rattles against its moorings. Here we find William deep in Gothic fantasies of human sacrifice and damp dungeons peopled by 'Strange forms ... white and tall'. Spirits are 'yelling from their pains' and the sound lures the poet close to a swamp where he beholds a 'grisly Phantom' with 'eyes of fire'. The idyll is revealed to be a haunted place, and William fears that his soul will either 'melt away with fear' or become so 'swelled to madness' that he will throw himself from a cliff. Imagination has brought the valley alive – not with happy memories, but with ghosts of folk and fairy tales.

After returning to Hawkshead from Penrith in August 1787 to prepare for Cambridge, William continued to work on 'The Vale of Esthwaite' – but the events of the summer had given him a different perspective on the place. The first section of 'The Vale' focused on the sensations of sublime fear and terror that Esthwaite evoked in William, but the reunion with Dorothy had brought about changes in William's understanding of the broader family's experiences and memories. When William returned to the poem, its tone shifted, and what had been a teenage Gothic fantasy became a portrayal of the keen truth of grief. The emotional power of renewing this relationship had a profound effect on William and the poetry he wrote.

The second section of 'The Vale' begins with a vivid account of William's experience of and reaction to his father's illness and death four years earlier. As winter winds whistled through a hawthorn hedge and sheep sought shelter, William, aged thirteen, stood alone on the rocks above Hawkshead, scanning the road below for a glimpse of his father's horse. It was a long and lonely vigil, one made with 'swimming eyes'. When the horse finally did arrive, it was to take William and his brothers to their father's deathbed. This is a memory pierced with desolation; the whole world is 'wintry', 'sharp', 'poor', 'cold', and 'bitter'.

Following conversations with Dorothy, William reflected on what this sorrow meant – not just for himself, but for his family. He noted that in remembering how he kept watch alone that cold December, he could relieve himself of 'the mighty debt of Grief', and he now contrasted this grieving with a sense of someone else's loss. A few months earlier, he had not considered another person's viewpoint, but now he found he could not omit it. 'She lost a home in losing thee,' he wrote, and 'She', of course, is Dorothy.

Dorothy's view of her role within the family at this time was as a tragic figure. 'Poor Dorothy' is how she referred to herself, flung upon the untender mercies of the Cooksons and deprived of the prospect of financial or personal independence not only by her youth but also by the problems with her father's estate. Her emotions were intense, dramatic, all-consuming – and familiar to her brother. Though loss and grief had been powerful forces in their early lives, in each other William and Dorothy found something to sustain them:

> 'What from the social chain can tear
> This bosom link'd for ever there
> Which feels whene'er the hand of pain
> Touches this heav'n connected chain
> Feels quick as thought the electric thrill
> Feels it ah me—and shudders still?'[17]

From this point, the siblings felt a kinship of sensibility that would define their adult lives.

'The Vale' also gives us the first glimpse of Grasmere through William's eyes. As a teenager, he spent a day walking from Hawkshead to Grasmere and back, a journey of about thirteen miles. As William walked down Red Bank, the hill that edges Grasmere's south-western side, the view of the valley dazzled him. Below lay a small, round lake, surrounded by woods and meadows: 'lovely *Grasmere's* heav'nly vale'. William sat among 'the wild field flow'rs' and lost himself in combining these 'sweet scenes' with 'faery dreams' of his imagination. Grasmere's living patchwork appeared to the teenage William like Paradise, and sowed the seed of a dream – not of Eden, but of a real place which, from this early encounter, offered him beauty, comfort, and imaginative stimulation.

3

These Living Mountains

'Happily we cannot shape the huge hills,
or carve out the valleys according to
our fancy.'

Dorothy Wordsworth, *Alfoxden Journal*,
15 April 1798[1]

In Suffolk, where no land rises more than 150 metres above the sea, your vision is bounded by the sky. Weather approaches visibly: cumulonimbus castles warn of storms, and hazy mackerel cloud-flakes drift from the sea promising change. East Anglian mountains are made and dissolved above your head, impermanent monoliths that form, reform, and float away, high above the porridge of sand, clay, and flint that constitutes the earth in this flat corner of the country.

Cumbria's mountains, on the other hand, are real, close, and adamantine. They demark each valley's natural perimeter, shrinking the sky to a handkerchief square. Grasmere is edged on every side by Loughrigg, Silver How, Helm Crag, and Dunmail Raise, and these hills will be the bounds of my new territory. Their hard sides frame the world, and to me their proximity feels claustrophobic. When I left Suffolk, I made a pact with my mother to give it a month and if I wasn't coping, I'd come home. Now I'm here, I want to feel that I can leave at will and remain connected to what lies at the other end of the paths that snake across the hillsides.

The hills in central Cumbria are the highest in England. Four summits rise above 3,000 feet, and mountain slopes cover around 900 square miles of the county. Primaeval seas once covered this land, leaving deposits of their life forms, and ancient volcanoes shaped this landscape. Slates grey, black, blue, and green now cut through the hills, mixing with lime- and sandstone. Copper, lead, and iron once veined these mountains, minerals long since dug out with picks or blasted from the rocks with dynamite. In winter the high peaks are often hidden by low cloud, but on clear days they rise, mantled imperiously with snow and mist, to command the heavens with the certainty of gods.

They even have their own name: fells. Though I've spoken English all my life, I'd only seen that word in print before I came to Grasmere. I had thought *fell* belonged to the waxy lexicon of poetry, but here I hear it everywhere, as unremarkable a word as pond or hedge or field. Fells echo round the staffroom as colleagues chat about their weekends, and call to me from bookshelves in the library and pump clips in the pub. At first I feel self-conscious saying the word 'fell' myself, wary of intimating an affectation to familiarity, but soon I realise that there is no better word to accurately describe these mountains.

Fell is an old word, first brought to the British Isles by the Norse. In Norwegian, Swedish, and Danish, *fjell*, *fjäll*, and *fjeld* are respectively terms used specifically for mountain areas where trees struggle to flourish. In England, fells are particular to the North-West, to the old counties of Westmorland and Cumberland, and the northern tips of Lancashire and Yorkshire. Originally *fell* meant high land beyond the treeline, rich with the promise of the wild. Fell soil cannot easily be cultivated and so is usually covered in moss, heather, bracken, and other low-growing plants. 'Frith' was the term for marginal woodland that often abutted this wilder land. 'Fell and frith', once a common figure of speech like 'up hill and down dale', contrasted two fundamental land types, but both words feel almost obsolete today.

Whilst I feel hemmed in by hills, Emily – the other intern from Suffolk – is full of exhilaration at their promise of adventure. Pinned on her wall is an old Ordnance Survey map of the central Lakes, its tallest summits picked out in red. She wants to become their familiar, to learn to recognise one sharp-edged sister from another. Eager to make the fells' acquaintance, Emily asks Mark what walks she can do from the door. The lumpy bulk beyond Dove Cottage is Nab Scar, he says, gesturing with a roll-up. Then it rises to become Lord Crag, and beyond that, Heron Pike and Great Rigg. If you follow the fells far enough, they turn back on themselves, and the wheel of mountains becomes the Fairfield Horseshoe. The tang of their names is lively on his tongue. I repeat them in my head, trying to pick up the knack of sounding like I know them. 'I'm going up there,' Emily says, and Mark tells her that if she goes as far as Alcock Tarn she'll be able to see the whole valley spread out below. 'Come with me?' Emily asks, and I hesitate, unsure of myself, but before my head can think of a plausible excuse, I'm pulling on my wellies, stuffing a bar of chocolate into my coat pocket, and following Emily up the coffin path.

Coffin path, corpse road, lych way – these names allude to this path's long-time use as the last roadway for the dead as they made their final journey to Grasmere's graveyard. There was no church in Rydal until the nineteenth century, so before then anyone who died there would be brought to St Oswald's church at Grasmere to be buried. Friends, neighbours, and relations of the deceased would shoulder the deadweight burden and bring the corpse to the village centre. Dorothy saw such a bearing in her first year of living in Dove Cottage. The Dawsons at How Top Farm hosted the funeral of pauper Susan Shadrake in September 1800, and men from the village bore her body down the corpse road to the churchyard. Dorothy wept at the sight of the coffin, moved not by the death itself (she had not known Susan), but by the contrast between the solitary body lying without relatives to mourn her and the bright, beautiful day on which she was laid to rest in this serene valley.

Emily and I turn off the lych way at Brackenfell, walking under oaks and firs that shade the path. Below us we can see the southern edge of Grasmere lake, and beyond it the snow-strewn flanks of Silver How. The lake makes a mirror of the hills and sky, doubling the clouds and sunshine until the whole place alternately glows and glowers, its mood changing with the wind. Water is everywhere, the fellside scored by streams cutting their way through the rocks. The Syke, Dunney Beck, Tongue Gill – new names for icy danger, for necessary waters.

After we've been walking uphill for a while, we stop beside a small pond and Emily turns to me and asks, 'Is this the tarn?' I answer with a breathless shrug – I do not know what a 'tarn' is, much less if this is the one we seek. This new-to-me world speaks an unfamiliar language. Sundry small particulars of a place require precise description, and *tarn*, like *fell*, has its origins in the Nordic world. Rooted in the Old Norse *tarnu*, meaning 'mountain lake', its earliest recorded use in English comes from the Westmorland assize roll of 1256. Cumbrian place names are distinct, retaining their connection to the ninth-century Norse, who saw similarities between their old and new homelands, and tarn remains the linguistic sister of Swedish *tjärn*, Norwegian *tjörn*, and Danish *tjern*.

All newcomers go through a process of learning the names of – and naming – the world around them. Place names often record this history like a palimpsest, as in the old tautologies of the river Avon, Bredon Hill, the Isle of Insh. Identical meanings are overlaid to make new names: Avon comes from the old Brythonic *abon*, meaning 'river'. In Scots Gaelic Insh means island, so the Isle of Insh duplicates the old name with the new. Bredon Hill is a triplicate tautology, combining Brythonic 'bre' with Old English 'don', which both mean hill, with the later addition of 'Hill' to distinguish the landform from the village borrowing its name. Finding the right word is not just satisfying, it is essential. If we cannot accurately describe the world around us, we run the risk of getting lost, of failing to see threat – or safety – in the landscape.

Following this track as it cuts along the hillside, I teach Emily the Japanese I learned that relates to Japan's forested mountain landscapes. Volcano is *kazan*, meaning 'fire mountain'. Goats are *yagi* – literally, 'mountain sheep'. Then there's *komorebi*, which has no equivalent in English, but describes the way light is filtered through the forest canopy, and *kogarashi* – cold winds that shake the leaves down from the trees. Emily's a poet, and immediately begins to make up some translations. We laugh at *shakebreeze*, play with *susuradiance*, and enjoy the feel of *leaflight* on our tongues.

I began to learn Japanese when I was twelve, the year I started high school. In our first few weeks, my best friend and I joined several new clubs – orchestra, choir, cricket – but the most exciting was Gonenkai. Meaning 'fifth-year club', Gonenkai was a lunchtime group run by a dedicated and enterprising maths teacher called Mary-Grace Browning. Its mission was to give young people in Suffolk the chance not just to learn Japanese, but to actually go to Japan – without having to pay for it from their own pockets. In 1999, it was as revolutionary an enterprise as it was when it had been founded by Mrs Browning thirty years earlier. As part of our membership, we hosted Japanese students in our homes and fundraised for the club. For five years we went on sponsored walks, ran cake sales, and just before Christmas every year stayed up all night to make a thousand origami cranes, which would be taken by the oldest members of the club that year to Hiroshima's Peace Memorial Park and left at the Children's Monument there as a wish for peace.

Learning Japanese was also a fundamental part of Gonenkai. For five years we studied the language during lunchbreaks and after school, after which everyone sat a GCSE Japanese examination. Fortunately, our performance did not determine whether we got to go to Japan, as the results came out only after our return. Going to Japan was a reward for welcoming people to England, not a prize to be won only by those who excelled at this very different language.

In Japanese there are three alphabets to master: two syllabaries, *hiragana* and *katakana*, and one system of pictograms originating from Chinese, known as *kanji*. Our teacher Mrs Browning began our first lesson by handing out a sheet of these little pictures. First there was a mountain, made of three simple pen strokes (山). Then there was a tree, its straight trunk and regular branches reduced to four straight lines (木). Two sticks licked with flames meant fire (火), and three rushing lines were a river (川). Then we were shown how each picture was joined with others to enhance its meaning: two trees meant a wood (林), three became a forest (森), and a tree with roots meant something's source (本). These were *kanji*, and within an hour of being introduced to them I was entranced by their minute, complex beauty. These tiny, beautiful riddles seemed a gateway to another world.

Nine years after that first lesson, I was scouring a map of Japan, looking for my new home. Seventy-three per cent of Japan's land is mountains, and most is dense, uninhabitable forest. The country's 125 million people live mostly on the islands' seaward fringes, where the sea's bounty is at hand but there is enough soil to till and space to live. I was asked if I would prefer an urban, suburban, or rural area, and I picked 'rural'. After three years of studying in a city, I was keen to be in the countryside. A few months later I was making my new home in Kikugawa. Most people went out of their way to welcome me. My house became full of little gifts: bags of oranges and persimmons, packets of unfamiliar sweets, even a handmade wooden box full of clinking bottles containing homemade plum wine. I may not have shared a mother tongue with my neighbours, but the language of generosity and kindness is universal.

Chief among these benefactors were Mr and Mrs Fujino. The Fujinos lived opposite my apartment in a tall, red-painted farmhouse they shared with their adult daughter and her children. From our first meeting, they were my self-appointed protectors. The morning after I arrived Mrs Fujino was waiting for me, her face creasing into welcome as I opened my front door. She pressed a soft bundle into my hand, and motioned to her forehead. I didn't understand her gesture and bowed uncertainly in response, but when I took the package inside to open it – in Japan, gifts are not usually opened in front of the giver – I found a packet of hand-stitched cloths, each in its own patchwork bag, beautifully made from softest cotton.

The Fujinos spoke little English, and this was before the days of spontaneous electronic translation, so to communicate we relied on a mixture of my schoolgirl Japanese, mime, and frequent consultations of the *denshi-jishō*, an electronic pocket dictionary. Mr Fujino, a sincere and educated man who had recently retired from his role as prefectural archaeologist, would spend several minutes painstakingly looking up word after word, before solemnly imparting to me a highly detailed, if grammatically unusual, piece of information about a kind of roof tile, flowering plant, or wayside shrine. His view was that nothing should be too difficult for me to grasp and that, although my Japanese was halting and peculiar, there was no reason why I shouldn't learn the word for funeral rite, atmospheric pressure, or caldera basin.

Mrs Fujino and I communicated mostly in a language beyond words. Reassuring smiles, pats on my arm, and a cornucopia of little gifts were her mothering tongue. No week went by without her appearing at my apartment with a packet of noodles, a box of sweets, or sometimes a bag of still-warm buns fresh from the oven. I learned to recognise the squeak of the Fujinos' mosquito screen as it swung open, and I'd race to pull on something tidy and be on my doorstep to thank her before she disappeared back into the house.

The Fujinos' daughter and grandchildren were quite shy and often busied themselves elsewhere in the house when I came round, but Mrs Fujino always ushered me to the table in the tiny kitchen and gave me tea or a cold drink, and often something small to snack on. She would talk rapidly as she worked, often reaching across to squeeze my shoulder or pat my cheek in a friendly gesture. I found her Japanese more difficult to understand than her husband's – it was fast and full of dialect, and I often wasn't sure I'd understood her – but the warmth of her welcome usually encouraged me to believe that she was happy to see me.

I needed Mrs Fujino's friendly reassurance. To not be Japanese but to live in Japan is to be a statistical anomaly: you are physically, linguistically, and culturally different from almost everyone around you. Japan has a notoriously strict immigration policy: only 2% of its 125 million inhabitants are not Japanese. In contrast, around 14% of the 67 million people who live in the UK were not born there.

I thought I had a reasonable grasp of Japanese, but even though I had mastered the basics, much of what happened around me was confusing, even mysterious. Japanese has several registers not found in English; what is appropriate for a situation varies with the age and status of both speaker and audience, and these nuances are reflected not just in vocabulary, but also in grammar. Children start by learning the casual forms of verbs used within a family. When they begin school, they need to develop a further, more formal register to show the appropriate amount of respect for their teachers. Once they are in the world of work, there is an even more decorous mode of speech to master: *keigo*, 're-spectful language', which oils the wheels of professional communication. Japanese also has several regional dialects, so words I heard around me in the village would be unfamiliar to someone from another part of Japan, much less another country.

I had been taught *teineigo*: polite, everyday Japanese acceptable in most situations. However, I was now teaching young children, who usually only knew the unfamiliar, informal version of the verbs I thought I knew. To go, to look, to eat: suddenly I didn't have the bricks-and-mortar speech I thought I'd mastered. I could order food in a cafe or talk to my colleagues about their hobbies, but trying to ask a child to pass a pencil was beyond me.

I also found I could barely read. Not just books or reports at work, but even simple things like road signs were often incomprehensible to me. Japanese place names are usually written exclusively in non-phonetic *kanji*, so even though I knew and could say the names of where I wanted to go, I couldn't necessarily identify them from their Chinese pictograms. Suddenly I wasn't just a slow reader, I was almost illiterate. Everyone else could see that the big grey building was the local government office and the left fork at a junction took you to the tip, but I felt like I was navigating using a map without a legend. Symbols were everywhere, but I only knew a handful, and frequently not enough to orientate myself in this unfamiliar landscape.

Every Monday the Fujinos took me to Japanese lessons in the city of Shimonoseki, where I worked hard to pair up the words and phrases I'd heard around me with the correct combination of *kanji* and *kana*. We were supposed to practise conversation too, but I preferred to hide in written words. I wasn't fluent enough to make or understand a joke, or to express myself in anything more complex than a two-phrase sentence. At home my language had been not just an expression of who I was, it *was* me. Without humour or the ability to tell others what was on my mind, I felt like half a person. As the months passed, my sense of self shrank to a skeleton. Who was I? I found I was no longer able to answer that question. Unmoored from my mother tongue, I couldn't resurrect myself.

*

Soon we are above the treeline. The path is steeper now and before long our lungs are burning. The unfamiliarity of the fells is as physical as it is linguistic: this is unlike any walk you could ever take in Suffolk. Emily leads the way and I follow, trying not to show how much I'm sweating. The path has become a staircase, rimed in ice that makes each footstep doubly hard won. The thick tread of Emily's boots confers advantage on this ground. I slip and slide in wellies. Until now the route has been clear, but halfway up the fell-side it divides, with one branch leading north and the other west, and so we stop to check our position.

Beside me Emily unfolds her map, but the wind immediately catches it like a sail, turning it into a paper billow of possibility. I weight one side whilst Emily wrestles the folds back to show the part we need. Before I came here, I never took much notice of which direction was north or south, east or west. I had hardly ever read a map, and because I could not drive, I often relied on other people to take me where I needed to go. Having a specific sense of my place within a landscape hadn't been important before, but now I need to be able to read the land to help me find the best way across the fells.

The map shows a footpath leading to the long lake at Thirlmere that lies to our north, and we see that the right-turning fork of this path is ours. We press on up the fellside, but suddenly the regular thud of Emily's footsteps ceases, and I hurry to see what's stopped her. There, up on this wild hillside, is a manhole cover. There are no houses needing drains up here – so what, then, is this? We peer at the rusted top, picking out the words 'Manchester Corporation' in the

ochred metal. At first all we can hear is silence, but as the
pounding of my heart slows I hear the distant whoosh of
water, like a faraway river. Beneath us is a pipeline taking
water from nearby Thirlmere to Manchester. Half of the
city's drinking water rushes from these fells.

There has always been water at Thirlmere. Its name means
'pierced' or 'binding' water, and what is now one lake had
once been two, a body each to the north and south joined
by a narrow waist of water. At the end of the nineteenth century, the lakes were turned into a single massive reservoir
to supply the Thirlmere Aqueduct with fresh water. The
aqueduct, then as now, carries 220 million litres of clean
water on a 95-mile journey that takes two days. There are no
pumps or pressurising stations to help it on its way; instead,
gravity alone moves the water at a speed of four miles per
hour – about the pace of a brisk walk. Thirlmere lies below
the swelling bulk of Helvellyn, the third highest peak in
England, taking the western catchment of its watershed,
where over a metre of rain falls every year. Becks, burns,
and gills all feed the lake, swelling it with their water every
winter. But in hot summers some of these dry up, the water
level drops, and the bottom of the lake offers up old secrets.

Thirlmere holds a drowned world. When planning the
reservoir, Bradford-born engineer John Frederick Bateman
calculated that the level of Thirlmere would need to
be raised by thirty-five feet to ensure a continuous and
adequate supply for most of Manchester. Such an increase
in capacity would swallow up fields, roads, and houses at
the lake's south-western side and at the narrow middle

where Wath Bridge stood. Two roads used to run along the lake, vital arteries for a scattering of hamlets and small farms: Wythburn, Armboth, May Green, Bank, and The City. Their flat fertile fields lined the valley bottom – but Armboth is no longer there, and all that's left of Wythburn is its church. Small and simple, its thick stone walls are painted white and a tiny bell hangs in the bellcote, waiting to summon congregations as it did long ago. A place of worship has stood on that site since 1554, on the high ground preferred by early masons for its stability and surety from flooding. It proved to be a sound choice, for almost everything else of what was Wythburn now lies beneath the water. Soon after the dam's first stone was laid in 1890, water rushed in to wash away the villages. The wood-covered rocky outcrops at Hawes and Deergarth became islands in a lake of urban need, and now it is only in the hottest, driest summers that the ruins of the old buildings become visible.

What we are looking at, high upon the fellside, is a cover that allows a person to enter the pipeline. The tunnel was designed with self-closing safety valves which automatically shut off the flow of water if the aqueduct cannot cope with a sudden increase in water volume (for example, following heavy rainfall), so as not to flood the towns and cities further down its course. Once a year these need to be reopened manually, and later Mark tells us a story about a man who drowned when a valve failed and water rushed along the tunnel as he 'walked the line'. That was years ago, but someone still must go down into the earth to check the pipes.

Below us the road snakes on to Keswick, a modern approximation of the route taken by the Wordsworths. The old road was well known to Richard, William, John, and Christopher, who would have passed through Grasmere as they travelled between Cockermouth and Hawkshead on their way to and from school, but there is no record of Dorothy coming to Grasmere until after she turned twenty-one, six years after the teenage Wordsworths' reunion in Penrith.

Following that halcyon summer of 1787, the Wordsworth siblings resumed their separate lives. Eldest brother Richard continued his apprenticeship to a lawyer cousin in Branthwaite, Cumberland; William returned first to Hawkshead before leaving that autumn to begin university in Cambridge. John, the least academic of the brothers, left Penrith to start work as a sailor on a ship captained by another Wordsworth cousin, whilst thirteen-year-old Christopher went back to Hawkshead to complete his schooling. Dorothy remained in Penrith until the death of her grandmother Cookson in 1788, after which she moved to Forncett St Peter Rectory in Norfolk with her favourite uncle William Cookson and his wife (also Dorothy), where William had secured a curacy.

A phrase Dorothy uses repeatedly in her letters to describe the Wordsworth siblings' situation at this time is 'squandered abroad',[2] a phrase borrowed from *The Merchant of Venice* meaning to be scattered widely, or to be away from one's home. It is a poignant phrase for Dorothy; though only John is away from England for any significant time (he made long voyages to India and the West Indies throughout the late 1780s and '90s), the remaining siblings are separated from each other.

Our language relating to the home carries the implication of ordinariness or unimportance. To describe something as 'homely' is to emphasise its plain or unprepossessing character. 'Homemade' or 'homespun' can carry the tang of amateur imperfection. 'Domestic' retains the same nuance: small-scale, small interest. Yet feeling 'at home' is to be comfortable, relaxed, accepted. To have a home is to belong; to not have one can spell disaster, foreboding a lifetime of searching. By the time they were teenagers, the Wordsworths were all effectively homeless because nowhere guaranteed them safe haven – and the search for such a place was to preoccupy Dorothy, William, and John throughout the coming years.

Between 1787 and 1794 William and Dorothy met only twice. The first time was in Cambridge in October 1788, as Dorothy and the Cooksons travelled to their new home in Norfolk. As an unmarried teenage niece, Dorothy's responsibilities there would be to teach Sunday school, look after the Cookson babies (one of whom arrived almost every year following the move), and tend to the garden and chickens. She also continued her studies and got to know her aunt and uncle's friends, including the abolitionist William Wilberforce, whose work she fervently supported and who in turn gave her money to donate to charitable causes of her choosing.

The second time was in 1789, during the university vacation, when William came to stay at Forncett, where the siblings reaffirmed the bonds between them that had developed at Penrith. William and Dorothy spent hours each afternoon pacing the rectory garden and talking, before going out together in the evenings to explore Norfolk on foot. The psychological impact of their developing relationship echoed the 'electric thrill' William had described in 'The Vale of Esthwaite' two years earlier. Dorothy delighted in this connection, but also noted that there were two emotional lodestars in her life, writing to Jane Pollard that 'Love will never bind me closer to any human Being than Friendship binds me to you my earliest female Friend, and to William my earliest and my dearest Male Friend.'[3]

Whilst Dorothy's inner life was bound up jointly with Jane and her brother, William was developing his own sense of himself, his needs, and his desires. After a promising first year at Cambridge (1787–8), William became increasingly disillusioned with academic work. The Cambridge curriculum focused on studying and translating classical authors, most of whom William had already encountered in the Hawkshead schoolroom. Realising that revisiting these authors would not hold his interest, William decided to create his own curriculum, centred on learning Italian and translating poetry not on the syllabus, including works by Virgil and Horace. He also continued to write poems, and in October 1788, around the time Dorothy and the Cooksons briefly visited him in Cambridge, began to work on verses later published as 'An Evening Walk'.

Dedicated to Dorothy, this poem paints a picture of William travelling, in his mind's eye, through the Lake District. Rich in topographical description and physical sensation, it transports its reader (and its author) into the Cumbrian landscape, revelling in a shared sense of oneness with the mountains, villages, and woods. 'An Evening Walk' (first published in

1793) also reinforces William's conception of Grasmere as a prototype 'happy valley' as portrayed in 'The Vale'. The poem contrasts the roaring waterfalls at Lodore with the 'peace [that leads] to Grasmere's lonely island' and its surrounding valley edged by 'willowy hedge-rows' and 'emerald meads'.[4]

The poem's other keynotes are loss and absence, and descriptions of the passing of childhood ('in youth's keen eye the livelong day was bright') are accompanied by an exploration of how the natural world enhances and reflects these losses. In contrast with the gloomy 'The Vale of Esthwaite', written only a year or two earlier, the place is reimagined as a lost idyll for 'a happy child' whose explorations 'endear my Esthwaite's shore, And memory of departed pleasures, more'. Though a sense of loss remains, 'An Evening Walk' replaces the Gothic-haunted, grieving child of 'The Vale' with an image of a young boy of prelapsarian innocence as he with 'thoughtless gaiety ... coursed the plain, And hope itself was all [he] knew of pain'. The loss of a father has been translated into the loss of childhood, of somewhere to belong.

The other palpable absence in the poem is Dorothy. Her distance from the poet and the landscape frames the poem (it is dedicated 'To a Young Lady' and its author describes himself as 'Far from my dearest Friend'), yet central to the poem's message is the promise of her presence in the future, embodied by a cottage whose walls catch the evening sun and '[w]here we, my Friend, to golden days shall rise'.[5] To be in this place with the poem's dedicatee is the poet's 'Sole bourn, sole wish, sole object of [his] way', a desire repeated in a letter William wrote to Dorothy that same year when he described the life they will have 'when we have stolen to our little cottage!'⁶

As well as dreaming of cosy cottages, William yearned for adventure. In the summer of 1790, he made a six-week walking tour through central Europe with his friend Robert Jones. Dorothy was not informed of his plans until they were under way; it was the time of the French Revolution (Robert and William arrived in time to see the first Fête de la Fédération on 14 July), and France was viewed as a dangerous place, though its Alpine scenery made a greater impression on William than contemporary politics. As he walked through the mountains, Dorothy was never far from his mind. He wrote to her 'I have thought of you perpetually; and never have my eyes burst upon a scene of particular loveliness but I have almost instantly wished that you could for a moment be transported to the place where I stood to enjoy it.'⁷ Both siblings dreamed of a shared future, but how would they make this a reality?

After returning from France, William unenthusiastically completed his degree in 1791, then spent a few indolent months in London with his brother Richard. It was not a happy time: William described the '*strenua inertia*'⁸ he felt at living in the city, reliant on his brother's largesse and unable to make much progress with his own vocation as a poet. After several indolent months, William returned to France in 1792. This time he went alone, and fell in love. He and Annette Vallon met at Blois, became lovers, and not long after Annette became pregnant with their child.

Returning to London in the teeth of revolutionary war a few months later – and shortly before the birth of his daughter Anne-Caroline – William once again had to confront his lack of money and career. His financial situation was precarious: he had no regular income, owed money to family and friends, and now had a common-law wife and child to support. His education fitted him for the traditional middle-class professions of church or law, but William wanted neither: 'What will become of me I know not, I cannot bow my mind down to take orders, and as for the law I have neither strength of mind, purse, or constitution to engage in that pursuit.'[9] He turned down the offer of a curacy, procured by Uncle William Cookson following the news that his nephew was to become a father, which led to a rift within the family. William was banned from visiting his uncle's house – which effectively meant also not seeing Dorothy, as she was still living there.

William was determined to be an author, and in January 1793 finally succeeded in publishing the two poems he had been working on since his early days at Cambridge. 'An Evening Walk' and 'Descriptive Sketches', a lyric based on William's earlier Alpine walking tour, were printed – but not rapturously received. William remarked to his university friend William Mathews that these poems 'have been treated with unmerited contempt by some of the periodical publications', and even Dorothy, who remained William's staunchest supporter despite her uncle's disapproval of him, thought they could be improved. She and their younger brother Christopher made a 'very bulky criticism'[10] of the poems, which they sent to William – who no doubt did not receive it with ecstatic gratitude.

Dorothy's criticism was pragmatic as well as literary. Although Dorothy had previously assured Jane Pollard that she was 'perfectly happy at Forncett',[11] by February 1793 this had changed, in part due to the feud between the two Williams. She had reached her majority on Christmas Day 1792 and was busy in the Cookson house but, 'kind as are my Uncle and Aunt, much as I love my sweet little Cousins', she finds that she 'cannot help heaving many a Sigh' as she realises that she has 'passed one and twenty years of my Life, and the first six years only of this Time were spent in the Enjoyment of the same Pleasures that were enjoyed by my Brothers'.[12] Her only chance to leave her aunt and uncle's household was if another relative could support her – as a woman without private income, and with the small inheritance she was due from her father still legally inaccessible, she had almost no autonomy over the direction of her life. Without someone else to support her, Dorothy would remain reliant on the clemency and approval of the Cooksons, so if William continued to write unpopular poetry, he would never earn enough to be financially independent of their relations – and thus she would never be indepenent of them either.

Dorothy's chief desire was to be together with Jane Pollard and William. Her daydreams were of sharing a companionable autonomy, where the three 'erect a little cottage and call it our own'. However, throughout the winter of 1793–4 Dorothy was thwarted in her attempts to visit, much less live with, either William or Jane. She waited at Forncett for a suitable escort (a Mr Griffith) to accompany her on a visit to Yorkshire or London; Mr Griffith disappointed, but eventually she made it to Halifax and the home of her aunt (now Mrs Rawson; Elizabeth Threlkeld had married in

1791) in January 1794. William soon joined her there – but for all that Dorothy regarded Halifax as the place most like home to her, she and William were to remain there for only a few weeks.

What the Wordsworths were seeking was not only kin but *kith*: a sense of being in their rightful place. Kith means one's own country, one's individual acreage. It refers not necessarily to land owned, but to somewhere a person feels that they belong, a place which is somehow part of themselves: the metaphorical cosiness of 'hearth and home' translated into landscape. A descendant of the word lives on in Scots, where *couthie* – meaning full of friendly warmth and familiarity – ties people to a sense of place. William and Dorothy had found blood-red kin in each other's company, but the suburban bustle of Halifax did not suit them. The Penrith reunion had given the two siblings half a sense of self, a yearning kinship recognised in 'The Vale of Esthwaite', but the years spent in London, Cambridge, and France made William realise another loss: that of his (albeit adopted) Lakeland home.

Just as 'The Vale' showed the importance of *kin*, contrasting the death of the Wordsworths' father with Dorothy's separation from her entire family, 'An Evening Walk' showed how much William longed for the Lakeland of his boyhood during his exile in Cambridge, London, and France. William's enthusiasm for returning to the Lakes was ardent and infectious – Dorothy described him to Jane as being 'fired with the idea of leading his sister to such a retreat'[13] – and in Halifax they quickly devised a plan to be 'alone together' in the county of their birth.

By April 1794 William and Dorothy were ready to act. Dorothy had been invited to stay with relations in Whitehaven on the Cumberland coast, so William announced his plans to escort her there. After taking a coach from Halifax to Kendal, they would complete the thirty-one miles to the house of friends near Keswick on foot, staying at an inn in Grasmere on the way. It would be a sort of walking pilgrimage to the mountains, lakes, and valleys of William's schooldays. As well as providing them with a chance to (re)visit the places about which Dorothy had heard so much, the excursion would also be a test, to see how far their idyll of companionship might live up to expectation.

That spring was to be a golden time for Dorothy and William. Nothing could dampen their spirits as they set out from Kendal on the eighteen-mile trek to Grasmere. They stopped at the little village of Staveley to rest and drink milk at an inn before skirting the edges of Windermere and Rydal Water as the sun made its way towards the horizon. Coming over the rise at White Moss, they saw the lake of Grasmere glow with the gilded light of evening as a 'rich yellow light on the waters' reflected the hills around. After a night at Grasmere, they walked the remaining thirteen miles to Windy Brow, the home of William's schoolfriends, the Calvert brothers.

'You cannot conceive of anything more delightful than the situation of this house,' wrote Dorothy to Jane Pollard a few days after arriving. Windy Brow was – and remains – an old farmhouse on the slopes of Latrigg, overlooking the Vale of Keswick. The views of Derwentwater and the nearby fells were sublime, and though Dorothy planned to be there but briefly ('I intended to stay only a few days'[14]), she found herself still there weeks later. This was in spite of written rebukes from Charlotte Crackanthorpe-Cookson, her aunt at Penrith, who, upon hearing that William and Dorothy had 'tramped' from Kendal, wrote to chastise them for having placed Dorothy in danger of 'moral corruption'. Emboldened by joy and freedom, Dorothy retorted that not only had she not been corrupted, but that she was benefiting from this experience: 'The country is so delightful, and, above all, I have so full an enjoyment of my brother's company.'[15]

Part of Dorothy's delight at being at Windy Brow was the feeling that her presence there was purposeful and wanted. Since her mother's death, she had often felt like an outsider, coming to believe in the 'painful idea that one's existence is of very little use'. But at Windy Brow, she both was with her longed-for brother and had creative purpose. She was already an early reader and critic of William's completed works – we know that she received a pre-publication draft of 'An Evening Walk' by post in 1792 – but the spring of 1794 marks the beginning of a critically important role for Dorothy in relation to her brother: as his amanuensis and poetic collaborator.

The notebook the Wordsworths used at Windy Brow shows that from this point the siblings worked in tandem to draft, copy, and amend William's poetry. This is the first time that Dorothy's handwriting appears on a surviving Wordsworth manuscript. Larger and loopier than her brother's, it records many lines of *Salisbury Plain*, an early draft of a

narrative poem inspired during William's travels in the West
Country in 1793. Because William disliked the physical
act of writing and preferred to compose poetry aloud,
ideally whilst walking outdoors, Dorothy's near constant
companionship could also be realised as a commitment to
his creativity: this poem, which had been alive in his mind
for months, could now finally be committed to paper. From
this point until his death in 1850, many of the drafts, copies,
and revisions made to the manuscripts of William's poetry
were in the hands of people other than himself.

Living together brought a second creative advantage. Just
as Dorothy had lent emotional insight to William during
their shared summer in Penrith, helping him to develop
a more thoughtful and less melodramatic second section
of 'The Vale', her sensitivity and experience could now
be applied to new works. Though the 'Corrections and
additions' to 'An Evening Walk' made in the Windy Brow
notebook are in William's hand, interleaved with lines from
Salisbury Plain in the handwriting of both siblings, the
change in emphasis between the 1793 and 1794 versions
hints at Dorothy's reflective and humanising influence on
her brother. Whilst the 1793 version describes the landscape
like a picture, focusing on its 'natural' rather than human
features, by 1794 the views have become peopled with those
who live and work in Lakeland.

Whilst 'The Vale' gives little insight into the psyche
of its characters beyond the narrator, the poems in the
Windy Brow notebook show a shift in William's interests
as for the first time they enable the reader to glimpse other
people's inner lives. People are no longer shadowy figures

or scene-setting devices that serve to move the narrative along; now their feelings and emotions are beginning to be guessed at and explored. As children race along the side of the churchyard in Grasmere, the poet wonders about whether they think about the contrast between the silence of those lying in the graves and the 'sensible warm motion' of their 'wild mirth'. He also reflects on his past and possible similarity to those children he now watches, recognising their shared humanity in the same 'spring of body once proclaimed to me'. Later we see a young woman passing the spot where 'crushed by falling rocks her lover fell' and feel the sharp contrast of 'passions thrilling fires' with 'her bosomed pain': William is coming to realise that his feelings and memories are indicative of a shared humanity, one that connects rather than isolates.

As well as beginning to develop a sense of emotional connection with the inhabitants of Lakeland, William also explores the idea of individual *kithship* with the landscape itself. There is a kind of spiritual pantheism, what he later describes as 'an active principle alive in all things' (a phrase first recorded in a notebook by Dorothy in 1798), which appears for the first time in the expanded 1794 version of 'An Evening Walk':

> 'A heart that vibrates evermore, awake
> To feeling for all forms that Life can take,
> That wider still its sympathy extends,
> And sees not any line where being ends;
> Sees sense, through Nature's rudest
>   forms betrayed,

Tremble obscure in fountain, rock, and shade;
And while a secret power those forms endears
Their social accents never vainly hears.'[16]

We cannot be sure which of these lines, if any, owe a direct debt to Dorothy. However, the Windy Brow notebook demonstrates her presence as an attentive and intuitive audience for her brother's poetic ideas in development as she became intimately acquainted with his creative process. Over time, this would come to influence her own creativity, but at Windy Brow the focus was on delight and possibility: the joy at them being together combined with hopeful promise of a shared future made real through William's writing.

Though it's hard work climbing up the hillside, I can feel the bite of wind and cold every time I pause for breath. After crossing the pipeline, the land begins to flatten. Frozen heather snags my boots, and just by the path, clumps of reeds mark out the edges of a little lake. The tarn mirrors the grey of the sky, a plate of pewter set against a tableau of wintry moorland. Rushes have their feet frozen into the water, the wind whipping their pliant stalks into a sighing, rushing choir. On the tarn's far side is a small pile of stones, little more than a thickening in the wall. It is a hint of this place's history, a trace that tells us there was once a boathouse at the water's south-western edge.

It's cold by the tarn, with little shelter from the wind. Now we have stopped, our labouring hearts no longer force their extra warmth through us. Cracking the icy edges of the water with our boots, we watch streamers of thin mist pass between us and the valley. Grasmere disappears for a moment then reappears in a glimpse, a meteorological magic trick. With it comes the sting of snow on my cheek. For all this landscape is new to me, there is familiarity in its bitter breath. The frost that rimes the reeds is like the salt that sweats from the old brick oast houses of East Anglia, the wind reminiscent of storms that cut across the Suffolk marshes, bringing winter from the east. In the gale-whine I fancy I can hear the phantom bell-tolls of doomed, drowned Dunwich. Memories of home are always with us: sometimes as ghosts to exorcise, other times like old friends we love to gather round us.

From the tarn we can see the lower slopes of Helvellyn, its flanks a mesh of interlinking tracks. In the low February light we pick out the broad belt of a path that we could climb to reach the peak of one of England's highest mountains. It follows Tongue Gill as it cuts into the hillside, and we watch it disappear into the clouds that hide the summit. Every landscape bears witness to its history; this route was a footworn path of necessity, cut by the tread of packhorse, shepherd, and peddler centuries ago in search of the quickest route between Grasmere and the Eden Valley. Its lower fork leads to Hawse Gap and on to Patterdale, whilst the upper crosses Dollywaggon Pike and snakes towards Helvellyn's top.

A sprinkling of snow is beginning to settle here, and the grey-pink light intimates that it already lies much thicker further up. Though the sun has stayed behind the clouds all day, we feel it sink behind the hill as the sky slips from silver to leaden grey and the air grows even colder. We don't go back the same way, but seek a quicker route back down the mountain. We turn, and trace our footsteps away from the tarn and down the steep gulley to the north. Above us the hawk-sharp profile of Stone Arthur juts into the sky, throwing long shadows down the gill to remind us that we need to beat the darkness home.

4

Flawed Coleridgeans

'It had all been going great; then:
Do you drink? *'Well . . . Yes,' I replied.*
Smoke? *'Affirmative.'*
I was somewhat startled by the questions:
Had I disappointed him already?
No water-drinking bard here:
Just another flawed Coleridgean.'

Mark Ward, 'Regret vii', *Thunder Alley* (2008)[1]

Tonight there is to be a Town End party, the first since our arrival. The Trust's graphic designer will soon be leaving for a new job in London, and everyone is invited to his house to mark his departure. None of the Trust's buildings are warm, but we've been warned that this one is almost uninhabitably cold. After a shower as hot as the terrace's Victorian plumbing will allow, I dress in an ankle-length kilt and layer three tops under my padded jacket. It's not what I would usually wear to a party, but normal social rules don't seem to apply here. Emily completes her outfit with a folded sheaf of poems tucked into her coat pocket, in case the moment might arise to read one.

Before I came to Grasmere, the parties I went to hardly ever involved poetry. Even in the febrile days of university, poetry stayed decorously away from entertainment, protected in the pages of books, or brought out for examination in the lamplight of tutorials. In Grasmere, it seems that no gathering is complete without someone reading a poem. Plenty of people want to perform, for as well as the current Poet in Residence, paid by the Arts Council to be inspired by this place, several of the museum staff are also writers.

Enabling poets to continue living in – or at least, very close to – Dove Cottage became a central concern of the Wordsworth Trust in the closing decades of the twentieth century. For beyond the house and its manuscripts, what makes this place itself? There is the physical space it occupies; the rocks and soil on which it stands. The trees that frame and shade it; the plants that grow and bloom and die. The colour of the leaves; the water that flows underneath them; the way the light reflects its turns and trickles. Human traces are important too: the bricks and stones, slate and glass, metal, wood, and concrete. But is there more? A spirit that resides? And if there is, how can this ephemeral essence be nurtured and protected?

Preserving physical relics of the past is not enough to ensure that poets from two hundred years ago will not be forgotten. For a love of poetry to survive, an active legacy of art and writing has to endure. In Grasmere, poetry is a living, breathing entity whose vital flame must be allowed to burn. From the 1990s onwards, artists and poets have come to find inspiration in the Wordsworths' world through a series of paid residencies. Living in the houses around Dove Cottage, intermingling with its employees, they have attempted to capture something of the spirit of the place through verse as the Wordsworths did before them.

This legacy of the living word began with Robert Woof, the Trust's first director, who worked for decades not just to preserve and cherish the bricks and mortar of Town End, but also to ensure its poetic inheritance. Though he was five years in the grave when we arrived in Grasmere, we feel Robert's presence like a ghostly force, a spirit of this place whose dedication was vital to what Town End has become. A larger-than-life bust of him sits beside the entrance to the archive, and when we walk through the museum, we can hear Coleridge's 'Kubla Khan', read in his warm Lancastrian tones, purring faintly from a pair of earphones. Rich dreams ring in every syllable as words slip through the air like water: 'For he on honey-dew hath fed, / And drunk the milk of Paradise.'[2]

It was Robert who, in the early 1960s, realised that the surviving Wordsworth manuscripts were in danger of damage and irreparable disintegration. Since their donation by Gordon Graham Wordsworth in the 1930s, the handwritten drafts and revisions of some of the greatest poems in English literature had lain stacked in old cardboard boxes in the Trust's library. Few had been read, let alone studied. Robert realised that expensive professional restoration was essential if they were to survive the ravages of the Cumbrian climate, otherwise these priceless manuscripts would be lost to the twin threats of damp and time. So Robert worked on ordering and organising the notebooks, loose sheets, and letters, before transporting them by hand to the world-renowned Cockerell Bindery in Cambridge. There, master paper restorer Sandy Cockerell carefully stabilised the pages on acid-free paper before transforming them into bespoke handmade books for Robert to take back to Grasmere.

As Robert didn't drive and the Wordsworth Trust at the time had scant budget for curatorial endeavours, these journeys were usually made by train, taxi, and lifts hitched in every conceivable type of vehicle. Robert's shabby briefcase carried these treasures half the length of England so that the Wordsworths' literary legacy might be preserved and cherished. Their survival has meant that successive generations of researchers have been able to study directly from the manuscripts, rather than from photographs or transcripts, in their quest to better understand the Romantic writers and their works. This contribution alone was tremendously important to ensuring the Wordsworth legacy, but it was just the beginning of Robert's all-encompassing commitment to securing the physical and creative life of Town End, the effects of which can still be felt – and seen – there today.

As William Wordsworth had two centuries earlier, Robert fell in love with Grasmere in adolescence. Born in April 1931 in Lancaster, he grew up on a farm that shared its land with the Royal Albert Institute, a residential home for people with learning impairments. Robert's father William managed the Institute's farm, his mother Annie was a housewife, and Robert was the youngest of their three children. A bright child who loved to read, Robert went to Lancaster

Royal Grammar School, and in 1949 won a scholarship to study History at Oxford University's Pembroke College.

Before he left the North for Oxford, Robert made a pilgrimage to Grasmere. Coming over the crest of the hill above Town End he stopped: the vale below bewitched him. He later said, 'By the time I got back home, it was burned into my imagination that there was such a place.' After taking up his place at Pembroke, Robert quickly transferred from History to English, completing his degree in 1951, and in September 1953 went to the University of Toronto to study for a PhD in the creative friendship between William Wordsworth and Samuel Taylor Coleridge. The move gave him access to a vibrant community of Romantic scholars and literary critics: Kathleen Coburn was doing groundbreaking work on manuscripts of Coleridge, whilst Northrop Frye held court as a vibrant and original literary theorist.

Robert returned to England in 1960 to take up the Lord Adams of Ennerdale Research Fellowship at what was about to become the University of Newcastle upon Tyne, then a college within the University of Durham. The fellowship became a lectureship in Romantic literature in 1962, and for the next thirty years Robert combined his lecturing responsibilities with being a Wordsworth Trustee, focusing his research and creative energies increasingly around Dove Cottage. In 1991 Robert took on the inaugural directorship of the Wordsworth Trust, a role he revelled in before dying of lung cancer in 2005.

A man of superhuman energy and dedication to the literary arts, Robert combined his work for the Trust with a full-time academic teaching career at Newcastle University. In addition, he was a central figure within Northern Arts and

Arts Council England, becoming chair of the latter in the 1980s, as well as serving as director of both English Touring Theatre and Theatre by the Lake. His knowledge, skill, and charm were legendary; Robert's vivifying enthusiasm for the world of words was a shaping force not just in Grasmere, but in the cultural life of England in the second half of the twentieth century.

Robert's love of others' words and worlds extended beyond the Wordsworths and their circle. The Romantics were only young and revolutionary once, but their belief in the vitality of freedom, their love of the world, and their fellow feeling became immortal. Robert saw that the inheritance of these Romantic forebears was as imaginative as it was physical, and so his central concern became the preservation of both Town End and its intangible poetic heritage. The best gift any writer can give is to open that mystic door of understanding for someone else, allowing them enough space into which they can squeeze the keystone of themselves. Robert saw it as his duty to fulfil this vision, creating a place for 'youthful poets, who among these hills / Will be my second self when I am gone'.[3]

Today this 'second self' is Neil Rollinson. The Trust's Poet in Residence from a few years ago, Neil has come up from Manchester for the weekend and there's a glint in his eye as he walks down the lane from the bus stop and opens the gate opposite Dove Cottage on Friday evening. It has been a while since he was in Grasmere, but things change slowly here, and the door code to House Two still lets him in. He knows where to find the coffee too, and by the time I see him the next afternoon he's leaning out of the window of the kitchen, a steaming mug in one hand and a half-smoked cigarette in the other. He's telling a couple of my colleagues that whilst looking in a cupboard for a mug he found a dead blue tit, its feet frozen as it scrabbled for a door it couldn't find. 'Write a poem about it, Neil,' remarks John wryly as he passes. 'Aye, that's not a bad idea Johnny,' Neil replies, pulling his head back inside the window.

Wendy, whose bedroom is closest to the kitchen, says Neil spent last night on their sofa. He's been out all morning, perhaps up the steep path to get the view from Helm Crag, or along the rocky route to Rydal, smoking roll-ups along the way. Even with a late start, Mark assures us that Neil could be round Fairfield and down to the Golden Rule in Ambleside before last orders. A pint of Robinson's followed by a whisky chaser, taken with a pickled egg or greasy pork pie slathered with mustard. Then back home along the coffin path, following the ancient dead and the badgers that come each night for chips provided by the pub at Rydal.

Tonight Neil's smartened up – not enough to shave, but he's put on a fresher T-shirt and there's a rumour that he's brushed his hair. He stands up and reads a poem about another party here, one that began with Baileys being poured into plastic glasses in the kitchen after work and ended only with the coming of the next day's dawn. Bass resounded through the soles of his feet, and raindrops glowed with the early-morning light. It was the green world of those who eschew sleep, who smoke joints down to the root before dancing in the empty road at daybreak.

We take our cue from the poem. Before long, bottles have been emptied into basins, and someone is scooping out mugs of 'Death Punch' – a heady cocktail of vodka, white wine, cider, and beer. The kitchen floor is sticky, and out in the hall people are sliding down a peculiar and inexplicably steep ramp that leads from the staircase to the living room. The graphic designer leans on the kitchen counter and looks down his six-foot frame at Emily as he passes her a swatch of paper samples. They're talking texture, thickness, feel, flirting with the dream of turning Emily's words into a book. His fingers lead hers across each page, teaching her fingertips to read the paper. She's grinning and he's laughing. They look like people who might end up in bed together.

The front door creaks open and in comes Tom. Jeff told us that his middle son was living at home after finishing university, but this is the first time that we've met. Though he's half a head taller, Tom looks a lot like his dad, with a thin, straight nose and broad lips, but where Jeff's hair is straight and sandy-coloured, Tom's is curly brown. His cheeks are very red – he tells me that they're not usually so bright, but he was out walking for most of the day and the wind and cold have whipped them into roses. 'Where did you go?' I ask, and he tells me he walked to the top of Helvellyn from Grasmere, following that snick of a path beside Tongue Gill that I'd seen with Emily.

I was cold even by the tarn, and Tom confirms the snow was deep and frozen solid higher up. I tell him that we looked at the path and were glad we didn't take it. I'm tuning my ear to the northern burr in his voice, and watch the way his eyes crinkle when he smiles. He says that on the summit it was so cold that the rain froze as soon as it landed, coating his body in icy armour – but he's grinning with the thrill of it. I am half impressed and half bemused: being filmed in ice does not sound like my idea of fun.

I go to get another drink and as I step through the kitchen door Mark passes me a spliff. I hesitate, but decide it's not a night to be restrained. I've smoked a bit before, but it had left me either unaffected or racked with paranoia that took all night to shake. Perhaps this time will be different, I think, noticing the blurry smile on Mark's face and feeling the warmth of his hand on mine. I take a few long, slow draws, and wait.

Before long I'm crying, and between each gulping sob I'm trying to describe how it feels to split from the reality that other people seem to share. Fortunately, almost everyone's as out of it as I am, and no one's really listening as I repeat the rather silly refrain, 'I have a dark past.' At midnight, one of my housemates decides to head home, and I go with her. On my way out, Tom waves goodbye. I know by the way my stomach jolts that I like him.

The next morning I'm awake just before dawn, convinced my heart has stopped. I lie in the dark and try to reassure myself by placing my hand on my chest to feel its regular tattoo. My mind is racing, and I can't seem to stem the horror. My fears are coming true: I think I'm dying, alone, and no one knows. I try to anchor myself back to reality with a cup of tea and piece of toast, but it isn't enough, so I pull on my wellies and coat and head out into the gloom to walk off the panic.

Passing the site of last night's party, I can see traces of excess glinting in the half-light. The recycling tub overflows with empty bottles, and a pool of vomit is slowly mixing with last night's rainwater as it drips from a downpipe. Someone's car is parked at a rakish angle on the hill, its back wheels nudging the double yellow lines. The smell of weed clings to my hair, and my heart thuds so hard my raincoat seems to rustle with each exaggerated beat. I can feel sweat in my armpits and know that it holds the bitter tang of drink. But at least I'm alive, my legs pushing me towards morning. If I keep moving, I know that the road will soon dip down to meet the lake's lip, where I can cross the boardwalks to watch a new day spread across the water.

Once it's light and I'm back in the terrace, I feel much better. However, the episode reminds me of a promise I made a few months earlier. Before leaving Suffolk, I had agreed with my doctor that I would continue to be in regular contact with medical staff once I moved. Though time, company, and new occupation have already given me back some of myself, I am still far from well. A small setback could see me spiral into disaster once again, and after this panic attack, I know I should make an appointment. Luckily, the doctor can see me tomorrow, when she'll be holding her weekly surgery in the village.

Having listened to a description of my symptoms, the doctor's sensible advice is to steer clear of weed. Brain chemistry is delicate, she tells me, and if I've had a bad reaction to a joint before, then it is likely I will have another. She tells me that many people try to self-medicate with drugs long before they seek more mainstream treatment for an illness, and I refrain from telling her that this isn't the only marijuana-induced panic I have had.

At university a friend and I decided to dress up as clowns for a party. I put on a tunic dress stitched from patchwork pieces, topped with a bright red bowler hat. My friend wore a white shirt and exuberant, outsized trousers held up with vivid braces. We painted our faces with abstract blocks of colour, obscuring the usual curves of nose, cheeks, and mouth, and she made us a fat joint to share. As it did with me, company could make her nervous.

When we arrived at the party, everyone else was dressed from head to toe in black, sipping white wine as ethereal jazz music wafted through the room. I became paralysed with fright: what was I doing here dressed like a clown? I gulped down a drink, hoping it would relax me, but instead I found I could not move. People came over and tried to talk to me as I perched on the arm of a sofa, but I became convinced they couldn't see my face underneath the psychedelic make-up. Eventually some kind person helped me up and walked me back to my room. After this, I'd sworn off weed, but somehow in the heady blur of a Grasmere night I'd forgotten the vow I'd made myself.

It was also at university that I first started experiencing dark, angry moods that descended quickly and left me breathless with their intensity. I'd chosen to study English Language and Literature because I loved reading, devouring any book I could lay my hands on. By the time I started sixth form I was going to weekly poetry-reading classes led by my English teacher, squeezing into the faculty storeroom to become acquainted with the work of authors not on the school's curriculum. Stacked around me in teetering piles were coverless, scrawled-in copies of fading books that had been read, studied, and scribbled on by previous generations of students, and I was free to rehome any I wanted. Each poem led me to another, and I gorged on them like honey, leaving with my rucksack crammed full of Larkin, Keats, the Metaphysicals. After the first session I came into the common room and cried with the magic of it all: poetry showed me the world, and promised me a place in it. The prospect of studying English literature at Oxford held all the heady promise of a dream.

Once I got to university the reality of studying literature came as a shock. In tutorials, which happened twice a week, it was made clear that we were here to pare things down. There wasn't time to enjoy reading, or luxuriate in language. Meaning was to be *got at*, stripped away, truths uncovered. Criticism was the thing. It was a competitive game, played at a giddying pace – but not to be taken too seriously. Dry humour combined with razor-sharp observation was the critical mode we strived to imitate. Every week we had to read, absorb, and analyse perhaps twenty books before turning this rushed reading into a couple of two-thousand-word essays. To squeeze enough time from the days to do this meant pulling regular 'all-nighters', and I often found myself staggering down the high street with the dawn to deliver essays ahead of 8 a.m. deadlines, before going back to bed to sleep away the morning.

The pace of work was relentless, and though my anxiety about producing essays lost its sting after that first manic term, the three years that followed were tinged with uneasiness. I had thought that I loved books, but at university studying them became a kind of torture. Pulling apart poem after poem to find their meaning or spot a clever dualism came to feel like I was ripping the heart from the words I used to love. As well as studying Victorian literature and critical theory in that first term, we also took a course in Anglo-Saxon poetry, and though it was thrilling to try to learn Old English in just eight weeks, by the time I came home for the Christmas holidays I was so exhausted I spent most of the holiday asleep. I should have been reading Joyce's *Ulysses*, but before I'd even opened it, I knew I hated the book. It had become just another thing someone was pressuring me to read.

College was demanding, and wildly different from life at home. Impressive, beautiful, commanding, my college had been the last formerly single-sex Oxford institution to admit female students. Thirty years later, almost all its Fellows were men. One tutor referred to a friend and me – two of only three girls on our course – as 'giggling fishwives', and another told me that I produced my best work when I was unhappy. During my third year, my mother was diagnosed with a chronic muscle-weakening disease, and in the weeks after this revelation and the urgent surgery that followed, during which time I returned home to look after my younger brother, I apparently wrote some good essays. A mental note: unhappiness might be part of the sacrifice necessary for success.

I won a scholarship at the end of my first year, but instead of buying me some psychic space, the reward for this achievement, beyond a small contribution towards my university expenses, seemed to be more work. Now I was expected – or maybe *I* expected – to turn out first-class essays every week, not just fluke them in examinations. In the year that followed I became prone to black moods that descended suddenly, making me feel sick to my stomach. Like a knife, they came sharp and hard, cutting me off from the world I wanted to be part of. They mostly felt like anger: a bubbling heat that swelled in my head and had me raging with a fury that seemed both righteous and disproportionate to what was happening. When these moods came, I took myself away, walking alone through the streets until the feelings passed. They always did – but I dreaded when the next would come.

Around this time I began to have recurring sleep paralysis and nightmares, waking drenched in sweat and unable to move after vivid dreams of corpses swinging by lighted windows. It wasn't an entirely unfounded fear; a few years earlier, the president of our junior (undergraduate) common room was found in his college rooms, his inert body hanging from the light switch. Suicide had been the official verdict, but rumours still swirled that implicated someone else, hinting at some kind of autoerotic sex game. I used to hate walking through college at night, as my eyes couldn't help being drawn towards lighted open windows. More than once I made myself almost hysterical by imagining that flapping curtains were bodies suspended from the ceiling.

Mental disquiet was rife at college: phone numbers for the Samaritans decorated the backs of toilet doors, and posters advertising counselling services papered the walls of the post room and the library. Two of my peers left abruptly during their first terms and were never seen again. Bulimia was common; its insistent purges had robbed one friend of her gag reflex, and drove another to search through the communal kitchen cupboards when she thought no one else was awake to gorge on cereal, bread, and uncooked pasta. Others self-medicated with cocaine, amphetamines, laughing gas – whatever they could get. Some used dealers they knew from school – after all, the college prided itself on a centuries-long association with Eton. Not everyone came up to Oxford with such connections. One night someone, another former state-school student, invited me round to empty bottles of Benylin, a cough syrup whose active ingredient is a mild antihistamine. Whatever high we chased, we were unlikely to find it there.

Most of us sought escape in the pub at one time or other. A favourite was The Half Moon, a small, dark bar close to college that only offered crisps for food but whose barman could be persuaded to keep serving past last orders if you paid him with a song. Others buried their discomfort by getting away: one friend would kayak miles along the wide rivers of the Chilterns each weekend, whilst others found solace in racing to Wales or the Peak District in search of crags to climb. Though I did not feel drawn to the water or the rocks, I shared the same soul-longing to be somewhere – or maybe someone – else.

The unsettledness of those transitional years, before we have anything more substantial than examination results and expectations to anchor ourselves to, can be dizzying. Working out who we are, what we want, and what we must

reject so that we can become ourselves is difficult work,
yet this giddy youthful period is often lauded as paradis-
iacal, free of responsibility. But how and where we will live,
what we will do – the pressure to answer those questions to
others' satisfaction is immense. A major reason for choosing
to move to Japan was to have an answer to the question 'And
what will you do after university?' Being able to say I had a
job and a place to go bought me more time to work out what
I wanted from my life. Finding an answer satisfactory to
myself took much longer.

The next day is Monday and I'm back at work and feeling
better. On these cold mornings my favourite place to be is
in Dove Cottage. I love being the first intern there, making
sure that the fire, laid the night before with sticks and twists
of newspaper, crackles in the houseplace grate. As I top up
water in the vases to slake the thirst of snowdrops and helle-
bores, I half-expect to find Dorothy at my elbow, or catch a
glimpse of William in the garden. There seems to be a sense
of benevolent possession, a feeling shared by Dorothy's first
biographer, Edmund Lee. Lee acquired the house in the
1860s because he felt that the spirit of the Wordsworths,
particularly Dorothy, was still resident in the building, 'every
room of which her presence fills, in this orchard garden,
every flower of which breathes of her, she is alive and
delightful, and beloved for evermore'.[4] Stopford Augustus
Brooke, the Trust's first chairman, who oversaw its purchase
of Dove Cottage, described it as 'the haunted place'.[5]
　Throughout the 1790s the Wordsworths were like
hungry ghosts themselves, searching for a home. After a

few halcyon weeks at Windy Brow, William and Dorothy visited their childhood home at Cockermouth, where they were dismayed to find it in a state of disrepair; no one had lived there since their father's death eleven years earlier. Dorothy spent the rest of the summer staying with relations across the North-West, with William joining his sister intermittently, but his other focus that summer was the health of his erstwhile schoolfriend Raisley Calvert. Calvert had consumption and his condition was becoming increasingly serious. In July William walked with Dorothy to Broughton-in-Furness before returning to Windy Brow at the end of September, where he found Raisley 'worse than I when I left Keswick'.[6]

Raisley was determined to go to Portugal in the hope his health would improve in a warmer climate, and William agreed to travel with him, but they only managed to get as far as Penrith before Raisley became too ill to continue. On 7 January 1795, William wrote from the inn where they stayed that 'my poor friend is barely alive';[7] Raisley died a few days later. Such was his belief in William's poetic power that he left him £900 in his will to be used 'in the purchase of one or more annuities for his use and benefit', with the codicil that William could invest any portion 'for the use and benefit of his Sister'.[8] This was the first concrete vote of confidence in William's creative talent, also offering the promise of financial security for both siblings.

This money could not be released straight away, and in the meantime Dorothy and William still had no home or income. They discussed moving to London, where there would be some opportunity for them both to earn money by writing, but Dorothy noted that the city atmosphere would not suit her brother: 'he is never so at home as when in a beautiful country'.[9] Their wider family also had concerns about the suitability of this plan. In March 1795 their aunt Elizabeth Rawson worried in a letter to her foster son that 'William and Dorothy have a scheme to live in London and plan to maintain themselves by their literary talents, writing, and translating', which she thinks is 'a very bad, wild scheme'.[10] William disagreed – the previous year, he had written to his friend William Mathews to say that as well as 'essays on morals and politics I think I could communicate critical remarks upon poetry &c, &c, upon the arts of painting, gardening, and other subjects of amusement'[11] – but he was emphatic that he would not 'prostitute [his] pen' by writing about anything which was not of 'sound and exalted Morality'.[12]

This 'bad, wild scheme' of a literary life in London was never realised, and by August Dorothy was back in Halifax to celebrate her friend Jane's marriage to John Marshall, a young linen manufacturer from Leeds whom Dorothy knew slightly from her time at the Hipperholme school. Dorothy attended the wedding and remarked in a letter to Jane a few weeks later that 'I know enough of Mr Marshall's character to be persuaded that the hopes you had formed of happiness would receive daily confirmation'.[13] Dorothy's life was also about to start a new chapter, for in the same letter Dorothy swore her friend to 'most careful secrecy': 'Know then that I am going to live in Dorsetshire.'[14]

The decision to move to Dorset came about because of two critical shifts in the Wordsworths' circumstances. After

Raisley's death and with the promise of the annuity to come, William travelled to London, where he renewed several friendships from his university days with the hope of finding some temporary work whilst the details of Raisley's bequest were finalised. They included his acquaintance with Basil Montagu, a contemporary at Cambridge and the illegitimate son of John Montagu, 4th Earl of Sandwich. Basil had recently been working as a tutor to John and Azariah Pinney, junior members of a wealthy Bristol family that had made its money through the sugar and slave trades, and introduced them to William. Immediately impressed by William's intellect and conversation, John Pinney readily offered the family's empty country house to this would-be poet, who apparently did not mind accepting assistance from sources of less 'sound and exalted Morality'. Fully furnished and with its own library, Racedown Lodge was a large red-brick country house where William could live and write without paying a farthing in rent.

The other development which made this plan possible was that William had taken an interest in Montagu's motherless three-year-old son, Basil Caroline, and had agreed to provide a home for the child at Racedown whilst his father remained in London. It was a surprising offer for a young man who had left his own wife and child in France, though perhaps William hoped that this would somehow balance the emotional debt of his separation from them. Despite the conflict, William was able to send small amounts of money to his French family, and Dorothy wrote regularly to Annette during this period. The two women dreamed that, once the war in France was over, they would set up a family

home with William and Anne-Caroline. Montagu promised
the Wordsworths an annuity of £50, on the understanding
that Dorothy would join her brother to look after the child.
Suddenly, the Wordsworths finally had not only the offer
of an income and somewhere to live, but the chance to run
their own affairs, far from the influence of their relations.
Dorothy described her excitement at 'the prospect which
at last opens up before me of having, at least for a time, a
comfortable home, in a house of my own'.[15] For William,
the move pragmatically offered, in Dorothy's words, 'such
opportunities of studying as ... will be not only advanta-
geous to his mind but to his purse'.[16]

At midnight on 26 September 1795, the Wordsworths
arrived at their new home in Dorset. Dorothy's delight in
being at Racedown is evident from her letters. She took satisfaction from running their household, writing to her friend
Jane to note 'I have all my domestic concerns so arranged
that everything goes on with the utmost regularity.' In the
same letter, she assured her friend that though they had only
'winter occupations, books, solitude and the fire-side', they
were 'never dull', describing young Basil as 'our perpetual
play-thing'.[17] Neighbours had called but Dorothy coolly
remarked that 'I do not think we shall be much benefitted by
their society' – to her, '[t]he greatest inconvenience we suffer
here is in being so far from the post office'.[18] Later that winter
she began a letter, unaddressed and unsent, saying that '[this]
country is delightful; we have charming walks, a good garden,
a pleasant house':[19] her cup of happiness appeared to be full.

The siblings were not, however, united in their delight.
While Dorothy described Basil as 'a lusty, blooming

fearless boy [who] dreads neither cold nor rain [and] is my perpetual pleasure',[20] William offered a more succinct and critical assessment: 'he lies like a little devil'.[21] Just days before Dorothy penned her first missive to Jane from Racedown, glorying in her new situation, William wrote a rather different letter to his friend Francis Wrangham. Its contents were 'melancholy proof of my procrastinating spirit'; William made almost no reference to his new life at Racedown, only acknowledging that 'it is an excellent house and the country far from unpleasant but as to society we must manufacture it ourselves'.[22] This was clearly unsatisfactory, as William's next sentence asked, 'Will you come and help us?'[23]

William's surviving letters from the rest of their time at Racedown repeated his desire for a broader range of company and acknowledged a slackening of his spirits. In January 1796 William wrote to Joseph Cottle, a Bristol publisher who he hoped would publish the only poem he had completed since coming to Dorset, to wish 'Best comp[limen]ts to Coleridge, and say I wish to hear much from him.'[24] On 21 March he wrote to his college friend William Mathews, requesting 'Pray write to me at length [regarding] any other information likely to interest me.' Of his own endeavours, he mentions only planting cabbages, wryly noting 'you may perhaps suspect that into cabbages we shall be transformed'.[25]

In contrast, Dorothy did not invite Jane Pollard to visit Racedown (though she does instruct Jane in finding it on a map). On 7 March, Dorothy wrote to her friend to say that the Pinneys had returned to Racedown and had stayed for the preceding month, and '[w]e all enjoyed ourselves very much', describing the young Azariah as having 'a charming counte-nance and the sweetest temper I ever observed', adding that 'he is well-informed, has an uncommonly good heart, and is very agreeable in conversation'.[26] The only hint of loneliness in any of her Racedown writings crept in six months after their arrival, when Dorothy remarked that '[w]e seem quite quiet now that we are alone again' and 'we have not seen Mr Montagu which has disappointed us a good deal'.

For Dorothy, Racedown offered the chance to regain a half-remembered, half-imagined past: 'You know the pleas-ure which I have always attached to the idea of home, a blessing which I so early lost.'[27] She delighted in Racedown's surrounding hills, 'which seen from a distance almost take the character of mountains', because they reminded her of the siblings' 'native wilds'. William did not mention any notable similarities between Dorset and the Lakes, only making the laconic observation that the countryside around Racedown was 'far from intolerable'. Dorothy's few cherished recollections from early childhood found seed-time here, where her chief treasure was access to an imagined familial infancy – one she believed lost – through being with William, and having the opportunity to recreate a childhood for their ward. She also thrilled at exploring a landscape very different from the flat, low fields of Norfolk where she spent half her adolescence. For Dorothy, Racedown was the place where she needed to believe that her dreams had all come true.

For William, Racedown never felt like home, and neither did it offer him sufficient imaginative stimulation. His low mood, likely brought about by a combination of long months of writer's block and regular yearning for the company of his friends (and perhaps guilt at the situation with Annette and his daughter), persisted throughout the spring of 1796. 'As to writing it is out of the question,'[28] he glumly reported to William Mathews in March of that year. To Wrangham he wrote plaintively that 'Your Letter had long been looked for', but perhaps not wishing to annoy or discourage his friend, he ended his letter by jokily remarking that as the Pinneys had gone 'I now feel a return of literary appetite' and will 'take a snack of satire'[29] by tackling the poems of Juvenal. William admitted to having been 'hewing wood and rooting up hedges' rather than writing, and again entreated Wrangham, rather whimsically, to pay a visit: 'Devonshire and Cornwall have many attractions, if they should be powerful enough to lead you this way you will not pass us by', adding that '[i]f you could muster the cash to come down, we should be glad to see you during the course of this summer'.[30]

Though the Wordsworths' search for a home had been realised practically and financially with their arrival at Racedown, it was not until more than a year later that William's mood seems to have become more buoyant. Simply being alone with Dorothy in 'a beautiful country' had not provided him with the anticipated sense of companionship, purpose, and inspiration. Something was missing from the picture of a life which he hoped would allow him to both realise his ambition and support the household through his writing.

The two notebooks that survive from the Wordsworths' time in Dorset bear witness to this creative trajectory. One (DCMS 11) is a small collection of handwritten sheets rebound many years later, containing jottings and brief notes about William's 1790 tour of the Continent and a small amount of revisionary work on *Salisbury Plain*, but no new poetry or substantial creative work. The other (DCMS 12) contains the first draft of a lengthy verse play which William finally began to work on more than a year after arriving at Racedown. In the late autumn of 1796 Dorothy was able to report that her brother was at last 'ardent in composition of a tragedy', a five-act blank-verse play called *The Borderers*, which he completed around the end of February the following year. William then began the poem 'The Ruined Cottage', and the Racedown notebooks show that long sections from the play and 'The Ruined Cottage' were copied out by someone else: Mary Hutchinson.

In the spring of 1796 William and Dorothy had received a 'melancholy letter' from Mary. They had remained in touch with her following the 1787 reunion in Penrith, and between the Windy Brow visit in 1794 and moving to Racedown, Dorothy lived with the Hutchinsons at Sockburn, the family-owned farm near Darlington where Mary, Margaret, Thomas, George, and Sara had moved in 1789. Other Hutchinson relatives, including sailor brother Henry, visited regularly, and Dorothy admired the supportive comfort the Hutchinsons gave to each other. The domestic arrangement at Sockburn was 'very different indeed ... from what it was formerly', for, aged twenty-five and twenty-three respectively, Mary and Margaret were now 'quite independent [of relations at Penrith] and have not a wish ungratified'. She concluded '[Y]ou cannot think what pleasure it gives me to see them so happy; situated exactly as our imaginations and wishes used to represent.'[31]

The bliss that Dorothy had observed at Sockburn the previous year had been short-lived. Margaret had become ill with consumption, and on 28 March 1796 she died, aged 24. On receiving Mary's letter telling the siblings of the news, Dorothy invited her grieving friend to come and stay with them. Henry Hutchinson promised to escort her the 350 miles to Dorset on his way from Yorkshire to his ship in Plymouth, and six months later Mary became the Wordsworths' first invited visitor.

Mary immediately became a vital part of the Racedown household. She was not a guest to be waited on, but a helpmeet who not only gave the Wordsworths practical assistance (all her life she was regarded as a 'good manager') by copying out drafts of William's poetry and helping Dorothy with housework, but also supplied new and vivifying companionship. On 19 March 1797 Dorothy wrote to Jane to say that her brother was now 'as chearful [*sic*] as any body can be; perhaps you may not think it but he is the life of the whole house'. Dorothy declared herself 'very happy in [Mary's] society'; indeed, she declared that the three of them were 'as happy as human beings can be'.[32] William's increased creativity coincides exactly with Mary's arrival, bearing out the emotional impact of her presence on his work – though *The Borderers* is generally regarded as one of his weakest works.

On 5 June 1797 Mary's six-month stay at Racedown came to an end. Thirteen years later, William remembered their parting within sight of the Malvern Hills, where he 'fancied that we should have seen so deeply into each other's hearts, and been so fondly locked in each other's arms, that we should have braved the worst and parted no more'. He fantasised – at least in hindsight – that they might have rested under the shade of a riverside tree: 'in that thicket we might have hidden ourselves from the sun … thus did I feed on the thought of bliss that might have been'.[33] For all of William's emotional closeness to his sister, it was the presence of Mary that not only served to break his writer's block, but also inspired him to write about the physical side of love. However, there is no explicit – or at least surviving – record of him having such physical feelings for Dorothy, though there have been many historical conjectures and fantasies about what might have been.

Dorothy and William certainly desired and needed emotionally close communion – but not exclusively with each other. Their letters demonstrated mutual intensity of emotion, yearning for increased connection, and a shared desire to be together, but their most passionate feelings on the subject of each other coincided not with sharing a life, but with that long second separation between 1787 and 1794, when Dorothy desired the company of Jane Pollard equally and together with her brother. By the time they were sharing a house at Racedown, William was yearning for other company, and it was the arrival of Mary Hutchinson and the prospect of visits from his friends which most gladdened his heart. In the summer of 1797, the siblings were to meet someone who would bring them a greater sense of creativity and companionship than anyone else: Samuel Taylor Coleridge.

5

Romance and Terror

'You passed the volume round, and poured
    more wine.
Outside your cottage lightning flashed again:
a Grasmere storm, theatrically right
for stories of romance and terror.'

Fleur Adcock, 'The Keepsake',
The Incident Book (1987)[1]

The cold weather stays with us into early February. The streetlamp that usually lights Town End is broken, and the cobbled lane between the houses is so dark that I walk with one hand outstretched in case I veer into a wall. Some nights it is quiet enough to hear the faint patter of frozen leaves falling on the slates. Then overnight the soundtrack to our lives changes as storms blow in from the Atlantic. In place of the clomp of feet on frozen stone, rain and sleet beat their clear tattoos on the windows. Culverts struggle to gulp down all the water, and in Dove Cottage slates squeak with dampness underfoot. On days like these, when clouds lid the valley and every surface drips with water, the tick-tock drip of the moss counts the daylight down. By four o'clock the windows of Dove Cottage are dark and shuttered. At this time of year the museum closes at nightfall, and after that our time is our own.

At least two nights a week we head to the pub after work. Tweedies has been a Grasmere institution since the 1970s, when its psychedelic dance floor drew would-be poets, farmhands, and the occasional aspiring hippy from a nearby commune. Staff from the Wordsworth Trust came down to nurse a pint or two, as did the trainee teachers from Charlotte Mason College in Ambleside. Back then, the Trust mostly employed young men, usually recruited fresh from university, to help organise and interpret the museum's manuscripts and artworks. If you wanted to supplement your drink with something stronger, someone could usually oblige, and small intoxicating packets were slipped from hand to pocket in the smoky darkness.

Now, there's a pub quiz on Thursday night, followed by the obligatory end-of-work trip on Fridays. Sometimes the staff get dinner here, but as interns we can't afford to order from the restaurant menu. Our pay is meagre, but if we club together we can afford enough chips, bread, and olives to keep pace with our drinks. We joke that a wedge of lime in a gin and tonic counts as 'one of our five a day', and that lemon-laced scampi fries and chilli peanuts make up another two. If we tire of Tweedies and omnipresent colleagues, there are the Reading Rooms, the Dove & Olive Branch bar at the Wordsworth Hotel, the Red Lion, and up at Town Head the Traveller's Rest, the valley's last outpost of hospitality.

Once we are settled with our drinks, the Grasmere grapevine assures us that Emily and the Trust's erstwhile graphic designer have – briefly – become an 'item', though in the dark it is hard to catch a glimpse of who goes where with whom. Several romances have been forged in Grasmere's backroom bars, and we are told plenty of stories of marriages made then broken in the crucible of communal living. Over the years Town End has seen its share of youthful passion, of midlife joy, and of hopes both raised and dashed. Listening to this talk of love, I feel my skin start to prickle.

For much of the previous year I'd felt haunted by memories, reminiscences of a boyfriend whose love sustained me during my last years at school and my first at university. He was much older than me, and worked in a job that had him climbing aboard ships and hanging from their railings in a harness. His family thought that I was far too young for him; mine, that he was much too old.

In isolation, we were each other's world. Our shared life began with the swing of the front door on Friday night and ended with tearful railway platform farewells on Sunday evening. Weekends were mostly spent in bed, alternating sex with sleeping, listening to music, and eating fancy food. When we did venture out it was for luxury. On our first trip away together, he took me to Selfridges to buy chocolates and stockings, then whisked me off for a restaurant meal that would have cost my mother half her rent.

My friends found him odd and overbearing on the rare occasions that they met. When we went on holiday – once to Italy, and several times to Cornwall and the Isle of Wight – we argued over everything. Whenever our cocooned world came up against reality, we failed. Our hobbies overlapped a little because we both loved music, but otherwise our lives and likes were distant. His housemates laughed at the tins of lobster bisque he'd buy for my visits, and my mother raised her eyebrows when I came home one weekend wearing a fur-lined coat that swept the floor. He read the *Telegraph*, and showed me the drawings he had made of the house he would build one day: all wooden panels and a sweeping porch overlooking a lake in Scandinavia or Canada. It was a delicious fantasy of a relationship, one that I knew would never really work, but it gave me somewhere I could rest, luxuriate, and hide whilst I got through other, harder parts of life.

As I grew up, I felt the old attachment to him ebb. By the time I was at university my adolescent closeness to him had gone. Soon I fell in love with someone else and started to spend my holidays with new friends. Nevertheless, our relationship limped on. His feelings had not shifted, so it was up to me to end things. For months that ran to years, I couldn't. Not only did I shrink from hurting him, but I wasn't sure I could cope without this steadying affection in my life. He had been there for as long as I had been an adult, offering an enjoyable escape when the pressure of university and home life got too much. Eventually it was me sleeping with someone else that broke us up, a concrete betrayal that told me, as much as him, that we shouldn't be together. I felt guilty about it for years afterwards – guilt tinged with regret, for holding us both back from living more truthfully and fully.

Emily's new romance reminds me that Valentine's Day is drawing near and, in the inky blackness of the lane one wet evening, I sneak out with an envelope in my hand. I have taken care to make the handwriting on it not too obviously like my own. Inside is a card with a sketch of an oak leaf on the front, accompanied by a poem. Not one of mine; I leave it to Geoffrey Hill to find the right words for my first anonymous valentine card. Nobody passes me as I make the short walk between my house and the cottage where Tom lives. As I lift the letter box I think I hear someone going up the stairs inside, and I stuff the card through quickly. I lift my feet as quietly as I can and walk away, my heart thumping so loud I half-expect that whoever is behind the door can hear it.

Though it still feels like winter, by the beginning of March there are signs that spring is not far away. When we finish work there is a little light in the sky above Silver How, and the vases in the cottage start to be filled with shop-bought daffodils, grown in the south of England, where warmer weather has already arrived. As the daylight lengthens so does the working day, and it can be half past five before we're closing the gate behind the last group of visitors. Where once cottage tours were necessary only once or twice an hour, now there can be people clamouring for them every twenty minutes. Everyone at the Wordsworth Trust can lead a tour. From the director to the shop staff, the curator to the interns, we can all tell the story that binds us to the stone cottage. How William and Dorothy came to live here, how they brought their friends and family to share the place with them, and how they were inspired to write about it.

As interns, we need to slough off our shyness and learn to lead our own tours. At first we follow the other guides around, soaking up their style and stories. Delivering guided tours requires mixing fact, legend, and interpretation with a splash of humour. Each person's tour reflects their own preoccupations: for Mark it is poetry, for the senior guide the history of the building – when it might have been built, by whom, and how. Others retell their own mix of stories: details of lives lived, literature created, the physical reality of *here*.

Each room in Dove Cottage has different stories, tied to the space and objects found within it. In the kitchen, some guides describe how Sir Walter Scott would climb out of a window to partake of a substantial breakfast at the Swan Inn after yet another bowl of oatmeal with the Wordsworths. On the stairs, many stop and point at a burned circle on the floor – this mark was not here in the Wordsworths' time, but nevertheless it records the cottage's lucky escape from conflagration when a later resident placed a bucket of hot coals upon this spot.

My favourite part of the tours comes towards the end, when we stand in an upstairs bedroom beside a window overlooking the garden. On either side of the frame are wooden shutters, locked back during the daytime and only closed after the last tour of the day. Keys have scratched away the glossy varnish around the locks. These are practical, almost unremarkable parts of the house which may not even have been here in the Wordsworths' day. Nevertheless, to me they seem like the heart of the place, the kernel of its purpose. For behind them is a hidden message, an accidental poem waiting to be found.

When Dove Cottage was bought in 1890, the original Trustees were obliged to undertake some repairs of the building. Most of this work has since been redone – the cottage underwent another renovation in the 1970s when it was found to be suffering from the tread of thousands of visitors every year – but one trace of the earlier restoration remains. Behind a shutter, someone left their mark, and I love to share it with anyone who's interested.

As I pull back the left-hand shutter, the visitors crane their necks to read words written there in looping pencil on 4 July 1891. The author, W. Martin, Paperhanger, was employed by the Wordsworth Trust to prepare the house for its first paying visitors. This relict of the house's restorer bridges the gap between the Wordsworths and today. After the rooms had been readied for their first opening, the shutters were locked back, and kept locked. It was only in the 1970s when the cottage was renovated again that they were opened, revealing this unexpected, ghostly message.

In the 1980s, the poet Tony Harrison visited Dove Cottage, and was so inspired by the words that W. Martin left behind that he used them as the concluding line for 'Remains', his sonnet to this place and those who have known it. Soon I have 'Remains' memorised as the finale to my tour. When I begin with 'Though thousands traipse round Wordsworth's Lakeland shrine', visitors sometimes exchange a knowing smile. By the time I've reached the penultimate line, 'in words from Grasmere written by the dead', they are silent, and I can see some shiver as my finger traces the paperhanger's 'one known extant line' which ends the poem: *our heads will be happen cold when this is found.*[2]

What do we look for when we seek out writers in the place they once called home? Entertainment, understanding, perhaps a common thread of experience, some shred of reality that might open another door into their lives? Perhaps it is a little of their genius we hope to gain, a sliver of understanding – that synapse snap again – to illuminate ourselves, to elevate our experience beyond the everyday. Or maybe we search for the unexpected, the gleeful exposing of feet of clay or cupboards full of dusty skeletons. For some it is a pilgrimage, for others a dalliance, and still more do not really know what draws them here. As guides, it is up to us to read each visitor and try to discern the nature of their yearning, providing answers to questions they might not know they had as well as to those they specifically seek to answer.

Many visitors are fascinated by the relationship between Dorothy and William, which had an intensity that can sometimes unsettle. Both siblings experienced their emotions strongly: in 1793, Dorothy confided in Jane Pollard about her brother's 'sort of violence of Affection if I may so Term it which demonstrates itself every moment of the Day when Objects of his affection are present with him'.[3] A decade later, Dorothy described in her Grasmere journal how she 'pillowed' William upon her shoulder and cherished his half-eaten apple. William's desire to be close to his sister was sometimes rendered in the uncomfortable language of a lover's tryst: 'how much do I wish that each emotion of pleasure and pain that visits your heart should excite a similar pleasure or a similar pain within me'. How do we make sense of this intense relationship within the context of a creative life – and within modern sensibilities?

Contemporary language for sibling attachment which includes an element of physical attraction or romantic intent bears a medical tinge. Genetic sexual attraction (GSA), a term first used in America in the 1980s by a support group for adoptees and their families, describes the kind of romantic relationship that can develop between siblings who have not grown up together. It is estimated that around half of adult reunions between close biological family members separated as children involve intense or obsessive emotions.[4] What has been termed the 'shock of familiarity', that jolt of realising that you are not alone and that there are other people like you in the world, has been observed to be a common, even normal, reaction to rediscovering one's natal kin. In the early twentieth century Finnish anthropologist Edvard Westermarck theorised that young children usually develop a strong sexual aversion to close relations, known as negative sexual imprinting. Termed 'the Westermarck effect', it is believed to have the evolutionary advantage of minimising the likelihood of inbreeding, critical for healthy genetic heterosis.[5] Without going through this stage of development, it is believed that people who have experienced separation from family members as infants can seek to recreate in adulthood a closeness they have felt missing. These theories do not, of course, reveal anything about the nature of the relationship between the Wordsworth siblings, but they do offer a different lens – and lexicon – through which to consider it.

Though the Wordsworths certainly desired closeness, that they should jointly seek a home together as siblings was not unusual for their time. Among their friends and social circle, Dorothy and William were far from alone in wanting – and needing – to share domestic arrangements and emotional support with family members. Long before the state offered financial assistance, accommodation, or even basic health care to its citizens, families were often the only safety net, through which people hoped they would not slip. Being close to one's siblings was important. For orphans like the Wordsworths, it could sometimes become a matter of life and death. Dorothy and William were familiar with the multi-sibling households of their childhood friends the Hutchinsons, and in 1795 William became acquainted with another extended family circle that included members of similarly literary inclinations: Coleridge, fellow writer Robert Southey, and the Fricker sisters.

Shortly before moving to Racedown in 1795, William visited Bristol, where he was introduced to 'two extraordinary young men'.[6] One was Robert Southey; the other Samuel Taylor Coleridge, already known to William by name as his younger brother Christopher had been friendly with 'S.T.C.' at university a few years earlier. After leaving Oxford and Cambridge respectively without completing their degrees, Southey and Coleridge moved to Bristol, where, as confirmed supporters of democracy and youthful radicals critical of the political establishment, they earned money by speaking and writing – predominantly about politics, including producing a three-act play, *The Fall of Robespierre*, in 1794. William met them the following summer, and the seed of friendship was sown: 'I saw but very little of [Coleridge]. I wished indeed to have seen more – his talent appears to me very great.' Southey also made a good impression on William: 'his manners please me exceedingly and I have every reason to think very highly of his powers of mind'.[7]

As with the Wordsworths, close creative and intellectual companionship was something both Coleridge and Southey were actively seeking. Throughout 1794–5, the two men had been planning to set up their own 'colony of like-minded spirits' – not in the West Country, but in America. From shared lodgings in Bristol, they dreamed of creating a new democratic society governed by ideals of equality, which the two men termed Pantisocracy, in the comparatively radical colony of Pennsylvania, where the Declaration of Independence had been drawn up twenty years earlier.

Founding this community with Southey and Coleridge would be the Fricker sisters Edith, Sarah, and Mary, educated middle-class neighbours who were able to support themselves with dressmaking following their father's bankruptcy and with whom the young men had become close. Southey became engaged to Edith, whilst impulsive Coleridge lost no time in declaring his love for Sarah shortly after being introduced to her by Southey, and the two couples wed in the autumn of 1795. Their friend and writer-democrat Robert Lovell had recently married the third Fricker sister, Mary, and the close-knit sibling-secured group believed that together they could build a new Eden.

The location of this new Paradise was chosen solely for the beauty of its name: Susquehanna.

Though this idealised community of philosophers never came to pass – none of its would-be members ever visited America, much less set up home there – Coleridge and Southey shared William and Dorothy's desire to draw a family of intellectual as well as sibling kinship around them. All had lost parents early in life, and felt the lack of familial closeness denied to them by these premature deaths. For years they had, out of necessity, been sometimes unwelcome additions to other households. Now in their twenties, they wanted to build their own worlds, both physical and imaginative.

By the spring of 1797, Samuel Taylor Coleridge was living a rather different version of the dreamed-of Pantisocratic idyll. He and Southey had fallen out some months before and, with Sarah and their baby son Hartley, he was living in Nether Stowey, a small village to the west of Bristol. The young family rented a cottage from Thomas Poole, a tanner and supporter of radical causes. Poole's home and Coleridge's cottage shared a garden and though Coleridge had dreamed of being self-sufficient in America, in reality his aptitude for working the land was slight and the garden remained untilled. The household was cramped and noisy, a fact exacerbated by the presence of their lodger, a young poet and mentee of Coleridge's called Charles Lloyd. Lloyd was prone to periods of mental illness derived, according to their mutual friend Charles Lamb, from 'an exquisiteness of feeling which must border on derangement'.[8]

William visited Coleridge at his cottage in March 1797, a meeting which may have helped inspire some significant changes he made to 'The Ruined Cottage' that spring, but it was not until three months later that Coleridge leapt fully into the Wordsworths' lives. Shortly after Mary Hutchinson departed after her six-month stay at Racedown, Coleridge came running across the neighbouring field, having walked forty miles with the intention of befriending the Wordsworths. His animated conversation and infectious enthusiasm made an indelible impression on the siblings; fifty years later, William wrote that he and Dorothy 'both retain the liveliest possible image of his appearance at that moment'.[9] Dorothy's opinion of their new friend was unequivocal in its admiration: '[Coleridge] is a wonderful man. His conversation teems with soul, mind, and spirit ... His eye is large and full, not dark but grey [and] it speaks every emotion of his animated mind.'[10]

It is rare to find such an enthusiastic and detailed physical description of anyone – besides her brother William – in Dorothy's surviving letters. Coleridge clearly made a vivid and electrifying impression, stimulating not only her intellectual interest but also her emotions. Coleridge was similarly delighted at getting to know Dorothy, noting 'She is a woman indeed! – in mind, I mean & heart ... her manners are simple, ardent, impressive.' Though he cannot decide whether she is plain or pretty, her curiosity and attentive nature are striking: 'her eye watchful in minutest observation of nature – and her taste a perfect electrometer – it bends, protrudes, and draws in, at subtlest beauties & most recondite faults'.[11] He compares her to Joan of Arc in innocence of soul, declaring in a letter to his publisher Joseph

Cottle that 'Guilt was a thing impossible in her'.[12] The epithet he reserves for William is 'the greatest Man', whose writings contain '*profound* touches of the human heart'.[13] With this engagement of hearts and minds began the most intensely creative period of the Wordsworths' lives so far.

As our knowledge of the Wordsworths increases, we start to lead tours by ourselves. This daily exercise in recreating worlds reminds me of how we are drawn irresistibly to stories. From the spooky lure of fairy tales to the compulsive spectacle of soap operas, the narrative impulse is as much a part of us as our heartbeat. Psychologically, we need narratives because we live inside them: not just the great, dramatic arc of history, but also our own story. Like the smallest doll inside a Russian *matryoshka*, this personal narrative is often obscured, and yet it is also the kernel around which we build our lives. Other stories weave around it – family tales, experience, education, relationships – but this central sense of self gives us the blueprint of the person we believe ourselves to be.

As experience shapes us, we craft and recraft this story, strengthening treasured memories and attempting to blot out bad ones, so that gradually we become the best fit for how we see ourselves. Whether this be as lucky or daring, wild or caring, cursed or blessed, the story of each of us is the driving force that can turn fortune to disaster, or tragedy into triumph. When we lose the plot, things start to fall apart. If our story doesn't quite make sense to ourselves, we can lose our sense of who we are. Without that narrative thread, our experiences can seem random, unenriching, even frightening in their unpredictability. We risk feeling reduced to someone things happen *to*, rather than one who makes them happen.

Leading tours requires a mix of levity and seriousness, coupled with a confidence in what you know that helps visitors to trust you. We have been surrounded by the Wordsworths' legacy for the last two months, and William and Dorothy now feel as real to us as neighbours, familiar as the cobbles in the lane or the hourly rattle of the Keswick–Kendal bus. We extend the same affectionate ribaldry that we share among ourselves to these literary siblings who, when they lived in the cottage, were not much older than we are now. Though we know we are not supposed to, some of us find some of Dorothy's Grasmere journal entries childishly funny. In private, we laugh over 'John had sodded about the Bee-stand'[14] and 'William rubbed his Table after candles were lighted [...] poor William wore himself & me out with Labour.'[15] We joke that it could be titled 'Dirty Dotty's Diary' – but we take care to hide our mirth, knowing the debt we owe to the people upon whose legacy our lives in Grasmere have been built. Though smutty jokes and silly humour contrast sharply with the world's view of the Wordsworths, we can easily imagine Coleridge smirking as we do.

Sharing the experience of being interns at the same time strengthens the bonds between the ten of us, particularly for those who share a sense of humour. One of these is Jane from Preston and, as with Mark, her Lancashire lilt is rich with words I do not know. Good things are 'gradely', and for lunch she might have a barm cake or butter pie. She finds my Suffolk expressions just as funny, and half-kills herself laughing when I apologise for being late by saying 'I'm on the drag' or describe Dove Cottage's uneven floors as 'on the huh'. Some she adopts: 'Charlie Big Potatoes' seems just the phrase for the neighbour who sometimes jogs past us in a gilet with a plummy shout of 'Hello ladies!' This makes us roar with laughter, and humour cements our friendship until it feels like sisterhood.

Jane and I also share an inclination to anxiety. One night we hear strange rattles and crashes coming from the upstairs bathroom. As we listen from the landing, we convince ourselves that a burglar has broken in through the window and is trying to force the door. A late-night visit from Jeff to check the premises shows our 'burglar' to be a work of fiction. Ancient pipes snaking through the bathroom cupboard are to blame, as they rattle when the water in the pipes is warmer than the freezing air. Coupled with my after-party panic, this episode is a reminder that my mind is not yet recovered from its breakdown of the year before, much as I might wish it otherwise.

Despite surges of worry that gnaw at me in pre-dawn hours, I am feeling happier than I have done for years. In those quiet mornings, as the sun begins to rise and night's dark grip begins to lessen, I think about how the narrative of the rest of my life will play out. Memories of my impatience with other people's – even my friends' – struggles haunt me. It feels cruel and silly to have been not just dismissive but angry with them.

Before I came to Grasmere, I'd had to confront the truth of my feelings after several months of evasion, medicine, and distraction had not improved my mood. My parents persuaded me to talk to someone about what I was feeling and, after two failed attempts at talking to psychologists I didn't like, I finally decided that I could stand weekly visits to a psychotherapist, whose attitude I found consistent and sympathetic rather than over-eager or conspiratorial. She held her ground; whatever I did or said had no bearing on her mood. This was important as my feelings were difficult, overwhelming, hard to 'solve': there was no easy way to return me to myself. I needed someone who could help me work through what had happened without being affected by the volatility of my emotions.

When my narrative came apart in Japan, it completed a process of unstitching me from myself that had begun years earlier. That feeling I had of being difficult – too inquisitive, over-emotional, unhelpfully sensitive – was something I had been aware of since childhood. I asked the sort of questions that adults found difficult to answer: why did Dad sleep on the bunkbed below my brother instead of in bed with Mum? When I was five, we had to leave our house under the cloud of bankruptcy as my father's business absorbed not only his energy, time, and money, but also our family home. The first I knew about this was when the police came round to arrest Dad. It was how Mum found out too. She suspected things weren't going well, but the news that we were about to lose our home came not from Dad but from these uniformed men standing on the doorstep. When I tried to ask her what was wrong, she cried. I couldn't bear her pain on top of my own anxiety of half-understanding.

Whilst Dad battled to shore up the business, Mum found us somewhere else to live. On the estate where she was doing a bit of temporary work to bolster the household finances, there was a small cottage standing empty. The width of a single room, the house had once been a dairy and its flint-and-brick walls were designed to keep the cold in. It didn't have much in the way of heating – an open fireplace in the living room combined with a few ancient storage heaters – but Farm Cottage was cheap – and empty – so we could move in straight away.

That winter we put our possessions into cardboard boxes and left our house behind. That was the end of either of my parents being able to own property or take out a loan. Bankruptcy hangs over a family long after court proceedings finish. It is grisly and drawn out. The assumption is you can't be trusted with money, that you shouldn't be able to persuade someone else to take a risk on your future. There is no possibility of a mortgage for at least a decade: the message is that your family do not deserve security in their future.

Farm Cottage could have been a turning point, and in a way it was, but our years there were marked by the breakdown of my parents' marriage. One night, someone drove up from London and slashed the car tyres whilst we were in bed: Dad's business still owed them money, and they wanted it back. Mum, brought to desperation in the bleak aftermath of bankruptcy and permanently in fear of someone knocking at the door demanding money, sought comfort and escape in a brief affair. For weeks, Mum was hardly at home, ricocheting between the sofas of friends and relatives whilst we remained at the cottage with Dad.

We spoke to her on the phone, but for a few weeks we didn't see her, and I was mad with fear that she would never come back. That summer, Dad made the elder of my brothers and I two swings. He hung long twists of rope from an oak tree by the farm gate and fixed pieces of wood to the ends for seats, and we spent days soaring up and down, reaching for branches with our feet and kicking the trunk as we spun into space.

Though my mother did return and her affair ended, from that time onwards our presence in the house felt temporary. My parents remained together for a further six years and had another child during that time, but unspoken stress and the ongoing trauma of the bankruptcy – creditors calling at the cottage and constant worries over money – became the constant background to our home life. When things got particularly bad, Mum would take herself away. I vividly remember her driving off without telling us where she was going, my brothers and I crying as the car disappeared in a dusty rattle down the farm track. Whilst she was away, we built presents from Lego to give her when she returned. My elder brother always constructed cars or motorbikes, but I preferred houses. The best one I ever made had a barrel-vaulted ceiling, meticulously shaped from a rainbow of tiny bricks. I made Mum lie on the floor and squint through its tiny door so she could marvel at its steps and curves. It wasn't enough to keep her there. By the time I was twelve she had found somewhere else to live, a council house in the nearby town, but this time my younger brother and I went with her.

I tell Jane my story as we walk around Grasmere lake one

, after work. As I talk, Jane runs her fingers along the wall that edges the path, picking at the moss that clings there. 'My parents stayed together until after I left home,' she says, 'but sometimes I wish they hadn't. Their relationship became so sour – I think we'd all have been happier if they'd lived apart.' It is a familiar sentiment. For all that I wanted my parents to get back together, I can see that Mum was more content once she had left Dad and Farm Cottage. Free at last from the threatening fallout of the bankruptcy and secure in a house provided by the council, she could take control of her life once more. Running a single-parent household brought its own difficulties, but at least Mum had the space to relearn how to carve out contentment for herself. And eventually so did I, for living with anxious, unhappy parents is a relentless, aching burden for a child.

If the adults who care for you are often stressed or short-tempered in your presence, it is hard to avoid concluding that you might have made them feel this way. Terse replies to probing questions feel like proof of childish stupidity, not the worried impatience of the adult who might not know how to answer. But once the adult seems content and can make time and space for the child again, that weight of causal misery is lifted. You can be yourself, test out your ideas and feelings without worrying that voicing your concerns will bring your parent further upset. We didn't have the words to talk about what had happened to our family: danger lurked in revisiting the past, so we got on with life in the present, hoping that what had happened would remain behind us. What none of us realised was that the past is the only territory we know. Laid out before us like a map, it is a landscape we revisit throughout our lives to navigate our way through the unseen future. The past may be another country, but it is the only land we feel that we possess. In the absence of a physical kith, it might be the closest thing we have to knowing where we belong – and where we want to go.

A few weeks after I post my anonymous valentine, Tom sends round an email inviting anyone who is not at work to go and help clear ditches. Most weeks he volunteers with a local conservation charity, and this week they'll be unblocking the land drains in Dora's Field at Rydal. Though it's a prosaic offer, I can feel excitement reddening my cheeks. The part of me that thought of becoming a thatcher still longs to work outside. I check the rota – it's my day off. Rydal is close enough to walk to and I set off after breakfast, my feet in wellies, and arrive as the church bell is tolling ten.

Tom gets there before me, along with a handful of other volunteers, all head to toe in waterproofs. The majority are a lot older than us, retirees with time to spend and a desire to preserve the landscape they have come to love. For most, moving to the Lakes has been the longed-for realisation of a dream. Tom is unusual in having grown up here. Young people can rarely afford to live in the National Park, and work outside the tourist trade is scarce. The Wordsworth Trust makes living in the Lakes possible for us both, ensuring that Grasmere continues to have a younger resident population than many Lakeland villages.

Working on the land feels like a way of strengthening my commitment to it, and I think this feeling is shared by the other volunteers. We're split into pairs, and Tom and I are tasked with clearing drains clogged with last year's bracken and moving stones brought down the hillside by the winter's water. As we scrape away the debris of the old year, I ask him what it is like to have lived his whole life beside Dove Cottage, how it is to have grown up in the shadow of the Wordsworths – has he come to feel as if he knows them, or does he need to slough them off like skin so that he can grow into himself?

Tom laughs at my questions. He tells me that he once won the Wordsworth prize at school for reciting a poem, but beyond this – with the exception of the occasional quotation in a birthday card from Jeff – poetry was not really a part of his life here. In their family, Wordsworth was synonymous with work and, like many children, he wasn't really interested in what his dad did. Even though his family lived a few metres from Dove Cottage, the goings-on of either the Wordsworths or the inheritors of their poetic legacy were of peripheral rather than central importance.

Far more vivid were the people whose job it was to keep the spirit of the Wordsworths alive. As a young boy, Tom remembered seeing the chief guide at Dove Cottage taking potshots from his bed, aiming his air rifle at pigeons, his pipe smoke casting a permanent miasma around Town End. Then there was the gardener who once beat a rat to death with a spade in front of Tom, and Hippy Jim, all long hair and tatty clothes, who loved climbing and could often be found halfway up the wall of one of the cottages. Someone else used to dig up potatoes by moonlight in their pyjamas, and there were tales of an assistant whose struggles with alcohol were so monumental that it became someone else's job to get them out of bed each morning.

As Tom and I move mud, stones, and leaves to keep water flowing down the hillside, I hope that we are doing good and not harm here. We have been asked to keep paths clear so that visitors will not mar more of the landscape with their footsteps, but nature seems to have her own plans. Today the sky is clear, but the forecast predicts two long weeks of rain ahead that will push more soil towards the lake and likely make our labours here redundant. Winter exerts strong forces on this landscape; to battle them feels like a ravage of its own.

We also learn to pleach the hawthorns that edge the field. Pleaching is the art of making a hedge from living trees. By cutting, bending, and weaving woody trunks and limbs, a skilful hedge-layer can persuade a line of saplings to defy gravity. It takes time and dedication to shift trees from vertical to horizontal, and hedges require annual persuasion to remain in parallel to the ground. The work is worth it, for within these webs of branches a world of small, important life abounds. Birds and small mammals need the guardianship of a pleached hedge, shielded by its tangled branches and fed with nuts and berries from hazel, hawthorn, spindle, blackberry, and beech.

Pleaching used to be an essential part of maintaining rural landscapes, but it is a dying art. In Cumbria it is one of a few traditional farming practices which endure because there isn't another, better way to farm these fells. This land is steep and the weather wetter than that of any other English county. Winds batter the hills year round, and yet this is no wilderness. It is a living, lived-in landscape that has been farmed for more than a thousand years. Hundreds of metres above the valleys, where no trees can grow, drystone walls mark boundaries and offer shelter for livestock. They look like they have been there forever, formed by powerful gods who moved those stones into improbably precipitous positions.

The truth of the survival of these walls and hedges is prosaic: they only exist because of regular and careful human maintenance. Now it is our turn to help them. Armoured in thick leather gloves, Tom and I are shown how to swing a borrowed billhook towards a clump of overgrown trees. Slicing through bark and wood, we stop short of chopping them down, leaving a latch of living wood, no thicker than a thumb, between the lower and upper trunk. From there we bend the trees until they lie parallel to the ground, then weave their limbs into the spaces along the field's edge. Cutting, bending, weaving: we are trying to keep the line of the living hedge true to itself.

6

Second Selves

'for the sake
Of youthful poets, who among these hills
Will be my second self when I am gone.'

William Wordsworth, 'Michael', ll. 37–9,
Lyrical Ballads (1800)[1]

After the chilly deluges of late winter, spring finally arrives in Grasmere in a burst of sunshine. As the air warms, the roads become edged with colour as spring flowers spill across the verges. The Dove Cottage shop gets busy. Its daffodil-decked cups, cards, and tea towels are designed to honour William's best-known poem, but visitors agree that they are just the thing for Easter gifts. On our tours we enjoy a little literary myth-busting, telling visitors that 'I wandered lonely as a cloud' owes more to Dorothy's observations than her brother's, and that Mary Hutchinson came up with that most Wordsworthian of couplets about the solace of memory, 'They flash upon that inward eye / Which is the bliss of solitude'.

The arrival of warmer weather also heralds the start of another season: the Trust's fortnightly poetry readings. A regular fixture of the Grasmere calendar, they draw audiences from across the country. Some are given by the Trust's Poets in Residence, past and present, whilst other writers are invited specially to Grasmere to read their poems. Seamus Heaney, John Cooper Clarke, Jackie Kay: all have come here to share their verse.

Grasmere's readings partly have their genesis in the Morden Tower poetry scene, set up in Newcastle in the 1960s by writers and activists Tom and Connie Pickard. Inspired by visiting Edinburgh, where they delighted in the creative vitality of the Festival Fringe and Jim Haynes's infamous Paperback Bookshop, the bohemian Pickards decided to set up a similar enterprise in their own city. The Morden Tower, a damp thirteenth-century turret room in Newcastle's city walls only accessible down a dark alleyway adjacent to the kitchens of several Chinese restaurants, was their chosen, if unlikely, venue.

Once described by a publisher's rep as being 'more suitable for breeding pigeons'[2] than for use as a literary venue, the Tower nevertheless became a vibrant hub for contemporary poetry. It had no plumbing or electricity, but at ten shillings a week it was affordable, and it was also less than a ten-minute walk from the city's main railway station, an important consideration for both audiences and performers. Readings there were memorable: the gas supply was frequently cut off, with poets sometimes performing by candlelight or the glow of an open fire. Nevertheless, it all added to the bohemian allure of the Tower, and soon poets in the ascendant flocked to read there, including Lawrence Ferlinghetti, Allen Ginsberg (who described it as a 'mediaeval tackroom'[3]), and Ted Hughes. Against the odds, it became one of the most iconic venues for poetry readings in Britain. In the words of critic and editor Eric Mottram, the Morden Tower was where 'the finest British and American poets read at a time when they were unheard elsewhere [in England]'.[4]

At the heart of the Morden Tower community was the edict that poetry should not, in the words of Basil Bunting, 'lie dead on the page'[5] but exist as a vibrant, living entity for anyone to access. Audiences were a mix of Newcastle's eclectic creative community – students, artists, academics, writers – and young, working-class Northumbrians, many of whom were on the dole but earned a little cash in hand as musicians and performers in pubs and folk clubs. As a young academic, Robert Woof was initially drawn to the fizz and fire of these readings and the alternative society they fostered. In the early years, the Pickards received several grants from Northern Arts, the regional board of the government-funded Arts Council of Great Britain, to cover the costs of the readings, but after a while relations between the funders, the university, and the organisers of the Tower readings cooled.[6] From the 1970s, Robert began to invite poets who had read in Newcastle to perform their work in Grasmere.

Some of these, including Seamus Heaney and Tony Harrison, became semi-regular members of the Town End community. Sometimes they stayed in local hotels, often alongside academics attending conferences or on research trips, but other times they would make use of the Trust's accommodation in Town End, where they delighted in what Heaney called the 'strange residual life' that flourished around Dove Cottage.[7] This was the beginning of the creative legacy Robert had envisioned, and by the late 1990s the Wordsworth Trust was running a regular programme of residencies and readings, as well as publishing contemporary poetry inspired by writers connected to Town End.

The Trust doesn't have a building big enough to host events for audiences of more than about thirty, so the sympathetic vicar of St Oswald's church in Grasmere now opens it to the poetry faithful once a fortnight. Every other Tuesday afternoon, the literature officer fills the back seat of his tiny car with rattling boxes of wine glasses and the boot with a microphone stand and two battered speakers. On the front seat are a box or two of books, and beside them a noisy tin of coins. This paraphernalia necessary for the business of poetry clatters slowly down to the church, and we follow in its wake to help set up.

Having laid out fifty light-bulb glasses and some bowls of peanuts across two trestle tables, Emily, Catherine, and I station ourselves beside the main and side doors, ready to welcome the audience. Most weeks the poets read in pairs, often a bigger name supported by an up-and-coming writer, but once or twice a year a superstar of verse comes to do a solo show, someone whose name is known not just among the small, passionate crowd who openly profess to love the written word. Perhaps Ian MacMillan, unofficial

Bard of Barnsley, or maybe a poet laureate: Andrew, Carol Ann, Simon – our colleagues know them by their first names, the way the rest of the world does Elvis, Bono, or Beyoncé.

Two poets – Josephine Dickinson and Jeremy Over – are reading in Grasmere tonight, and fifty, maybe sixty, people have squeezed into the wooden pews to hear their verse. As we wait for the reading to begin, conversation hums and shoes squeak on the old slate floor. People arrive wrapped up in anticipation of the cold draughts that sometimes haunt the church, but tonight the heating's working, and before long the building echoes with the sounds of scarves being unwound and coats unbuttoned. Beside me in the pew Mark is telling us about the poets, both of whom he has heard read before. He mentions that Josephine once used 'the hard stuff' – opioids – though not for creative stimulus. In fact, taking methadone did the opposite, dulling her experience to the point where creative expression was impossible.

Drug taking is something we talk about in our cottage tours, for in one of the upstairs bedrooms in Dove Cottage is a cabinet containing a tiny bottle of black liquid labelled 'Genuine Black Drop'. This was a local brand name for laudanum, a preparation of opium grains dissolved in wine and flavoured with sugar and spices. In the eighteenth and nineteenth centuries opiates were available without prescription and recommended for almost every ailment or distress, including to soothe and calm young children. Laudanum was particularly popular; Dorothy took it for various aches and pains, marking such events in her diary (for example, on 24 November 1800 she 'had the tooth-ach in the night – took Laudanum', after which she was 'very sleepy – slept all night').[8]

Whilst William almost never imbibed laudanum or its sister sedatives, Samuel Taylor Coleridge was familiar with a wide range of its effects. It is likely that he, alongside many others, was first was given opium as a child, and by the time he was at university he was self-medicating with laudanum on a semi-regular basis. Initially it seems he used it as a physical analgesic; however, by March 1796 he was also taking it as a tranquilliser, particularly when anxiety left him unable to sleep. Later that year he started to experience neuralgia in his face, and by the time he walked to Racedown to meet the Wordsworths, he was administering himself with twenty-five drops of laudanum every five hours.

As well as deadening pain, opium can bring about other sensations. Coleridge observed in himself a '[d]eep self-possession, an intense repose ... relapses into bliss',[9] and openly enjoyed the 'reveries' or euphoric dreamlike states it can cause. Whilst under the influence, he saw 'phantoms of sublimity' in smoke rising from the fire, and noticed that 'liquid convolutions of hope' ran through him as he watched them. He found this dreamy drowsiness delightful, referring to it as 'inchantment'. One poem was composed directly in response to it; 'Kubla Khan' was written in the autumn of 1797 after taking a few grains of opium on a walk near Nether Stowey. It remains a wildly vivid poem that passes on this enchantment to its readers.

Whilst hazy reveries like these were welcomed by the poet-dreamer, Coleridge's use of opium was beginning to create more problems than it solved. The sleeplessness and neuralgia that had dogged his days and nights became more frequent during his time in Nether Stowey. He found it increasingly difficult to focus on his writing, was constantly ill with diarrhoea, and some days would ingest hundreds of drops of laudanum. If he reduced this dose, the immediate consequences were as bad: his bowels remained unreliable, his body broke out in boils, and his testicles became grotesquely swollen.

At first the Wordsworths did not realise Coleridge's dependence on the drug, for the impact of their developing friendship was itself intoxicating. Almost as soon as their first radiant Racedown meeting was over, Coleridge borrowed a cart to take the Wordsworths to his cottage at Nether Stowey. He introduced Dorothy to his family and to the rolling Quantock hills, and together the friends explored the wooded coastline that lines the south side of the Bristol Channel. Days later, the Wordsworths arranged to rent grand Alfoxden House – which they could ill afford – so that they might remain close to this new and exciting friend.

The feelings shared between William, Dorothy, and Coleridge were intense and transformational, and the creative impact of this proximity was immediate. Between the summers of 1797 and 1798, William composed more than twenty poems. For any writer, much less one who had spent years working on a handful of verses, this was phenomenal. Walking in the Quantocks with Dorothy and William likewise inspired Coleridge to write *The Rime of the Ancient Mariner*, a verse epic that charts a journey of a sea captain and his dramatic, supernatural encounters. The poem grew rapidly in the winter months of 1797–8, and before it was finished the three friends had decided to publish *Rime* as part of a shared endeavour: *Lyrical Ballads*, a collection of 'experimental verse'.

The nineteen poems William contributed to the *Ballads* were almost all written at Alfoxden and based on the lives and experiences of real people. Two, 'Lines left upon a Seat in a Yew-tree' and 'Expostulation and Reply', had their roots in William's boyhood on the shores of Esthwaite, but many more – 'The Female Vagrant', 'Goody Blake and Harry Gill', 'Simon Lee', 'Anecdote for Fathers', 'The Thorn', 'The Mad Mother', 'The Idiot Boy', and 'Old Man Travelling' – had been inspired by stories told to William in Somerset. Most use a simple lexicon and a regular rhyming structure that make them memorable and easy to follow – something not popular in poetry at the time. William later added a Preface to the *Ballads* to explain that he had deliberately chosen to write 'in a selection of language really used by men' because their 'simple and unelaborated expressions' form 'a more permanent, and a far more philosophical language, than that which is frequently substituted for it by Poets'. Poets, William believed, wanted to see themselves as special, 'conferring honour upon themselves and their art' by indulging in 'arbitrary and capricious habits of expression, in order to furnish food for fickle tastes, and fickle appetites'.[10] In other words, poetry should not aim to follow fashion, but should speak truthfully about universal human experience.

William's poems sought to champion the voices of those not usually permitted a poetic platform. In 1797 the experiences of the poor, of women with post-natal psychosis, of

children with learning difficulties were not thought fit subjects for poetry. Yet in them William saw valuable truths and
a relevance and commonality missing from popular literature
of the time. His *Ballads* are verse stories with transparent,
compassionate, humane – and at the time, radical – moral-
ities which took years to become widely accepted but now
form the basis of the provision of social and health care
in the UK. *Lyrical Ballads* not only championed ordinary
voices, it also made the case for personal freedom above
social convention, and did so in a new style of verse that was
intentionally plain, with the aim of being straightforward to
understand.

Another important manuscript was begun at Alfoxden
when, on 20 January 1798, Dorothy began to keep a journal.
She had long been an attentive correspondent, but as her
brother and Coleridge were fervently busy with poems for
Lyrical Ballads, she was inspired (and encouraged by them)
to start her own literary endeavour. As far as we can know,
the Alfoxden journal was the first time she wrote anything
on her own account besides letters. Full of acute observations of the natural world, the journal was also a witness to
her own experience. As well as making a physical record of
the connection or triple bond that had been forged between
the three, it provided vital inspiration for William and
Coleridge as they tried to turn the stuff of their lives into
immortal verse. The journal bears witness to the moment
when the creative friendship between William, Dorothy, and
Coleridge became a vital crucible for the Romantic revolution as they 'together wantoned in wild Poesy'.[11]

Their friendship was forged in the heat of Coleridge's

virtuosic creativity, and as they got to know each other, William came to view himself and Coleridge as 'Twins almost in genius and in mind [...] Prestin'd, if two beings ever were, / To seek the same delights.'[12] For his part, Coleridge felt that being with William and Dorothy was to become 'three persons and one soul'. This triumvirate of youthful potential, enamoured of what they saw of themselves reflected in each other, had – though it was not acknowledged then – begun to change the history of literature.

Though the Wordsworths experienced a kind of creative 'homecoming' in their move to Alfoxden, by late spring of 1798 they had realised two things. The first was that they could not afford to continue to rent this rather grand house; the second, proximity to Coleridge was now essential for William to realise his poetic vocation. But by the summer of 1798 Coleridge's creative output had slackened considerably. When he first met the Wordsworths, Coleridge had been the more prolific writer, as well as the more dynamic speaker. But now he was having difficulty not just with poetry, but also in producing prose essays, the publication of which provided a core part of his income. At the same time, his expenditure on opium was increasing.

William and Dorothy were increasingly concerned for Coleridge – and for themselves, aware of the interdependence of their poetic vocation and shared commitment to finishing *Lyrical Ballads*. Perhaps going abroad, something they had often discussed and dreamed of funding through sales of the *Ballads*, would lessen their friend's temptations whilst improving their own precarious financial situation, as life on the Continent was apparently cheaper than it was in England. As the lease on Alfoxden came to an end, Coleridge visited the siblings one last time there, where they made, in William's words, 'a resolution: Coleridge, Mrs Coleridge [his wife, Sarah], my Sister and myself of going into Germany'.[13]

Living in Germany had been a long-held dream for Coleridge. He spoke German fluently, revered German philosophers and writers like Kant, Schiller, and Goethe, and believed that the kind of intellectual and social freedom he – and the Wordsworths – wanted was only possible on the Continent. Their initial aim was to 'pass the two ensuing years in order to acquire the German language, and to furnish ourselves with a tolerable stock of information in natural science'. They also had an idea of the geography or landscape they would prefer: 'Our plan is to settle if possible in a village near a university, in a pleasant, and, if we can a mountainous, country.'[14]

Though William and Dorothy spoke little German, Coleridge assured them that they would quickly become proficient once abroad. He also convinced them that he and William could soon secure paid positions at German universities. When the lease on Alfoxden expired in June 1798, the siblings did not renew it, and instead spent a peripatetic summer with friends in Wales, Shirehampton, and Bristol whilst they waited for Coleridge to finalise plans for going to Germany. William also continued to work on poems for inclusion in *Lyrical Ballads*; 'Lines written a few miles above Tintern Abbey', the collection's concluding poem, was written that July. By September, just days after the anonymous publication of the *Ballads*, the Wordsworths and Coleridge, accompanied by the latter's wealthy friend John Chester, set sail from Yarmouth for new lives on the Continent. Perhaps abroad they could find a home to share, and continue the reciprocal creativity that had allowed each to feel like the best version of themselves.

As the clock strikes the hour, the church quietens, and into the expectant silence come Josephine's words. I have never heard poetry spoken like this before, and it is beautiful. Her voice is clear as water, the syllables rising and falling into place like bells in a peal. Between each word is the tiniest gap, an infinitesimal pause that works the acoustic so that sentences form like chords, each word oscillating in the minute word-swim of the last. Josephine sounds her words like music, and once the applause fades she tells us that she has been deaf since childhood and that before becoming a published poet, she had a career in performing and composing classical music – though writing poetry has been an important part of her life since she lost her hearing at the age of six.[15]

It seems oxymoronic – a deaf poet and musician? – but as my lazy brain forms the thought Josephine shatters it. Ears – highly efficient though they are at turning sound pressures to neuro-electrical signals for the brain – are only a small part of our ability to hear: our entire bodies resonate with sounds of different frequencies. As those who have felt the bass vibrating through them from speakers at a music gig will know, listening to music can be a sensory experience that involves the entire body.[16] Researchers at the Department of Information and Communications

Engineering of Tokyo Institute of Technology have shown that sound energy from live music (as well as from loud-speakers) can vibrate the body through the air, as well as through chairs and flooring.[17] These vibrations, particularly at lower frequencies, are an important part of the experience of 'hearing' music, demonstrating that sound is experienced by far more of ourselves than simply our ears.

Even comparatively quiet, unamplified speech affects us at a sensory level, for the physical sensation of words moving through the air is perceptible to us all, even though we may not consciously realise it. This is most apparent in aspirated plosives – the 'p' of 'poet' and 'performance' – when the tiny puffs of air formed by the lips brush our skin. Researchers from the Department of Linguistics at the University of British Columbia have shown that when they applied inaudible air puffs on participants' skin, syllables heard simultaneously were more likely to be misinterpreted than when the same experiment was repeated without the air puffs.[18] Our bodies sense language in ways that go beyond what Wordsworth termed 'the mighty world / Of eye and ear'.[19]

As Josephine continues reading, I sit silent and statue-still, trying to tune in to the frequencies of her voice. My body seems to tingle as I imagine the words echoing through me, and in my chest my heart feels like it is retuning itself to follow the beat of her words. Around me the audience sit entranced as the old church takes each syllable and raises it to the heights.

The last poem Josephine reads is titled 'Do I Sleep with You?', a sonnet about her relationship with the man who became her husband. Josephine moved to Cumbria at the end of a very low period in her life during which she took methadone. There, she met and fell in love with Douglas Dickinson, a local farmer. Douglas was more than forty years Josephine's senior, and they were married for six years until his death at the age of ninety-two.

At their first meeting, he recognised the symptoms of drug dependence and withdrawal, but instead of blame or disapproval, he offered tea, and before long their friendship turned to love. On paper they were not much alike: he was a Cumbrian farmer, she a composer and student of the classics from urban southern England. Yet at heart their loves were twinned: he too loved poetry and words, and the world of farming became a new love for Josephine. The poems that their shared lives inspired explore the bond between people and a landscape, between physical realities and imagined futures, between what is real and what is feared.

The heart is our tireless, overworked synonym for love. Falling in love is fierce, and this metaphor of vertiginous abandon is no accident. Nothing more than a glimpse or word is needed to launch a person's heart into that wild abyss of longing. Stomachs drop and palms sweat. Nerves tingle with tense anticipation, a heightened awareness of another person's presence. Thoughts and daydreams intermingle as the heart demands attention to these feelings. Once kindled, love is hard to quench, and with good reason.

Before coming to Grasmere I had been in love twice, and been loved twice. After my first boyfriend, there were two others: one adored me, the other I adored. These were the imaginative passions of late adolescence, fired by hormones that shape our brains at a time when we realise that we can be different things to different people. The future is amorphous and sometimes we cannot divine our own shape in it. We need to test ourselves against others, to see how our idea of what we might become fits in with the rest of the world.

The one who loved me unrequitedly told me how and why he felt the way he did. This declaration came in a letter that arrived one summer morning during my last weeks at university. As soon as I saw my name on the envelope, I knew what it said. I recognised the handwriting, and a flicker of instinct told me what was inside. The letter, detailing almost a decade of semi-secret adoration, showed me how it was possible to be haunted by the ghost of who you thought you might have been. Those hand-inked words offered me a gateway into someone else's heart, but it was one through which I knew I could not pass. I would have to turn aside the love those words proffered. My stomach twisted and I could feel my nerves tense in anticipation of the action I knew I must take. Dizzy nausea swam in my ears, for which of us likes to think of ourselves as the inflicter of a heart-wound?

Heartbreak is no idle metaphor: medical research has revealed that sometimes our hearts become so misshapen by grief or distress that they simply cease to beat. First described in Japan in 1990, takotsubo cardiomyopathy is also known as 'broken heart syndrome', where the left ventricle of the heart is weakened or damaged by stress. This causes it to balloon dangerously on the lower left side, and the heart comes to resemble a *tako-tsubo*, a traditional pot used by Japanese fishermen to catch octopuses. This is metaphor made real: grief or shock can literally reshape the body until it cannot function.

When depression had me in its grip, my heart felt like it had been cut from my chest. The body is a literalist: our hearts speak our body's language with each pulse and squeeze. They supply our whole selves with everything we need to live, picking up chemical messages from our blood and transmitting them to the parts of ourselves that need to listen. Heart cells are the only cells that are present throughout our lives: from the first beat to the last, they do not have time to rest and regrow as those in our bones and muscles do. They are our oldest cells; none know us better.

My own heart shattered the same summer that I dealt out heartbreak. Though that outpouring of adoration left me with a kind of shivered guilt, the fact that I was leaving for Japan in a few weeks' time drove me to attempt a declaration of my own. For most of the last three years I had fancied myself in love with someone at college. We had shared a group of friends and a few inebriated kisses; I thought there was a chance he felt as I did.

Once we went to a performance of lieder in a little concert hall not far from college. It was autumn, and we walked there under the turning leaves to hear a warm baritone voice singing words that made me ache: 'The heavens had silently kissed the earth. So that in a shower of blossoms, she must only dream of him.' That afternoon fed a thousand fantasies – though all of them were mine. On my last night at university, I tried to tell him how I felt, but he didn't share the sentiment. I drowned my sorrows in a binge of booze and laughing gas and ended that night, and my student days, in bed with a friend who professed to prefer men. Though it wasn't love, I like to think we gave each other a gift in that tensioned, heady time.

As Josephine finishes her reading, the church is momentarily silent, before its walls echo with cacophonous applause. Leading it is the Wordsworth Trust's president and Robert Woof's widow, Pamela Woof, whose slight, upright frame commands a front-row seat. Editor of the definitive edition of Dorothy's journals and author of several essays on the Wordsworths and their circle, Pamela listens to poetry with an ear that is flattering in its intensity. After each reading her hand shoots up and, as she leads the conversation around the poem in her precise, clear voice, her eyes twinkle with a shared communion. Inspiration, intimation, consolation: they are all there, if the listener's ear is tuned to them. The best poems shorten that gap between *them* and *us*, *then* and *now*: rooted in personal experience, they nevertheless transcend time and space because, as William wrote, 'we have all of us one human heart'.[20]

How literature helps us manage what it means to be human – to learn, to feel, to love – has been a central part of Pamela's life. Born in Padiham in Lancashire, she won a scholarship to Accrington High School for Girls and went on to study English at St Hugh's College, Oxford in 1949. In those post-war years men outnumbered women five to one, so whilst she worked hard and graduated with a First, there were also plenty of young men whose company she

could enjoy on Oxford's tennis courts, and in its tea rooms
and dance halls. Pamela began postgraduate studies of the
poetry of John Donne, but, discouraged by a dismissive
tutor, she left and returned home, where for a short time she
taught at a convent school. After Oxford, life in suburban
Lancashire felt stifling – the acme of her mother's dreams for
Pamela was to marry the local bank manager – and Pamela
realised she had to escape. Her older brother had gone to
work as an aeronautical engineer in Toronto, so Pamela told
her parents she was going to visit him. What she did not
reveal then was that she had a one-way ticket – and no plans
to return.

Canada held the promise of another life, though at first
Pamela struggled to find it. After a while she found herself drawn to the lively academic atmosphere of Toronto's
university community, so she took a job at the university
bookshop. The initial aim was to earn enough money to buy
a car, as her brother lived fourteen miles from the central
campus, but she soon realised that she would need another,
better paying job to realise her ambition. Approaching the
Mother Superior of a local convent school to ask if there
was a vacancy for an English teacher, Pamela – on the
strength of her accent – was asked if she would coach basketball instead. Knowing nothing about the sport, Pamela
nevertheless agreed to take on the job, but soon devised a
system whereby the more proficient players in her classes
would demonstrate to the others, leaving her free to earn
extra money marking undergraduate English essays for
the University of Toronto in the relative peace of the
changing rooms.

Though basketball coaching wasn't very suitable work for this lover of the written word, neither at first was grading essays. The Canadian university system was markedly different from the one Pamela had experienced at Oxford, and on her first assignment she failed eighty per cent of the scripts. Upon returning them to the English faculty Pamela was told that this would not do, and it was then that she found her 'knight in shining armour'. Robert, working towards his PhD in the same department, stepped in and agreed to show her how to grade papers according to University of Toronto guidelines.

These two young people – northern grammar schoolboy and girl, both passionate about the world of words – fell in love and, in 1958, got married. Their first child was born in Canada in 1960; shortly after, the family moved back to England for Robert's fellowship in Newcastle. At first Pamela and Robert rented a university flat, but halfway through the two-year fellowship Robert secured a lectureship and they were able to buy a terraced house in Jesmond – a necessity, since more children soon arrived: two sons in 1963 and 1965, and a second daughter in 1968.

Though Pamela had won the Wordsworth prize at school and studied Romantic literature at university, it was Robert's scholarship that brought her to the Wordsworth Trust. She knew the Lake District from family holidays and teenage youth hostelling adventures, though her fondest early memories of Grasmere were of the scones served in the tea room opposite Dove Cottage. The Wordsworth Trust's manuscripts were increasingly becoming the focus of Robert's time and attention and, as Robert had never learned to drive, Pamela helped him make the long journey to Grasmere. The basketball coaching and essay marking had paid off: she now had a Morris Minor, and though she was then mostly at home looking after the children, Pamela would often take Robert to the West Road on the outskirts of Newcastle so that he could hitch a lift the rest of the way to the Lakes. Trains and taxis were expensive, and in those early years infrequently used.

At this time most Trustees visiting Dove Cottage, including Robert, would stay in Miss Borwick's guesthouse, run from the terraced house where I now live. After her death, Robert persuaded the Trust to buy the old farmhouse at Sykeside. The adjacent barn was already being used as the Wordsworth Museum; acquiring Sykeside meant that Trustees would have somewhere free to stay when they came to Grasmere, as well as preserving the building which had been home to the Wordsworths' neighbours. The house was eventually purchased in 1968, and from then on Sykeside became Trust accommodation.

Sykeside was very different from the tall Victorian terrace where the Woofs lived in Newcastle. The original farmhouse rooms were small, and some had been subdivided further during the nineteenth century using wooden partitions that had once been part of Grasmere church. The beams between the floors were – and still are – unceiled, leaking light and sound from room to room. In the sitting-room ceiling was a knothole in the wood so large that one could observe what was going on in the bedroom on the floor above. Other additions since the Wordsworths' time were running water, electricity, and a small extension containing a bathroom and kitchen, complete with a range which, on the occasions that Robert had taken a taxi from the station, he would persuade a loyal taxi driver to light for him.

Now that there was somewhere for them all to stay, it fell to Pamela to drive the whole family the hundred miles to Grasmere. They came as often as they could (despite protests from the growing children, who longed for the sun and sand of the Mediterranean), fitting in visits around school and Pamela's own busy schedule: in 1970, she secured a teaching post with the Department of Continuing Education at Newcastle University. It was a job she held for the next three decades, and one in which she delighted, sharing the works of Shakespeare, the Romantics, and Milton with adults returning to education. So whilst much of the Woofs' life was in Newcastle, Sykeside became their home at Grasmere – in Pamela's words, 'the loved and frequent delight of us all'.[21]

From the kitchen window at Sykeside, standing at the sink as she worked her way through the washing up, Pamela would watch the kaleidoscope of Town End life. It was an ever-changing parade of human emotion, one where anything could – and did – happen. She became familiar with the constantly changing and considerable number of people who came to contribute to the work of the Trust, which by the late 1970s had transformed into a kind of *genius loci* for the Romantic spirit as well as for studying the Romantics. A frequent guest at Sykeside was the charismatic Jonathan Wordsworth, Wordsworth scholar at Oxford University, William and Dorothy's great-great-great nephew, and chairman and later president of the Trust. Town End was a stage upon which grand dramas played out – stories of love and

disappointment, of triumph and despair, of the struggles
of turning hopes and dreams into a lived reality. Romances
between staff and volunteers, Trustees and students, local
residents and poets: Sykeside bore witness to them all.

The borders between love, creativity, and friendship are
flexible, porous; Robert Woof's studies of the relationship
between William, Dorothy, and Coleridge had demonstrated
that. Since coming here we have heard how many young
people have been drawn to Town End – and particularly
to Robert, with his passion for Dove Cottage and its literary legacy. One of these, the poet Paul Farley, arrived in
Grasmere one February day to take up a poetry residency in
High Sykeside, one of the little nineteenth-century houses
close to Dove Cottage.

Paul had first visited the Lake District as a child, when
he experienced it as a kind of magical land, 'a place apart'
from his daily life on an estate in South Merseyside. After
studying at Chelsea School of Art and living in Brighton,
Paul was in his early thirties when he returned to Cumbria,
invited by Robert and Pamela to become the Trust's Poet in
Residence at the turn of the millennium. He had recently
won a Forward Prize for Poetry and a Somerset Maugham
Award, and been named *Sunday Times* Young Writer of the
Year; the offer of an opportunity to live and write as the
Wordsworths' latter-day neighbour was imagined as a gift
for both the writer, still developing his poetic voice, and the
Trust, for which paid poetry residencies were a relatively
recent innovation.

At first Paul found Grasmere life strange, even

discombobulating. In contrast to the hum and buzz of urban life, Town End's February quiet seemed deafening. High Sykeside had not a stick of furniture in it and, aside from an ancient storage heater in one bedroom, the only source of warmth was an open fire – if you could set it. Sally Woodhead, one of Robert's assistants, had to show Paul how to kindle light and heat in the old fireplace, and for several weeks he spent hours kneeling at that domestic altar, coaxing it into life.

It seemed to rain every day that spring, filling the air with the kind of damp coldness that seeps into your bones. Clouds obscured the surrounding fells, adding to a feeling of claustrophobia for this self-termed 'typical townie', who at times felt he had stepped on to the set of the cult film *Withnail and I*. Its eponymous protagonists, a pair of jobbing actors from London who have come on holiday to Cumbria half by accident, lurch between inebriated euphoria and hungover despair as they search for the good life – or at least an open pub – in a landscape dominated by swirling mists, brusque farmers, and heavy rain.

The stunning revelation of a sunny May morning three months later swept away any feelings of lonely desperation like an outgoing tide. Finally robed in sunlight, the Vale of Grasmere shimmered like a vision as beautiful as William's poetry had promised: 'a blended holiness of earth and sky'.[22] Over the winter Paul had been deepening his knowledge of those Grasmere poems, guided by Robert and Pamela, who lived a stone's throw away at Sykeside. They were inspirational neighbours, generous in helping younger writers to better understand the lives and writing of the Romantics. Robert in particular seemed like a force of nature who never slept, staying up late after long days at work to drink whisky, read *The Prelude*, and lead animated discussions about life, art, and poetry into the small hours. Robert accorded with Wordsworth's 'never-failing principle of joy'[23] in exploring philosophies of delight: exploring what elevates our experience beyond the quotidian was as central to his life as it had been to William as he worked on his poems here in Grasmere.

During firelit evenings at Sykeside, 'offcomers' (to use the local term for those not from the district) like Paul saw how they could become guardians of something both physical and intangible: the beauty of place, the essential human expression of feeling and thought. Robert became their friend as well as an affectionate mentor, someone whose search for joy was exceeded only by his intellectual strength and tremendous capacity for seeing, in Wordsworth's words, 'into the life of things'.[24] He encouraged them in both their creative work and their academic studies, and there were aspects of those Sykeside evenings that were a continuation of the fertile, curious ground trodden here by the Wordsworths and their remarkable friends two hundred years before.

A few people first brought to Dove Cottage by Robert are still in Grasmere and working for the Trust, somewhat older but in a sense continuing his aim of passing on that torch of understanding regarding the value of words and poetry in teaching and consoling, alongside caring for the physical papers upon which those words were written. They learned from him the vital importance of touching the minds and hearts of busy people involved in the activities of living in the world, and understood through him the eternal quality of humanity's growth through time, the voyage that we must all make from birth to death. Though Robert's influence permeates Town End – from the buildings that house us to the museum and archives in which we work – in another way his more important legacy has been passing on the knowledge of how our shared experiences connect us to, rather than separate us from, everyone who has gone before and will come after.

After the poetry reading we head down to Tweedies and, after a few sips of my first pint, I can feel a lightness giddying through me. My mind, delicately balanced after months mired in depression, can easily tip into overdrive, and sometimes my tongue can hardly keep up with my dizzy head. I'm all jokes and flirtation – and in Tweedies, anyone's a valid target. Thursday night is usually when I'm at my best (or worst): it's pub quiz night, when we try to win that week-same prize: a gallon of beer, redeemable against eight one-pint tokens. We have some success, though when we have won we usually dispense with the prize before last orders.

Tom and his younger brother Laurie often come to the quiz, and I always hope that we will be on the same team. One Thursday night I spill Tom's entire fresh-pulled pint across our table, a boozy cataract that soaks his shirt and jeans. Though I am mortified at my clumsiness, part of me thrills at seeing him peel off his T-shirt to reveal taut muscles honed by climbing. Jane catches my appraising look, and with a wink lets me know that she knows how I feel.

Tonight Josephine joins us in Tweedies, and though I feel we are initially awkward conversationalists, trying to position ourselves so that she can read our lips and attempting not to talk over each other as we often do, a drink relaxes us, and before long we are listening to her and Mark discussing the difference between reading poems on the page and performing them aloud. Whereas listening to a poem is an aural communion between at least two people, reading and writing are far more solitary endeavours, usually taking place in silence. In a way, we hallucinate words on the page into sounds in our heads when we read. This phantasm of sounds, of ghostly echoes of words we've heard – or never heard – happens so fast that most of us are unaware of it. But in our heads, all the time the ghost orchestra of reality plays on, feeding into that silent space where, like a shadow theatre, the voices of everyone we've ever heard might suddenly grab our inner ear and startle us into listening.

As I listen to Josephine describe her experience of writing poems, I feel an eery prickle down my spine. The loudness of my own internal voice had been a constant, cacophonic companion the year before I came to Grasmere. Only audible inside my head, this voice had tortured me since before I left Japan, turning every tiny thing I did into an indictment of how bad, or wrong, or stupid I was. The voice almost always sounded like my own – familiar to the point of boring – though occasionally it would be joined by echoes from other people, repeating phrases remembered from long-ago conversations. An endless tragic chorus commenting on my every failing, the voices spoke so fast that just keeping up with their diatribe exhausted me. The only place I could escape their angry refrain was in sleep.

At least I knew I wasn't alone in hearing voices like these. My friend Michelle had talked about the incessant and beguiling clamour of depression, and its sister tintinnabulation, anxiety. For her it was no black dog or pervasive doomy cloud, but a noisy bird that sat screeching on her shoulder, echoing the same grating phrases learned in her childhood. Her bird was yellow, vivid, abrasive; I immediately saw that mine was black. A dark and silky crow, glossy and seductive, possessed of a voice that drove every sensible thought from my head and left me with a shadowscape of picked-clean corpses. It knew everything I'd ever done, every selfish choice I'd made, every failure to be kind or good, and it repeated them until I felt like putting a bullet through my skull to shut it up.

Self-recrimination on this scale was exhausting. It was, quite literally, eating me up: I lost weight without trying or even noticing. As one aunt said, laying a conspiratorial hand upon my arm, there's nothing like anxiety for slimming. Frantic mental gymnastics take up a lot of energy. My head was so busy it became hard for me to sit still. I paced and tapped my feet, and when I was alone I searched for something to wind around my neck. I found several ties – the belt of a dressing gown, the cord from a drawstring bag – but I only ever busied myself with one end of these would-be nooses, which would be wrapped around my neck, the other left to dangle. I didn't really want to die, however much my self-sickness made me think I did.

Nothing felt as real as the panic that welled in my chest when I listened to these voices. Everything they offered was a failed solution, a missed opportunity for a better life. If only, if only, if only – every choice I'd made was wrong. My voice, a vindictive conductor to a phantasmic choir, led the chorus. One person I read about could only escape by listening to the cello suites of Bach. Something in the rhythm and beauty of the music gave them psychic distance from their own horrors, a life raft to cling to when the roaring sea of themselves threatened to overwhelm them. Sound opens the gate into ourselves, lifts the latch which seems to separate us from the rest of the world, and floods us with the proof of things.

As I sat in the pub that night, glowing with poetry and beer, something clicked in my head. Pamela was quizzing Josephine about the influence of 'Tintern Abbey' on her work, and I remembered the first time I came across that poem. It was in the same room where I'd read 'Westminster Bridge', trying to find some sliver of connection to a poem that felt alien to my own experience. I could not tune my impatient ear to the nuance of its blank verse, or feel a kinship with the kind of memory it describes: 'Five years have passed; five summers / With the length of five long winters!' My life felt pacey; university terms were intense, dizzy roundabouts of essays and all-nighters that left me breathless, and the movement of my life was intensely forward-looking.

'Tintern Abbey' is the last poem in *Lyrical Ballads*, written at the end of the Wordsworths' time in Somerset and just before they left for Germany in 1798. Unlike the rest of the *Ballads*, it is an autobiographical poem in blank verse, written in the first person. Though it describes a very different place from the Lakeland vistas of 'The Vale of Esthwaite' and 'An Evening Walk', it is in many ways their successor, a poem where William explores and tries to understand the importance of the connection between a writer, the natural world, memory, and the development of their own psyche. Its opening refrain of 'five summers' refers to the time that has passed since William's last visit to Tintern in 1793, when he first walked through the Wye Valley with his university friend Robert Jones, contrasting that experience not only with the intervening years but also with returning to this landscape with Dorothy. Where once he had arrived 'like a man / Flying from something that he dreads', now he 'sought the thing he loved'.[25] This time he experienced the countryside not just as he saw it, but for what it had contributed to the landscape of his mind.

For William, Nature is not merely external scenery, it is also a spiritual force guiding his moral life. It is an external 'sense sublime' which can be felt like 'a motion and a spirit, that impels / All thinking things'. The poet, whose heart is made heavy by 'hours of weariness' amid 'the din of Towns and Cities', finds physical repose in 'that blessed mood' engendered by memories of places like Tintern, when 'even the motion of our human blood' seems to have been suspended and instead 'we are laid asleep in body, and become a living soul'. The experience of 'tranquil restoration' is intensely physical and spiritual, bringing a 'deep power of joy' that allows the poet to 'see into the life of things'.[26]

In the wake of my breakdown, those words seem right and beautiful. They give voice to my overcoming of the tiredness and dread, what the poem calls a 'Joyless daylight', which had been the keynotes of my previous year. Here were other words for 'the fretful stir / Unprofitable, and the fever of the world' which 'hung upon the beatings of my heart'. But the poem lifts us beyond despair, for ultimately 'Tintern Abbey' carries a message of enduring love. For William, it is Dorothy's voice which rekindled 'the language of my former heart'; she was the messenger from William's past self, urging him to delight again in the world. This love, a kind of self-delight which renders the world joyous, is something we all carry with us.

In Japan I found out how time slowed in that joyless daylight when one was unmoored from the verbal world. Yet Josephine, in becoming spontaneously deaf when she was six, had to carry that once-heard world in her head. It was more than language that had cast me off, more than words that I had lost. The isolation I had felt in Japan wasn't just from language – I was homesick for myself.

7

Spots of Time

'There are in our existence spots of time,
Which with distinct pre-eminence retain
A renovating Virtue, whence, depress'd
By false opinion and contentious thought,
Or aught of heavier or more deadly weight
In trivial occupations, and the round
Of ordinary intercourse, our minds
Are nourish'd and invisibly repair'd.'

William Wordsworth, ll. 258–65,
Book XI, *The Prelude* (1805)[1]

As early summer arrives everything gets busier. Now that we are in May, the first cottage tour of the day can begin before nine in the morning, and some evenings we stay open after six to let in late groups. They come from all over the world – India, America, China – and, whilst not everyone is excited to be here, for some it is the culmination of an almost lifelong acquaintance with William's poetry. Many visitors can recite verses learned in childhood that they still know by heart, whilst some are drawn here because the fells are familiar to them from pictures in Beatrix Potter's books: Squirrel Nutkin's lake was Derwentwater, Mrs Tiggywinkle lived in Newlands Valley, and Peter Rabbit nibbled vegetables at Near Sawrey.

Several tour groups come from Japan and many speak very little English, so knowing some Japanese means I can help them navigate their visits. At first I speak haltingly, unsure of what I thought I knew, but soon the familiar phrases I once used every day come back and I enjoy the look of surprise on Japanese visitors' faces when I overhear their questions and tell them that the toilets are opposite the door to the museum, or that the next tour will start in twenty minutes. It is a facile trick, but useful too – I know the power of being understood when all is confusion in a foreign land.

In Japanese there are many terms for feelings of homesick longing. The most common is *natsukashii*, which describes a fond melancholy that holds a similarly bittersweet emotion to nostalgia. Something that is *natsukashii* evokes the not entirely unpleasant ache for something lost, where memories are wistful daydreams in which the passage of time is viewed as more precious for its impermanence. There is also *kyōshū*, meaning 'home town distress', and *chitogokoro*, a portmanteau of 'parents' home' and 'heart'. *Kaikyū* means a yearning for your village, and *kishin* describes your heart upon returning home. *Hōmushikku*, the English word 'homesick' transliterated, was the term I used to describe how I was feeling to the other psychiatric patients. They seemed to understand, and one woman, her warm eyes wet with tears, sang 'Les Champs-Élysées' to me in a sweet, high voice. It was her own offering of comfort: a foreign song for this tearful foreign person.

Although 'homesickness' might seem an insufficient term for the severity of what I experienced in Japan, in one way it is an accurate description. In English there is no equivalent of *hiraeth*, that evocative Welsh term for a nostalgic, heartsick longing for one's country. Perhaps our loss of kith is why: our collective sense of something being missed confuses place with time – in English *hiraeth* is sometimes, limitedly, glossed as nostalgia. Turning to history rather than landscape for comfort, we yearn for what is now behind us, rather than seeking to protect places that might not yet be lost. We can only see what has gone before, the terrain of our past laid out in memory. Something there calls us to search for that welcoming, familiar nook. Some of us spend a lifetime seeking and never make it home.

Once cognate with 'homesickness', nostalgia is a word whose history maps our changing relationship to place across the centuries. Just as *kith* denoted a once more widely recognised need to belong to a place, *nostalgia* was first applied to a longing not for the past, but to return home. The first recorded term used to describe this sensation was the German *Heimweh*, meaning 'home-woe', which in 1688 inspired Alsace doctor Johannes Hofer to coin the medical term *nostalgia*. A portmanteau of the Ancient Greek *nostos*, meaning 'coming home', and *-algia*, denoting pain or distress, this word was described by Hofer as 'the pain which the sick person feels because he is not in his native land, or fears never to see it again'.[2]

Hofer was the first person to analyse and treat homesickness as a medical malady, presenting it thus in his thesis of 1688: 'Until now, Heimweh, this often fatal illness, has not been described by physicians, although it very much deserves to be.' He had observed symptoms of this psychological pain in Switzerland, including the memorable case of a young man who moved from a village in the canton of Bern to the city of Basel. Since leaving home, his illness had progressed from 'dejection' or depression to continuous fever, anxiety, erratic heartbeat, stomach ache, and general debility. Death appeared imminent, but when an apothecary was called, he recognised the symptoms of *Heimweh* and instructed that the young man be sent home. Such was the relief at this diagnosis – and cure – that the patient recovered before even reaching Bern. Merely the promise of returning to his kith was enough to revive the patient.

Twenty years later, Swiss scholar Johann Jakob Scheuchzer (1672–1733) observed a kind of inverse altitude sickness, again in Bern, affecting those who usually lived high in the mountains when they came down to the valleys. He theorised that an increase in atmospheric pressure might be the cause,[3] but Basel physician Theodor Zwinger (1658–1724), reprinting Hofer's work in 1710, believed there was another reason: they missed their mountain homes. He observed that symptoms were triggered by the hearing or singing of *Kuhreihen*, herdsmen's songs, evocative of life in the mountains. The sound could induce melancholia so acute that it came to be regarded as an illness.[4]

Hofer also saw *Heimweh*-like symptoms among Swiss troops serving in France, though he was not the first to observe nostalgic distress in a military context. During the Thirty Years War (1618–48), soldiers in the Spanish army in Flanders were reported to have suffered *el mal de corazón* ('an illness of the heart'), described as 'a state of blank despair'. The other term for it was *estar roto* – to be broken – and Spanish army records show that at least six soldiers were discharged because of it.[5]

Hofer believed that this *'Maladie du Pays'*[6] resulted from the impact of different or foreign customs upon a 'disordered imagination', combined with other factors, including previous illness, chronic ailments, and atmospheric changes (such as coming down from mountain villages to the valleys). The 'vital spirits', Hofer's term for the neurological pathways connected to memory, were being constantly employed, and thereby unable to stimulate appetite, blood flow, and other normal physiological functions. He noticed that the 'persons most susceptible to this disease are young people living in foreign lands' and believed that '[e]xperience shows that imagination alone can cause all this'.[7]

Though it continued to be associated with Switzerland (another term for it was 'the Swiss disease'), nostalgic homesickness was recognised in Britain from the middle of the eighteenth century.[8] The first recorded case of nostalgia in England dates from 1787, when a Welsh soldier was made ill with longing for his homeland – *hiraeth* made manifest. In the 1760s, the Scottish doctor William Cullen included nostalgia in his *Synopsis Nosologiae Methodicae*. Unlike Hofer, Scheuchzer, and earlier physicians, Cullen did not class nostalgia with melancholia as an illness of the mind. Instead, he grouped it with anorexia, bulimia, pica, and other maladies he termed *Dysorexiae*, 'false or defective appetites'.[9] We know that William and Dorothy Wordsworth read about nostalgia as a medical condition in Erasmus Darwin's *Zoonomia* in the 1790s, where it is described as a 'disease of displacement', but their own relationship to home and homesickness was still to receive its greatest, and most transformative, test.

After leaving Yarmouth in September 1798, the Wordsworths, Coleridge, and Chester made their way via Cuxhaven to Hamburg, where Coleridge was delighted to find that his German was as good as he had hoped. This discovery, which should have been a benediction of the friends' shared venture, in fact served to separate the party. With autumn approaching, Coleridge and Chester decided to take up residence in the fashionable lakeside town of Ratzeburg. They envisaged a winter of skating and high society, bolstered by Coleridge's linguistic fluency and Chester's money. William and Dorothy, comparatively impoverished and unable to easily join in German conversation, were not included in these plans. Instead, the siblings decided to head for the small market town of Goslar in the Harz Mountains, where they hoped to live frugally whilst improving their German.

The dream of sharing a life with Coleridge shattered that winter in Goslar. The Wordsworths had no friends there, or within a hundred miles of the town. In addition, the weather across Europe in the winter of 1798–9 was extremely cold, with temperatures lower than they had been for almost a century. The lodgings William and Dorothy eventually found with widowed Frau Deppermann were so cold that flies froze to death as they crawled closer to the stoves for warmth. On the occasions when the Wordsworths left the building for bracing walks, Dorothy wrapped herself in heavy furs, whilst her brother donned a black dogskin cap and a green gown lined with fox fur 'in which he looks like any grand Signior'.[10]

Though Dorothy revelled in her brother's grand appearance, the siblings were not well regarded by their new neighbours. At that time, the term 'sister' was widely understood to mean 'mistress', and the Wordsworths found themselves in social exile. They had no company beyond each other, and little opportunity to acquire books to read, in English or German. With hardly any money and the weather too cold for travel, there was no prospect of their situation changing until the spring. The forthcoming winter must have seemed a dismal prospect.

'As I have had no books I have been obliged to write in self-defence,' wrote William to Coleridge that winter. The previous year, the pair had spent much of the winter devising a poetic epic, something which could rival Milton or Shakespeare in its scope and style. Known as *The Recluse*, it would introduce a whole new way of looking at the world: 'the state of man and society being subject to, and illustrative of, a redemptive process in operation, showing how this idea reconciled all the anomalies, and promised future glory and restoration'.[11] It was Coleridge's dream that such a work could exist, and his belief that Wordsworth would be able to write it.

In beginning *The Recluse* in Alfoxden, William had tried to grapple with the universal in an epic assessment of man and nature. Now, away from books which might help him research such a poem, he could only turn the magnifying glass of his attention to his own life. The verses he produced – that 'self-defence' against boredom, inertia, and possibly homesickness – became the first lines of what the Wordsworths called 'the poem to Coleridge', the verse epic we now know as *The Prelude*.

Whilst Coleridge delighted in using Chester's money and his own conversational abilities to make a niche for himself in Ratzeburg, the Wordsworths felt the absence of their friend keenly. It was not just his interesting and humorous companionship they missed, but also his acute critical eye and imaginative faculties. The desire to write, both poetry and prose, had been rekindled in them the previous summer, and they wanted to regain this creative closeness. A little while after they arrived in Goslar, Coleridge had written to them describing the glories of living in Ratzeburg, including the beauty of having 'a lake daily before [his] eyes'. Reading this, the Wordsworths decided to reply with their own rapturous descriptions – not of life in chilly Goslar, but of that in the Lakeland fells.

Astonishingly, the letter they sent has survived the intervening two hundred years, and it is one of my favourite objects in the Wordsworth Museum. Penned on a single piece of paper, the letter is creased with folds where it has been reshaped into an envelope. Around the central name and address a spill of dark ink blots one corner, whilst in the place where today we would put a stamp reads the printed word GOSLAR and the number 26. The legend *An den Herrn Coleridge, Ratzeburg* was all this letter needed to reach its audience, which it did one cold December day in 1798.

What is now referred to as 'the Goslar letter' contains several sections of poetry newly composed by William, carefully chosen by Dorothy to mirror in his impassioned, effervescent missive the enthusiasms expressed by Coleridge. In response to their friend's 'raptures of the pleasure of skating', Dorothy included William's description of frozen Esthwaite Water, where as a boy 'All shod with steel', he and his schoolfriends had 'hissed along the polished ice, in games Confederate'. In a somewhat acid comment appended to the verse, Dorothy hoped that such a race with William upon his native Lakes would give the heart and imagination 'something more Dear and valuable' than the thrill Coleridge felt at seeing titled ladies on the ice at Ratzeburg. Two further passages were squeezed on to the page, one about rowing on Ullswater at night ('twenty times I dipped my oars into the silent lake') and the other about gathering nuts near Hawkshead: 'move along these shades / In gentleness of heart, with gentle hand / Touch – for there is a spirit in the woods'.

The Goslar letter was, for the Wordsworths, an attempt to rebuild the emotional proximity that had existed at Alfoxden. As well as choosing passages of poetry in response to Coleridge's current passions, Dorothy also drew a vision of a landscape the Wordsworths hoped their friend would come to love. By choosing vignettes from 'the North of England amongst the mountains whither we wish to decoy you', Dorothy looked forward to a time when they would 'explore

together every nook of that romantic country'. The friends
had a mutual need for sympathetic and creative kinship in
their lives; now they were developing a sense of the importance of having their own kith too.

When I left Japan I had been speaking Japanese every day
for almost a year, but as soon as I arrived back home it began
to fade. Although a few cultural tics lingered – bowing when
I saw people, and making a low 'nnn' sound of agreement
during conversations – the language began to slip away
from me. On a whim of kindness, Judy, a friend of my parents who worked as a teacher, suggested that I could run
lunchtime Japanese language classes at her school. In truth,
I was too ill to take on this responsibility, but nevertheless
Judy saw that I needed something and, a few months later,
offered me a home.

As well as being my mum's friend, Judy had also become
my dad's landlady and housemate after the estate I'd grown
up on in Horringer was sold and he had been forced to leave
Farm Cottage. She owned a large house in a small nearby
market town, a tall Georgian building that had once been
rather grand but was now in need of renovation. Judy had
raised her children there, but now they were grown up the
house seemed empty, too big for one person. Hearing of
Dad's loss of house – and job – she offered him a room at
hers. Three other bedrooms lay icy cold and empty, but
at least the two of them could share some company – and
the bills.

One of these bedrooms would, for a time, become mine
in the aftermath of my breakdown. I had not shared a house

with Dad since I was twelve, though in my early teens I would go to stay with him for two nights a week, usually Thursday and Friday nights. These visits were not always enjoyable, for I did not then find my dad easy to talk to, particularly about personal or uncomfortable matters. I remember the agony of needing to tell Dad to get a bathroom bin because I had started my period and didn't want to walk through the house to find one. I couldn't bring myself to explain this, and so Mum interceded. In my later teenage years he moved even further to the periphery of my life as I filled my evenings with parties and pub trips with friends – a distancing not unusual as adolescents practise versions of their adult selves, but one heightened by the emotional space that already existed between us.

Neither of my parents wanted to talk about the past – about what had happened with the business or about the time at Farm Cottage. We had to look forward, move on; picking over the bones to find out what had gone wrong was far too painful. If I did try to talk to Dad about Mum or their separation, he angered quickly. His most frequent insult – which should not have been an insult at all – was the phrase 'you're just like your mother'. Sometimes the implications were that I was selfish, someone who shirked their familial responsibilities. Repeated many times in the years following their separation, these words reliably reduced me to tears. I hated it that they upset me so much, but I hated it more that they were used like a weapon, the concluding blow in any argument. Of course I was like my mum – I couldn't help it – but was that such a terrible thing? Dad seemed to want me to be more like him and less like her, but dividing the two parts of myself along these lines felt impossible.

Growing up is a painful, peculiar, and lifelong process, at its most intense as we shift from child to adult. Being like – or unlike – a parent can be a shaping force. As I grew and started to become my adult self, the meaning of being 'like Mum' shifted. Sometimes it meant showing when you were worried, whereas Dad preferred the keep-your-chin-up school of pretending to cope. Being 'like Mum' could also mean behaving in ways that were creative at the expense of earning money: Dad was vocal in his disapproval of people who didn't have full-time jobs but instead spent their time 'dabbling' in art, dance, or music.

Once Mum and I moved into the council house, the offer of which had been the practical catalyst for her to leave Dad, there was no other adult in our home. All decisions, good or ill, were now Mum's to make. This could be a heavy burden, and it was one which, like many eldest children, I unquestioningly helped to shoulder. My younger brother, who also came to live with us, was only three years old, so before long I had assumed the role of the second parent, helping us to navigate this new life. At twelve, I felt quite grown up, and set about making good where I thought I could.

From having been a dreamy child who lived half in the world of her imagination, I became a practical, driven, conscientious teenager. Mum worked part-time, sometimes as a supply teacher and at other times as an arts tutor for the council, so I picked up the domestic slack around her hours, taking my brother to nursery on my way to school, picking him up afterwards, and later giving him his tea.

At my new school I threw myself into every opportunity on offer. Language exchanges to Germany, France, Japan; extracurricular music lessons after and sometimes before school, coupled with concert tours in America and Italy. My violin playing, which started when I was seven but which had always been rather half-hearted, rapidly improved and I gathered grades like medals. Choirs, orchestras, a string quartet – all squeezed in around as many subjects as my timetable would allow. I also became confident, making more friends than I'd had at either of my earlier schools. Life was busy and I was determined to make something of myself.

There had been a quality of displacement to my illness in Japan, the old kind of nostalgia, but coming home did not return me to myself. Deep valleys of depression competed with vertiginous anxiety. Caught between extremes I felt storm-tossed by uncertainty. Though I had returned to live with Mum, being back there felt all wrong. Living in that house, in the room where I'd slept and read and dreamed since my parents' separation twelve years earlier, felt unbearable. Before I went away, I'd been content enough – it hadn't been perfect, but it had felt like home. Now I couldn't stand to be there, surrounded by reminders of who I used to be.

Mum and I became uneasy housemates. Neither of us knew how to navigate our relationship now that I wasn't functioning as a responsible adult and couldn't help her to manage her worry on top of my own anxiety. Mum's concern for me was born of love, but it threatened to overwhelm me at a time when I felt like my sense of self was vanishingly fragile. She tried everything to make me better – therapeutic drawing, volunteering with her friends, helping out in local gardens – but I baulked at them all, becoming angry at what felt like an incessant drive to 'fix' me for the sake of her own peace of mind. Perhaps I never would be well. So I turned to Dad, whose idea of a therapeutic activity was throwing old plates at the garage door. Just then that suited me, and it was at his and Judy's that I hunkered down for the winter.

One thing Mum did manage to do was persuade me to regularly see a psychotherapist. Once a week, Dad drove me to a little village deep in the Suffolk countryside, where a kind woman would listen to me talk. Nothing shocked her: she was sympathetic and gently practical, and together we went over everything I'd feared would come true about my life, followed by everything I wanted it to be. Between sessions, Dad, Judy, and I would sit round the kitchen table, close to the Aga, and read or listen to the radio. As I woke early, mind racing anxiously, Judy would encourage me to join her for a walk each morning, and as the winter frosts held the town in an icy grip I felt a slight loosening of the pressures in my mind, enough to fill out the form for the internship in Grasmere.

Pottering about with Dad and Judy helped me stand my ground against the bleak thoughts that dominated my waking hours. Living there wasn't exactly a happy time – I was too consumed by the phantasmagoria in my head for that – but being with Dad and Judy did bring a measure of contentment. They believed that I would get better, and they let me live with them without making me feel worse. Whilst Mum worried that the internship would be too much for me, they encouraged me to apply, and when Jeff told me by telephone that I had got a place they cheered and celebrated.

As the warming weather brings the Lakes to life, Dad and Judy come up to Grasmere to see how I am getting on. To invite them here feels like a gift returned. After months of the cold and damp, it is a joy to show them the fellsides as they bruise with bluebells. Wild garlic edges the paths where a few weeks ago daffodils made their loud trumpet, and the birch wood a few hundred metres from Dove Cottage suddenly riots in neon green. It rains overnight, the days stretch out long and sunny, and I find myself quoting William in *The Prelude*: 'Bliss was it in that dawn to be alive / But to be young was very heaven!'[12]

The idea of coming to live in the Lakes was not straightforwardly appealing to the Wordsworths upon their return to England from Goslar. The area was comparatively remote, a good day's journey from the arterial Great North Road that linked London with Edinburgh and promised the conduit of friends and books. They disliked – and were disliked by – their surviving maternal relations near Penrith, the Crackanthorpe-Cooksons; there was no ready home for them there. Wordsworth cousins still lived at Whitehaven and Broughton-in-Furness, but William and Dorothy had now managed their own household for four years, and were in no hurry to return to living with their relatives.

Instead, it was to the Hutchinson farmhouse at Sockburn that William and Dorothy went after reaching England. Arriving in early May 1799, they received a ready welcome – not just from Mary, to whom they had been promising a visit since she left Racedown in May 1797, but also from Joanna and Sara. Thomas and George were there too, along with their uncle, who owned the farm. The Hutchinsons extended their jokey, familial affection to the Wordsworths: Dorothy was 'Dolly', a nickname used by her own father and by Jane Pollard, whereas William was nicknamed 'the Great Poet', a soubriquet imbued with a healthy measure of teasing. For the returning Wordsworths, Sockburn seems to have been the place that felt most like home.

Though they stayed with the convivial Hutchinsons for the rest of the year, William and Dorothy knew that they could not remain there indefinitely. The question of where to make their next home brought no obvious answer. In late June, William wrote that 'as yet we are not determined where we shall settle'.[13] Around the same time, Dorothy wrote to Tom Poole, a friend from their Somerset days, to ask if he knew of somewhere in the South-West they might rent. Coleridge, by then back at Nether Stowey, hoped they might return to his neighbourhood, writing 'I would to God, I could get Wordsworth to retake Alfoxden' in his own letter to Tom Poole, but this was not possible as the house was already let and the Wordsworths' finances remained precarious. Being near to the Hutchinsons was another consideration, and later that summer William wrote that he and Dorothy were thinking of taking 'a house near to Northallerton',[14] a town ten miles from Sockburn that was also on the main coach route to London. After the isolation of Goslar, the siblings longed for company and connection, to be part of a community bigger than themselves.

The time at Alfoxden had convinced the Wordsworths that proximity to Coleridge was essential for William's creativity, but their experience in Goslar had shown that expecting Coleridge to provide such *genius loci* for them was a fallacy. What they needed was their own home, ideally a place which could exert a kind of magnetic power, drawing their chosen kin towards them. In the autumn of 1799, William – accompanied by Coleridge and their publisher Joseph Cottle – set out to find it.

Arriving from Bristol, Coleridge and Cottle met William at Sockburn, and from there the three men set off for the Lakes. They only made it twenty-five miles to Greta Bridge before the weather forced Cottle, travelling on horseback with his rheumatic legs 'hugely Muffled up',[15] to return to London. William and Coleridge continued on foot, covering more than fifty miles before arriving at Temple Sowerby, close to the home of the Crackanthorpe-Cooksons. Here they met William's brother John, just returned from attending the funeral of the despised Uncle Christopher, a family gathering William had chosen to avoid. Overjoyed to see his brother, John took little persuading to join William and Coleridge on their adventure.

The three men had hoped to walk over the fells from Haweswater to Ambleside, but the weather was too wet and cold for this ambitious plan. Instead, they walked down Longsleddale to Kentmere, and from there to Bowness-on-Windermere before turning their footsteps towards Grasmere. Here they stayed at the inn for nearly a week. William and Coleridge were 'enchanted' with the landscape and Coleridge was determined to rent his next home at Keswick, where a new house was 'being built and was to be let this midsummer'.[16] John shared their enthusiasm, offering his brother £40 towards building a house in Grasmere if he wished to do so.

The brothers seemed at home in the county of Westmorland, and Coleridge noted that William did not appear as awkward as he had sometimes seemed to his friends in the South. He was confident and relaxed, something which Coleridge believed stemmed from sharing 'small Sympathies ... such as Voice, Pronunciation, &c'[17] with the people who lived here. The sharp, short-vowelled savour of *beck* and *gill* was part of William's mother tongue. He felt at home with the Brythonic burr of *blen* and *crag*, of *penn* and *cair* and *din*. These were shibboleths to him, proof that he had found his kith. Grasmere now became the focus of his hunt for a place to live.

In a letter to Dorothy sent that November, William wrote 'You will think my plan a mad one, but I have thought of building a house here by the Lake side.' He also noted that there was an unfurnished cottage for rent on the edge of the village, a 'small house at Grasmere empty ... which perhaps we may take'.[18] These ten words, the first reference made to coming to live at Dove Cottage, encapsulated the promise of their future. Early in the morning of 17 December, a crescent moon bright above them, William and Dorothy set off from Sockburn for their new life on a pair of horses borrowed from the Hutchinsons.

Along with George Hutchinson, who rode one horse with Dorothy whilst William took the other, they crossed the Tees at Neasham Ford and headed west past Richmond. Eight miles into Wensleydale, George turned the horses for home and bade the siblings goodbye. Dorothy and William continued on foot towards their future.

It took the Wordsworths three days to travel the remaining sixty miles to Grasmere. The unmetalled road was frozen solid as they followed the river Ure through Wensleydale, and they reached the inn at Askrigg a little before sunset. When the self-proclaimed 'Wild Wanderers'[19] woke the following morning, the ground glowed softly with newly fallen snow. They left their rooms before sunrise, and before long the eastern sky had begun to turn 'a delicious pale orange'.[20] The midwinter sun was at their backs as they walked, snow showers buffeting them, and after a while they were able to hitch a ride with a pair of carters driving ponies along the valley.

Though their feet and ankles ached from travelling on the frozen roads and the wind worried their bodies, the Wordsworths' overriding feelings about this journey were ones of joy and wonder. After parting from the carters, they rested at the inn at Hardraw and warmed themselves by the fire. Scrambling along the path behind the inn, they found that icicles encased the surrounding rocks, turning the waterfall there to a fantastic sculpture. In the cave behind the falls, William and Dorothy came across a grotto draped with moss and ferns that sparkled with rime. Thrilled with this discovery, they dreamed of returning in the summer, when they might lie down on the moss and be lulled to sleep by warm sunshine and the water's companionable chatter, before making their way to the small town of Sedburgh.

The following day the bitter weather continued. The frozen road was no less hard under their feet, and the siblings covered the last eleven miles from Sedburgh to Kendal as quickly as they could. Both were good walkers – Dorothy later boasted of being able to cover 'sixteen miles in four hours and three quarters, with short rests between, on a blustering cold day, without having felt any fatigue'.[21] In Kendal they bought furniture for the new house, and arranged to take the post-chaise for the final stretch of their journey to Grasmere in the morning. At half past four in the afternoon on 20 December 1799, they climbed down from the carriage to set up home at Dove Cottage.

It was not an auspicious start. No one was there to greet them, though before long Molly Fisher, a neighbour who lived across the turnpike road, came out to welcome Town End's newest residents. It was Molly who had laid a fire in the grate, having lit one every day for the preceding two weeks as she hadn't known exactly when they'd arrive. They immediately engaged her for 'two or three hours a day to light the fires wash dishes &c &c',[22] plus 'scouring' on Saturday, for the sum of two shillings a week.

During that first week the weather remained cold and frosty. One of the fireplaces 'smoked like a furnace', both siblings had 'troublesome colds', and Dorothy was in agony with toothache after William 'tempted her forth' to see Jupiter shining above 'the top of the hugest of the Rydale mountains' late one chilly evening. She hardly left the house for several days, burying herself under mounds of fabric as she sewed new curtains to hang around their beds. Meanwhile, William expressed his intention to explore the area, borrowing a pair of ice skates so that he could give his 'body to the wind'[23] as he whirled across frozen Rydal Water.

William was keen to share the thrill of living here with someone who wouldn't be disheartened by tales of insalubrious lodgings (as some of his extended family would no doubt regard the cottage, far more modest than the family homes at Penrith and Whitehaven), but who would respond to the beauty of this place's potential. Coleridge was that person – and William wanted him to come to Grasmere as soon as possible, and to take the house at Keswick which he had admired in the autumn. As William was painting a picture of Lakeland delights in his letter to Coleridge, Dorothy was composing a more melancholy correspondence. This wistful missive – unaddressed and never sent, but drafted during those first days in Dove Cottage – describes not Grasmere but Racedown as 'the place dearest to my recollections upon the whole surface of the island'.[24] Not only was it 'the first home I had', but the surrounding landscape held Dorothy's heart, with its 'lovely meadows above the tops of the combs, and the scenery on Pilsden, Lewisden, and Blackdownhill, and the view of the sea from Lambert's Castle'.[25] Icy Grasmere, flanked by brooding fells and far from the coast, would take time to feel anything like home for her.

One warm May evening a gaggle of us are heading off for our customary post-work walk around Grasmere lake when we come across Polly Atkin, another writer who lives in Town End. Walking towards the car park with a towel tucked under one arm, she pauses to tell us she's off for a swim in a small, clear pool, tucked away in a crook of the hills above

Rydal. 'Come along if you like,' she says, and we rush to get our swimming things together. In order to reach Buckstones Jump before the sun's waning rays leave the water we'll need a lift, and so after grabbing towels and costumes we pile into Polly's little car and race off along the road.

Polly parks on the steep slope at Rydal and leaves the car in gear, but whether its brakes will hold until we return is debatable. To make sure it doesn't end up at the bottom of the hill, we place heavy stones behind its back wheels. Polly promises it is little more than a twenty-minute walk from here to Buckstones Jump. Above us the Fairfield Horseshoe keeps benevolent watch as we push through bracken and stamp over stones. We pass a barn full of silage, steaming in the sunshine, and the tall stems of foxglove buds nod to us as we walk by. As soon as their first petals open, the countdown to the end of summer will begin, but for now they are flags of good weather, portents of warmth and sunshine.

On the map Buckstones Jump is little more than a thickening in the river, but this small blue bulge belies a swimmer's paradise. Edged on two sides with smooth grey stone, perfect for sliding down into the water – or for jumping from if you're braver – Buckstones is an aquatic amphitheatre, filled with water flowing from the fells. Polly gets in first, languidly splashing as she dips beneath the water, as we scramble into swimming costumes to join her. The water's cold, but we're so hot from the walk up the hill that it feels more reward than punishment. I can't see underwater without my glasses, but Jane and Emily dive to the bottom and tell me there are fish there, nibbling moss that clings to the stones.

Though this mountain pool lies a scant two miles from Town End, it feels a world away. All around, the fells are basking in the last of the day's light, glowing greenish gold in the early-evening sun. From our high nook we can see Windermere, lying smooth and still below us like a giant's bathtub. Its islands are dark silhouettes against the still-light sky, and Jane tells us that one of them, Belle Isle, used to belong to her ancestors, the Curwens. 'You should reclaim it!' Emily exclaims, and soon we are planning a flotilla of small boats to retake the island.

As we talk the shadows lengthen all around us, and before long the pool is cloaked in shade. By now we're shivering, and we pull clothes on over our half-wet bodies to head down the hill for tea. At the bottom of the hill the track turns into a road, and soon we are on the steep slope beside Rydal Mount. Everyone else climbs back into Polly's car, and she gestures for me to get in too, but the night, all soft summer stillness and silhouette, persuades me to decline. I'll walk home instead.

The gardens at Rydal are filling the air with summer flowers, and in one of them I spot Keith, the electrician who has spent the last few weeks repairing the wiring at Dove Cottage. He recognises me and waves, and moments later he's walking down the path with a flower in his hand. Handing me a single stem, he smiles as I inhale the sweetest honey smell from the huge pink cups of rosy petals. 'Can I take this home?' I ask, and he nods in brusque assent.

Walking back along the coffin path, I stop twice as badgers cross in front of me, making their hasty, heavy way down the hillside to the Badger Bar, named for the animals that are bribed with chips to eat there in the evenings. The air seems golden and the last of the day's warmth hangs in it, rich with the promise of tomorrow. By the time I'm lifting the latch at Lake Terrace the air is streaked with the flight of bats, and from the other side of the wall I can smell that Mark is working his way through a joint. Up in my room I fill a mug with water, in which I place the rose so it can drink its fill. Its perfume pervades my room, and my mind leaps immediately to Tom: I want to share its honey-sweet scent with him.

Two days later I get my chance. Amy, the Trust's Exhibitions Officer, has offered to pick Tom up from Windermere station and asks if I want to come. He's been in Edinburgh for the day, being interviewed for a postgraduate degree he hopes to begin in September. His brother Laurie has already bagged their shared car for a night out in Keswick, but Amy and her little Peugeot are free to collect him. It's after nine by the time we're pulling into the station, but the sky is still light and the air warm. It's the sort of day you want to last forever. As he throws his bag in the boot, Tom suggests going home via Langdale: there are a pair of boulders on the valley side that are perfect for a scramble.

I've not yet seen Tom climb, but the others have been out with him to explore the nearby boulders. One day he and Emily walked to the top of Helm Crag, where they dared each other to climb up to the highest pinnacle and sit with their legs swinging over the abyss. Jane has also joined him on nearby crags, pitting herself against the rocks in Tom's spare harness. I want to go climbing too – but I'd like to know my body's limitations before testing them in front of Tom. I also need to be sure that my mind can cope. Since recovering from my illness I've not been sure I can trust myself in the world of rocks and winding ropes.

Made of andesitic tuff, the Langdale boulders have been in this place close to the hamlet of Chapel Stile since at least the late Neolithic or early Bronze Age. Thousands of years ago, human hands scored their surfaces: the east face of the larger one is patterned with circles and chevrons. Eleven rings form one concentric circle and angled lines point to another. At this time of night these shapes are clearer to the hand than to the eye, and our fingertips thrill at the closeness of the people who made these marks millennia ago.

The stones feel warm to the touch, still radiating solar heat into the darkness. Patches of climbing chalk glow white against the grey stone, and above a rowan tree spreads its narrow fingers into the sky. Tom steps over the stile and starts to climb; Amy gets out her camera and takes pictures of his silhouette. Under the overhanging rocks, it looks like he is suspended in the night air, caught improbably between sky and stone. I do not think I can hold my body with my fingertips, but fortunately the other side of the boulder slopes more gently, and I can scramble my way up.

On top there is a flattish slab, and I lie down here on my back, luxuriating in the rock's radiant warmth. Above the rock tiny flies and midges dance; they don't seem interested in me, but I can hear Tom cursing as they nibble his sweating skin. I see Amy down by the river and hear her muffled singing drifting towards me on the still summer air. I am aware that this is one of those moments that William called 'spots of time': a memory so physical and poignant it feels as though it will be with you forever. A scene to return to on subsequent summer evenings, or to revisit in winter, a reminder that warm weather will come again.

William developed the idea of 'spots of time' in Goslar when he wrote down the first lines of what became *The Prelude*. Isolation had forced him to turn inwards; without the company of friends or books, his inner world became both inspiration and distraction. In 'Tintern Abbey', written just before leaving for Germany, William had begun to connect the passage of a few years and the interplay of memory with one's experience of revisiting the same place. Now, he was delving back further, examining memories of childhood and exploring the effect they had on his identity.

Modern psychotherapy aims to understand a person's inner dialogue by questioning their past, and William was undertaking a similar self-analysis by constructing a coherent narrative of his own emotional development. He was twenty-eight years old; the challenge of writing *The Recluse*, with its encyclopaedic focus on the condition of humanity, felt overwhelming. In the unfamiliar surroundings of Goslar, he struggled to write – but reflecting on his childhood offered a creative way forward, through memories of bathing in the pools of the river Derwent at Cockermouth as a four-year-old; of ice skating and rowing a boat as an older child; of surrounding himself with the spirit of the hills, woods, and heathlands of the Lakes. William believed that these reminiscences 'love to intertwine / The passions that build up our human soul' and that they are an antidote to 'the mean and vulgar works of man', purifying and distilling our experience until we recognise a 'grandeur in the beatings of the heart'.[26]

Over the coming weeks and months, William explored these questions further. If these memories were important, what was the connection between them and his vocation as a poet? As well as being forces shaping our internal landscape, were they also the wellspring of creativity, the means by which 'imaginative power' is fed and restored? The answer came quickly: yes they were. But their power is not all benign, for some of our most powerful memories can come from times when our lives have been at their darkest, or most imperilled.

When we're getting back into the car, Amy says, 'Shall we go to the Old Dungeon Ghyll for last orders?' Soon we are sitting on a bench outside the pub with pints in our hands, resting our backs against the old stone wall. The air is full of rose and honeysuckle, and above us the last light slips from the sky behind the hills. Their silhouettes are splendid, and Tom can name each one. Pike o' Blisco rises to the south, edged by Wrynose Fell. Due west are Crinkle Crags, Great Knott, Bow Fell. Against their dark bulk I see a few flashes of light – head torches of walkers following footworn tracks that zigzag across the fells. Langdale is a wilder valley than Grasmere, and there is no road beyond the Ghyll. Tracks lead up to the last farm in the valley; beyond that only narrow paths and sheep tracks climb the fellside.

To me these routes seem exciting, unknown – even dangerous. I cannot picture where they go, but for Tom it is the knowledge of where they lead that brings enchantment. The remoter valleys of Borrowdale, Eskdale, Wasdale; the summits of Glaramara, Esk Pike, Bow Fell, their names a kind of incantation. Tom points out a worn notch that cuts below the crags: that one would lead you all the way to Scafell Pike, the highest peak in England. Once Tom spent the whole day on its summit, making and selling bacon sandwiches as a fundraising stunt. 'I'll take you there this summer,' he says, and my heart thrills at the promise.

After draining our glasses, we squeeze back into Amy's little car. When we get back to Town End Amy drops us by the house and goes to park. As we stand in the still-light night, I say that I've got a present for him, but he has to come to my room to get it. Raising his eyebrows he agrees, and soon we're heading upstairs as my housemates giggle in the living room. As the door to the staircase closes behind us, I can hear whispering and hope that Tom isn't as embarrassed as I feel.

My room is large and untidy, 'the opposite of the white cube aesthetic' according to one housemate. The walls are covered with postcards, carefully pinned at their corners, and on every surface are my 'treasures': tiny jewellery boxes, odd-shaped stones, tins and pots of pens. The bookshelf is stuffed to the point of bursting, and so is the wardrobe. Heaps of clothes spill across the floor, and though the bed is made, its end is still piled high with the blankets necessary in winter.

I lead him to the mantelpiece and ask him to close his eyes – the rose's smell is best all on its own. He does, and I lift the bloom up to his face. A smile breaks across his lips, and seeing it I decide to add one further present to the day. Leaning forward, I place my lips on his and hold them there for a kiss. He doesn't kiss me back, but neither does he pull away. We say nothing as he leaves the room, but my heart's hopeful tattoo lets me know how much I want him to return.

8

A Heart to Enjoy

'in which every man has a right and
interest who has an eye to perceive and a
heart to enjoy'

William Wordsworth, *Select Views*
of Cumberland, Westmorland, and
Lancashire (1810)[1]

June dawns in an explosion of roses and hot weather. The bracken unfurls its fiddleheads in an exuberance of summer, blanketing the fellside. Spires of white and purple foxgloves pierce the green, the fall of their petals counting down the summer days. The front wall of Dove Cottage froths with roses and honeysuckle, and under the beech trees in John's Grove the bluebells and wild garlic wilt and go to seed. Tourists swarm through the village like bees, delighting in the long days and the smells from the gingerbread shop. Walking to the Co-op and back at lunchtime, something we usually do in twenty minutes, now takes longer than our official break time, as we must thread our way through battalions of tour groups and fight with picnickers and their overflowing baskets for the last tomatoes.

As summer heat bakes the village, those of us on guiding duty gravitate from the warmth of the houseplace fire – lit on all but the very hottest days – to the shade of the cottage garden in between tours. Our wintertime desire for sooty comfort is replaced by a longing to lie in the shadow of the tumult of roses or beside a bright patch of columbines. The lattice casements are open as wide as they will go, and the edges of ferns and Welsh poppies nod against their sills like tired walkers propping themselves on the public bar in Tweedies.

The possibility of making a garden around Dove Cottage was one of the things that most appealed to Dorothy when she and William arrived in Grasmere. In his first letter to Coleridge, written in late December 1799, William described how she had already begun to make plans for the 'little domestic slip of mountain' that is to be their garden: 'D is much pleased with the house and *appurtenances* the orchard especially; in imagination she has already built a seat with a summer shed on the highest platform.'[2] From the beginning, the siblings anticipate that the garden will provide them with shelter and stimulation.

William and Dorothy had first gardened together at Racedown, from where in the winter of 1795–6 Dorothy proudly wrote that 'we have charming walks, a good garden, a pleasant house. My brother handles the spade with great dexterity'[3] – though William's letters indicate

that he felt less thrilled about this 'cabbaging'. The following spring, he wryly noted that he had been busy 'hewing
wood and rooting up hedges' (something he described as
'the penalty of Adam', though 'no bad employment')[4] and
that he and Dorothy had 'lately been living upon air and
the essence of carrots cabbages turnips and other escu-
lent vegetables, not excluding parsely [*sic*] the produce of
my garden'.[5]

When they arrived at Dove Cottage, however, there was
no such vegetable plot. The land – then as now – sloped
steeply. William described an 'orchard' of fruit trees, but
otherwise there was nothing structured or recently cultivated. The boundaries of their 'garden' were also flexible:
William noted that they 'mean to enclose also two or three
yards of ground between us and the road, this for the sake
of a few flowers, and because it will make it more our own'.[6]
This was done the spring after their arrival, and Dorothy
and the neighbours planted beans, peas, radishes, and potatoes in this 'little Nook of mountain-ground'.[7]

Instrumental in helping the Wordsworths make the
garden were the Fishers, their closest neighbours. John,
Aggy, and Molly Fisher lived at Sykeside, across the
turnpike road from Dove Cottage, and gave William and
Dorothy invaluable practical support in working their scrap
of land. Dorothy often mentioned that they were digging,
planting, and weeding in the garden, and a regular entry in
her journal was 'Molly washing'. Molly's droll humour and
brisk expressions appealed to Dorothy's acute ear: snowy
weather was 'a Cauld Clash', and when a neighbour was
sick Molly remarked 'poor Body! she's very ill but one does

not know how long she may last. Many a fair face may gang before her.'[8]

The ties the Fishers had to Grasmere were deep and lasting. They and their kin had long been bound to the area, for unlike the feudal system which dominated in the South, in the Lakes 'statesmen' farming meant that all but the very poorest lived and worked on their own land. Rather than tying labourers to their work and home through feudal obedience, Cumbrians were connected to the hills because they farmed them for themselves. On his first visit, Coleridge saw this heritage borne out in the way 'every Brook, every Crag, almost every Field has a name'. People belonged to this landscape as much as it belonged to them, something Coleridge interpreted as proof of 'a Society more approaching in their Laws and Habits to Nature' than elsewhere in England.

Like many farming families, the Fishers had witnessed great changes taking place around them in recent years, as land which had for centuries belonged to local farmers was sold off, forcing people to seek work in distant towns and cities. This was a common occurrence across England at the time; from the 1750s, enclosure by parliamentary Act had remade landscapes – and people's relationship to them – across the country. Between 1604 and 1914 over 5,200 enclosure bills relating to over a fifth of the total area of England were passed by Parliament. Where there were once large, communal open fields, land was now being hedged and fenced off. Enclosure forced those at the lower end of rural society, agricultural labourers without the security of their own acreage to till, to leave the land permanently and seek work in the towns. It was an economic landgrab that began a nationwide process of severing people from lands they had known, worked, and depended on for generations.

With their land and homes deeply intertwined, Lakeland farmers had perhaps more to lose as a result of these socio-political changes. Many of the Wordsworths' new neighbours were being wrenched from their kith; Peggy and Thomas Ashburner, who rented the cottage opposite Dove Cottage, had also been forced to put their farm up for sale. Thomas then set up a modest business as a carrier, often bringing the Wordsworths' coals and taking letters to and from Keswick in his cart. Thomas Ashburner's legacy lives on: his cart shed is now Tom's family home, having been converted in the twentieth century into a five-room house which bears the name 'Carrier's Cottage'.

The long-standing relationship that the Fishers and the Ashburners had with the land was very different from the excitement of discovery William and Dorothy felt at moving there. Both were a kind of love, but whereas the Wordsworths' had the heady whoosh of romance, theirs was the incremental ardour that came from knowing and living in a place for several lifetimes. But the lives of these rooted people were changing – and so were the landscapes that they loved and farmed. Dorothy recorded in her journal that there had been 'sad ravages in the woods', 'slashing away in Benson's wood', and instances of large houses being built around the lakeshore, indications of a landscape and a people under threat.

The garden at Dove Cottage allowed Dorothy to make her own claim to this place, to develop a new sense of kith as she worked this little piece of land. It provided useful, practical employment, a welcome counterpoint to writing – both her own (for she began her Grasmere journal in May 1800) and the many poems her brother had been inspired to work on since coming to the cottage. Gardening and writing often intermingled: on dry days Dorothy and William used the garden as a kind of outdoor office (much brighter than inside the house), finding inspiration for their creative work from the plants around them. William's poems from this period are peopled by the garden and its inhabitants – 'To a Butterfly', 'The Redbreast and the Butterfly', 'To the Cuckoo' – and Dorothy begins her new journal noting plants she has seen nearby, described with a horticulturalist's eye: 'Geranium – scentless violet, anemones two kinds, orchises, primroses. The heckberry[9] very beautiful as a low shrub.'[10] The same day she 'set some slips of privet' in the garden, and the next morning she 'hoed the first row of peas, weeded, &c &c'. The following day she '[t]ransplanted radishes after breakfast' before taking books to William Gell, a young man who had recently built a cottage across the lake from Town End. Dorothy 'carried a basket for mosses, & gathered some wild plants', and her wish was 'Oh! that we had a book of botany'.[11]

Dorothy frequently took plants from the hillsides to replant in the garden. Her gathering was extensive: in May and June 1800 she collected plants roughly every third day, and soon the area surrounding the cottage was bedecked with London Pride, mosses, ferns, daisies, orchids, alpine strawberries, golden globeflower, thyme, wild columbine: small native plants that are happy on rocky slopes. She also rehomed plants from the gardens of acquaintances. In May 1800, Dorothy described going into Jenny Dockwray's house near Underhelm on the Easedale side of the village, where she 'got white and yellow lilies, periwinkle, &c, which I planted'.[12] Three days later, she wrote that 'I got such a load [of plants] that I was obliged to leave my Basket in the road & send Molly for it.'[13] Molly, born in 1741, was then almost sixty years old – twice Dorothy's age.

Some visitors have been inspired not just by the spirit of Dorothy's endeavours, but by her methods. We hear a story, passed down from former chief guide George Kirkby, of a visitor apprehended by Dove Cottage staff, who had been caught with a trowel and a polythene bag ready to receive plants she had uprooted from around the cottage. The visitor cheerfully admitted that her aim was to recreate this garden in her own[14] – and it was hard to condemn her, as she shared more with Dorothy's method of gardening than with the niceties of modern conservation.

The garden around Dove Cottage is now a fair approximation of the one existing when the Wordsworths lived there. This was in part due to George's work on it during the 1980s and '90s; rhododendrons and other large exotic species had been introduced to it after William and Dorothy left, so George and subsequent staff worked to return the land immediately around the cottage to a style of garden more sympathetic to the Wordsworths' ideals. Like Robert Woof, George died a few years before my arrival, but his presence in Town End is palpable – albeit in a very different way from Robert's. George's picture hangs on the wall of the little cottage staffroom, and from there he watches us with a wry glint in his eye, a hat low over his brow as he leans on the cottage gate. He is there in the damsons and sloes slowly disintegrating in cork-stopped bottles along the ginnel between two of the Trust cottages, and in the myriad stories we hear about a man who was fiercely protective of Town End's particular character.

George's life was rooted in Grasmere. Born in 1936, he had grown up in the village, where his father had been the warden of Thorney How youth hostel. The Kirkbys lived in the hostel, in the shadow of Helm Crag, and George had known Emily Kirkbride when she was the Dove Cottage caretaker and guide, learning from her stories of the Wordsworths passed down from her mother and grandmother – another link in the chain connecting the village to the Wordsworths.

When George first came to work at Dove Cottage in the 1960s, he was struck by how un-Wordsworthian the garden was. In addition to the introduction of Victorian exotica, cultivated daffodils grew everywhere, quite different from the small *Narcissus pseudonarcissus* made famous in the Wordsworths' writings about their walks at Ullswater. George, who knew the journals and the poems well, set about putting this to rights – he wanted, in his words, to restore it 'to its former self [...] Wordsworth wanted his garden to have wild things in it.'[15]

To George, William's poem 'A Farewell' (1802) was 'a real gardener's prayer', with its emphasis on the importance of sun and rain for the plants: 'Sunshine and shower be with you, bud and bell!' For over thirty years, he tended to the garden, welcoming visitors and restoring the flora that Dorothy had brought to this 'most well-documented quarter of an acre in English literature'.[16] Echoing Dorothy's labours, George re-introduced wilder plants: climbing woodland honeysuckle, Osmunda ferns, dusky Lenten roses. He passed his love for the place on to Ann, a young member of staff with whom he fell in love. A skilled conservationist in her own right, Ann became head gardener and senior guide after George's death. We had seen her at the great January clean-up, a small, strong woman who I remember helping Mark to move the big chest that stands in the houseplace.

In Grasmere you can feel the trace of many generations of hands upon the land. George's connections wound like social mycorrhizae through the village, extending for miles and decades. He liked a joke, and several staff have told us the story of Coleridge's testicles. Once on holiday by the sea in Dorset, George stumbled across an unusually shaped piece of seaweed: two shrivelled purses, their skin wrinkly and pimpled, hinged together with a thicker flap of sea-leather. George wrapped them in tissue, put them in a box, and sent them back to Grasmere. With them was a letter purporting to be from a descendant of the poet, who had suddenly decided to bequeath them to the Trust. It was a while before George's colleagues began to question the likelihood of Coleridge's testes having been preserved for all these years.

Gardening – cultivation of the wild impulse to grow – roots you to a place. Gardens nourish you as you nourish them: tending plants forces you to spend time with the soil, which comprises the building blocks of life on earth. The minerals and elements present are transported into us through the plants we eat and the animals we eat that also eat those plants; anything grown bears the trace of its root origin. Dove Cottage garden gave sustenance to William and Dorothy, nurturing them creatively and physically, whilst giving them space to grow, think, and write, as well as providing focus and solace to their brother John, who joined them at the cottage in the spring of 1800.

Ever since I was five or six years old, gardens – and gardeners – have played an important role in my life. When my mother searched for work and a house in the aftermath of the bankruptcy, it was a garden that provided both. Mum did some weeding, digging, and helping out on a private estate – and it was here she found solace from the difficult situation at home. The man with whom she struck up a relationship told her about a now-empty worker's cottage close to the estate farm which might house our family. Though my father, when he found out about their affair, went round and beat him up, the suggestion of Farm Cottage was a good solution to the problem of where we would live. In time, it also answered the question of what my dad would do for work.

A year after we moved to Farm Cottage Dad secured himself a job as the estate's head gardener. He had no formal horticultural training, but had been gardening since he was old enough to hold a trowel. My grandfather had had two plots of rented land, as well as the garden next to the family's council house, where he kept pigs and chickens and grew fruit and vegetables to feed their family of seven, and the children were all expected to pitch in and help. After Dad's motorcycle engineering business went bankrupt, he'd cycled round the nearby villages looking for work. Stopping to buy an ice cream from one little post office, he saw a sign pinned to the village noticeboard: 'Gardener Wanted'. Though he had little recent experience, he reckoned his childhood had prepared him for such work, so he wrote the accompanying phone number on his hand and decided to try his luck. It held: he was invited to an interview the following morning.

The next day he arrived at a large nearby house, breathless after racing a pair of Dobermanns down the length of his potential employer's drive. When he finally escaped them, the appropriately named Mrs Root sat him down with a cup of tea and fixed him with a steely look. 'What do you know about growing show chrysanthemums?' she barked. Dad gulped, and answered, 'Nothing.' Mrs Root smiled. 'Excellent – you can start tomorrow.' 'But I don't know anything about them,' Dad persisted. 'Neither did any of the others, but they all pretended to. I can't work with liars,' was her smart rejoinder, and that was how Dad's horticultural career began.

For the next two years, he served an informal apprenticeship with Mrs Root's head gardener, a respected chrysanthemum grower whose incipient Parkinson's disease meant that he could no longer do the heavier gardening work himself. Here was someone who could hardly hold a rake, but whose ears could tell when a chrysanthemum needed watering from the tone of its pot when tapped by a cane. He could pick a winning bloom almost from the moment the flower bud formed, and he passed on to Dad everything he knew.

After this training, Dad got a job on the estate in Horringer, where we were living. Now he wasn't only watering chrysanthemums and mowing lawns: Horringer House had a walled vegetable garden, fruit cages, heated green-houses, an orchard, a chamomile lawn, two acres of mixed woodland, a boating pond, and a small fir plantation. Dad relished the freedom to run this verdant empire, and the opportunity to challenge himself. He had some books left to him by a bachelor uncle who had been involved in the work of the Royal Horticultural Society, and one of these Victorian tomes included instructions on how to grow pineapples using heat from rotting horse manure. No one seemed to be using this method in 1992 – and so Dad became the first person in Britain in a hundred years to grow pineapples in this old-fashioned way. *The Times* sent a reporter, and a few weeks later a two-page article with my dad's face at the centre appeared on breakfast tables across the country.

The gardens were as much my brothers' and my domain as Dad's. At Easter we climbed into the gnarled goblets of old apple trees to eat our chocolate in secret, secure in their blossomy embrace. In summer Dad let us pick armfuls of sweet peas to tie in posies, and in winter the thick yew hedges gave us deep, dark dens in which to hide from rain and snow. We gorged on what that garden grew, and Dad sold any surplus produce at a little local market. On Tuesday afternoon, we'd help him weigh and bag beans, plums, toma-toes, apples, and onions, ready to take to the stall before school on Wednesday. We could eat any that weren't quite perfect – each mouthful a tangy taste of home.

The background to this idyll was the gathering storm of our parents' worsening marriage. Mum would sometimes disappear for days on end, only to reappear without explan-ation. Dad pretended not to care that she wasn't there, though his answers to our questions about where she had gone were terse. Neither parent liked to shout, but the bitter silences interspersed with curt remarks were worse than the clarity of vivid rows. For my brothers and me, the garden became a refuge. Home may have been uneasy, but the farm, fields, and gardens gave us all the gentle welcome we could want.

As summer comes to Grasmere, I miss having a garden. I want somewhere to dig, to put my hands into the soil, to feel the curious aridity of earth on my fingertips. As interns, we have little to do with Dove Cottage garden. Responsibility for it falls to the senior guide, aided by Mark, who provides the necessary muscle for tasks that once a year include placing spadefuls of lion dung (donated by a nearby zoo) around the garden to deter deer from getting in to eat the plants. Occasionally one of us might help with a minor task like clearing drains, but otherwise the garden is not our domain. However, across the road from Dove Cottage is a patch of waste land known as The Allotments. A ragged stand of Leyland cypress shields it from the road, and a cluster of overgrown fruit trees divides it from a neighbouring pair of cottages. Garden rubbish and bags of leaves and grass clippings are brought there from across Town End and heaped in one corner to moulder into compost, but most of the little patch of land is covered in scrubby grass and weeds. This semi-wild spot is ours to use if we want to – and I do.

The Allotments also boast a greenhouse, where a sole determined vine clings to the rotting frame. Its growth has shattered panes of glass as thickening tendrils have reached for air and light, and though the door is locked, time and rust have dispensed with its usefulness. I could open it with nothing more than a gentle push, but I do not like to. Despite knowing that nobody else wants to grow things here, it feels like a transgression to assume that I could. Using someone else's greenhouse would be like breaking into their home and making myself comfortable on the sofa.

Instead, I claim one of the rectangles of rough ground closest to the road as my plot, and set to work. Looking for a cheap way to mark out different beds, I remember the gooseberry patch at Horringer, which had been edged in thick green glass. The recycling boxes outside the Town End houses are never short of wine bottles, and so I decide to frame the beds with them. Buried neck down and tilted slightly forward, they form a wobbly dividing line between the path and the soil. One day when I am busy digging them in, a woman calls to me from the roadside. She has been watching me work: am I trying to deter moles? No, I say, just making a border for the bed. She tells me that her father had half-buried milk bottles in their garden when she was a child. He placed them bottom down, so that the wind would blow across their tops, and the ensuing whistle was said to deter small animals. I reply that I would welcome them, and she walks away with eyebrows raised at my novice folly.

By the time the year approaches midsummer, The Allotments take on another role. One morning the whole Trust receives an email from Mark – a rare occurrence, since he doesn't have much cause to use a computer in the cottage or garden. Titled THE GREAT FEAST, it reads:

'Aristotle noted that earth, air, fire and water – the four elements – were combined to produce the first artificial substance – pottery; and it's this type of vessel in the form of earthenware bowls and fine china clay platters that will be required for the Great Feast in The Orchard this coming Saturday. Barbeques would also be useful for the more advanced amongst us who like our meat cooked. Rhymers, thespians, fiddlers (both musical and numerical) are also welcome, along with just about anyone else who possesses an eye to perceive and a heart to enjoy.'[17]

What Mark grandly termed 'The Orchard' is really the small piece of semi-derelict land squeezed between The Allotments and the two small cottages across the main road from Lake Terrace. Apple trees had been planted there some years before, but as they have been long neglected, their canopies now sprawl across the sky, and their roots are insulated by a thick blanket of weeds and grass. In warm, wet years they fruited well, but usually their bounty grew only on the uppermost branches, far from the reach of hungry hands. Now, under their wildness, we will raise our voices, hopes, and glasses to the sky.

As the Town End community is small and close-knit, everyone is invited to its parties, from our most senior neighbour Pamela Woof to our colleagues' school-age kids. As well as the ubiquitous house parties held to mark birthdays, anniversaries, the publication of poetry pamphlets, and other milestones, there are reports of raves in the caves at nearby Rydal, where Tom's brother Joe, a DJ making a name for himself with dubstep music, sometimes bounces drumbeats off the hard, sharp stone. This former slate mine, a relic from what was once an important industry throughout the Lakes, becomes the backdrop to the tension between the natural world and urban need as people dance around its mossy fissures.

Rhythm is cell-deep: our heart's tattoo is our metronome and clock. Its cells are the oldest in our bodies: they are the first to develop, and their in–out pulse is detectable on the scan of an embryo at just six weeks gestation.[18] The beat of its mother's heart is the first music a foetus hears, the first rhythm to which it moves. Music alters the chemistry in our brain by encouraging the release of dopamine, the neurotransmitter that makes us feel engaged and relaxed, motivated and happy. In turn, this chemical increases the efficiency of cell communication, improving the heart's function. It relaxes arteries, making blood flow more easily, and increases the heart rate, making someone able to both exercise better and recover from exertion more easily.

It isn't just Joe who needs heart-shaking beats: Jeff loves them too. Back in March, we threw a birthday party for him – not in a cave, but inside Dove Cottage. The furniture was moved to stand against the walls and a keg of beer set up in the buttery, just as it would have been in the days before the Wordsworths. Some of us wrote a silly spoof song to celebrate, and all of us delighted in the chance to party in the cottage. John plugged his disco speakers into the house's ancient electrics, so the place resounded with the screech and roar of the Clash and the Ramones. This too was for Jeff's benefit: punk rock is his favourite kind of music.

The Great Feast in the orchard is planned for Midsummer's Eve, the night before the year's longest day.

It feels right to celebrate this solar and metaphorical high point: across northern Europe, pre-Christian communities cherished the long summer days, and later the date was appropriated for the Mass of St John the Baptist, a counterpoint to Christ's at Christmas. In Scandinavia, garlands of flowers, bottles of aquavit, and towering bonfires still mark the summer's height, and here, amid the fells and after what has felt like my own longest winter, a celebration of summer seems both right and good. Mindful of Mark's (and William's) invitation to anyone with 'a heart to enjoy', I decide to invite some friends from university who I think will revel in such a night.

Parties have long been an undisputed and important part of Grasmere life, and this one echoes a midsummer celebration held by Coleridge and the Wordsworths in June 1800. Though that party was a smaller and more impromptu gathering, it marked the beginning of a new phase in the Wordsworths' – and the Coleridges' – lives: a time when both family groups were living in the Lake District. Coleridge had decided to rent Greta Hall at Keswick at the same time that William arranged to move to Dove Cottage, though it took him six months longer to realise the plan. This was partly because at the beginning of 1800 the Coleridges discovered that Sarah was expecting a baby. Coleridge, who had not taken his wife with him to Germany and had left her to cope with the birth, illness, and death of their second son Berkeley alone, was keen to relocate, but Sarah did not want to move away from her family in Bristol. There was also the possibility that William and Dorothy would not remain at Dove Cottage – after all, they had not stayed long in Alfoxden, Racedown, or Goslar – but by March Coleridge wrote to Tom Poole to say that William 'will never quit the North of England – his habits are more assimilated with the Inhabitants there'.[19]

Coleridge eventually arrived – alone – in Grasmere the following month, but by late June the whole Coleridge family were on their way to a new life in the Lake District. After staying for three cramped weeks at Grasmere, Coleridge and the Wordsworths rowed to the island in Grasmere lake, where Coleridge recalled that they lit a fire with 'our kettle [swinging] over the fire hanging from the branch of a Fir Tree', before making 'a glorious Bonfire' on the water's edge: the friends delighted in 'the Image of the Bonfire, & of us that danced round it – ruddy laughing faces in the twilight – the Image of this in a lake'.[20] Coleridge left Dove Cottage the following morning, and though for the rest of his life his family's main home was at Greta Hall, he would spend almost as much of his Lakeland time in Grasmere as he did in Keswick.

One of the Wordsworths' most enduring pleasures was the tremendous binding joy they felt in sharing this place with family and friends. John, who had been with his brother William when he decided to rent Dove Cottage, was the first to arrive in January 1800, just a few weeks after William and Dorothy. A year Dorothy's junior, John too had spent his adolescence away from his family. As he wasn't thought to be as academically gifted as Richard, William, or Christopher, the Wordsworths' guardians decided that at the age of fourteen John should end his schooling to become a sailor. A sea-captain cousin – also called John Wordsworth[21] – secured for John a midshipman's berth on his ship, *The Earl of Abergavenny*, and over the following fourteen years John rose to the post of commander, travelling to Brazil, India, and the West Indies in the company's employ. Like William and Dorothy, he remained essentially homeless; between voyages, he had to rely on his relations for a place to lay his head.

Being in Grasmere delighted John as being together at Windy Brow five years earlier had thrilled his siblings. Dorothy detailed how John had been 'exulting within his noble heart that his Father's Children had once again a home together', adding that 'he was so happy by the fire-side ... any little business of the house interested him, he loved our cottage, he helped us to furnish it, and to make the gardens – trees are growing now which he planted'.[22] For John as well as his siblings, the house held the promise of anchorage and haven. Coleridge, who first met John in 1799, noted to Dorothy that 'Your Br. John is one of you, a man who hath solitary usings of his own Intellect, deep in feeling, with a subtle Tact, a swift instinct of Truth & Beauty.'[23]

A quarter of a mile up the road from the cottage lies a wood, today mostly of beech trees, but in the Wordsworths' day a grove of firs. Dorothy named it 'John's Grove' for her brother, as it was John who marked out a path between the trees. After he left Dove Cottage in September 1800, some of the nearby trees were cut down by a local landowner. When he heard of this destruction, John wrote to Mary Hutchinson to say, in uncharacteristically strong terms, 'I wish I had the *monster* that cut them down in *my* ship & I would give him a tight flogging.'[24]

Just as Mary had been the first invited visitor to Racedown, she was also the first person to stay at Dove Cottage who wasn't a member of the Wordsworth family. A month after John's arrival, Mary came to stay for several weeks. As they had with John, William and Dorothy made her presence permanent in the landscape. A spit at the lake's foot became known as 'Mary Point', and William also made and named a stone seat for her on the hillside. In giving Mary her own space within this place, the Wordsworths attempted to build the community they sought, blending the affinity they felt with this landscape with the kinship they felt with those they most wished to share it with.

Across the water from Mary Point was 'Sara's Eminence', named for Mary's younger sister Sara Hutchinson, who also visited the Wordsworths at their new home in 1800. She was again commemorated on the lane opposite John's Grove, where 'Sara's gate' marked the place and time this visitor first stopped to admire the view of Grasmere. 'Sara carved her cypher upon one of its bars,' wrote the Wordsworths to her sister Mary, adding that though 'this gate was always a favourite station of ours; we love it far more now on Sara's account'.[25] The original gate has gone, but its tall stone gateposts still stand sentry over Grasmere.

William's urge to name was mirrored by a desire to immortalise his wished-for community in verse, and just as Mary's presence had inspired his creativity at Racedown, it had a similar effect in Grasmere. After a quiet winter, the spring of 1800 saw William busy composing poems that were published as 'Poems on the Naming of Places'. These locations were not necessarily the most spectacular places, but, rather, sites 'where little Incidents will have occurred, or feelings been experienced, which ... have given to such places a private and peculiar interest'.[26] In doing so, William pierced the 'spirit of the place' to the page, making permanent a landscape-community that had become vitally important to him.

Two of the places in the poems were named by William and Dorothy for each other. The first, set on 'an April morning, fresh and clear', describes a shady hollow by the beck in Easedale, the valley on the opposite side of Grasmere from Dove Cottage. It is a poem alive with the joyful rush of spring: in the sound of running water, William hears 'The spirit of enjoyment and desire, / And hopes and wishes, from all living things'. He named the spot 'Emma's Dell' – Emma and Emmeline being pseudonyms he sometimes used for Dorothy. When they first came to Grasmere, Dorothy had renamed the last of the fells to the north of Dove Cottage that 'parleys with the setting sun' for William. Although known locally as Stone Arthur, Dorothy determined that 'this lonesome Peak' should be renamed for her brother, who then wrote a poem in its honour. We laugh when we discover this, for the hill's striking silhouette, visible from Town End, has reminded all of us of portraits showing William's distinctive nose and chin.

The final poem in the group – though the first to be written – is an ode to Mary Hutchinson. Though it is set in the woods on the hills above Rydal, its metaphors are not of wildness or natural grandeur, but of home. For Mary's place has 'a slip of lawn' with a 'small bed of water in the woods', and William fantasises about building a cottage here, so that he can 'sleep beneath the shelter of its trees, And blend its waters with his daily meal' – this place has a spirit of calm order, a spirit of the daily rhythms of making porridge, gardening, and peaceful sleep.

Such a place, replete with images of domestic comfort, would become so much a part of the poet's heart that he believed 'in his death hour / Its image would survive among his thoughts'. In naming this spot for Mary, William dedicated himself to both person and place. Beauty, constancy, and comfort embody both, and it was here, in the spring of 1800, that William revealed he believed lasting happiness would come from making a home in Grasmere with Mary. The poem reads like an engagement vow: in place of a ring or other token, the offering William makes to Mary is the gift of shared kith in this landscape.

Falling in love, and sharing love, seem to be intrinsic to this place. As well as William devoting himself to Mary, John Wordsworth also seems to have placed his heart into Mary's keeping. The nature of the relationship between John and Mary can only be glimpsed at in a handful of surviving letters, but the little that we do see is an emotional connection rooted in tenderness and affection, combined with a love for this new shared home.

The two became close when they were together in Town End in the spring of 1800. This was the first time they had seen each other since the Wordsworths came to Penrith in 1787, and Dorothy recorded that the pair walked everywhere together: they were 'exceedingly attached to each other'.[27] Mary had 'a tender love of John and an intimate knowledge of all his virtues', and William wrote that Mary 'loved John with her whole soul'.[28] From January to September 1800 John lived at Dove Cottage and left only once, to visit Mary Hutchinson at Gallows Hill near Scarborough after she moved out of the cottage in April.

When not together, they wrote letters to each other. Mary's have been lost, but some of John's survive. Whilst they do not contain outright declarations of love, they are full of small courtesies and affections that go beyond anything John shared with anyone else – even his sister. In place of the common 'you', John addressed Mary with the old-fashioned intimacies of 'thee' and 'thou'. He writes more to her than he writes to anyone else, including his siblings, even as he confesses to dislike letter writing. The value of her replies is evident from his assertion that 'my dear Mary there is nothing that thou canst write but what will give me pleasure & to be with *thee* I read thy letters over a *dozen* times in a day'.[29]

This love-strengthened friendship seemed to pass unnoticed by William and Dorothy. When Dorothy broke the news to John of William and Mary's engagement, which had taken place when he was away at sea, she was apparently unaware of the effect such a revelation might have on him. Handing him a letter from Mary which contained the announcement, she offered him half a sheet of paper, on which she had already penned a letter to her future sister-in-law, for him to add congratulations. Struggling to summon the right words, John marked the page with false starts, errors, and corrections, before finally writing:

I have been reading your Letter over & over again My dearest Mary till tears have come into my eyes & I

known [*sic*] not how to express my[s]elf thou ar't [a] kind
& dear creature But wh<t>at ever fate Befall me I shall
love thee to the last and bear thy<y> memory with me to
the grave.[30]

John did not write directly to Mary again. On 29 September
1800 John's joyous summer in Grasmere came to an end, and
Dorothy and William accompanied him on the walk up
Greenhead Ghyll as far as Grizedale Tarn. On returning,
Dorothy noted that it was 'a fine day, showery but with sunshine & fine clouds – poor fellow my heart was right sad', even
though 'I could not help thinking we should see him again
because he was only going to Penrith.' John never returned
to Grasmere, and never saw Mary Hutchinson again. He met
his siblings a few times in London, but for the next five years
he spent most of his time at sea. In 1805 he drowned when
his ship went down within sight of Weymouth and Portland
Bill, and his little-known story portrays the other side of
Grasmere's giddy heart-givings.

Coleridge also lost his heart – and perhaps his head –
during those heady Grasmere days. Part of the reason for his
regular visits to Dove Cottage was the possibility of meeting
someone for whom he was developing increasingly strong
feelings: Mary Hutchinson's younger sister, Sara. Coleridge
had first met Sara at the end of his Lakeland pilgrimage the
previous year when, after parting from William at Penrith,
he visited the Hutchinson farmhouse in Sockburn. Shortly
after Coleridge's arrival, twenty-four-year-old Sara came
rushing into the house after a horse ride. 'A little over five
feet in height', she had 'a delicately fair skin and a profusion

of light brown hair', and an effervescent humour which immediately charmed him. As she went to change from her damp riding habit into clothes more suitable for entertaining, Coleridge caught a glimpse of her déshabillé. His mood was already buoyant – when Catherine Clarkson had seen him a few days previously she remarked that 'C. was in high Spirits and talk'd a great deal'[31] – and was alert to sexual possibility. Unbeknownst to the Clarksons, Coleridge had also been busy amusing himself when staying at their house by comparing the 'round fat backside of a hill' reflected in a nearby lake to female genitalia, recording gleefully in his private notebook that 'I never saw so Sweet an Image!!'[32]

In the days following his first meeting with Sara something happened which, for Coleridge, came to take on enormous personal significance. After 'Conundrums and Puns and Stories and Laughter' round the fireside, Coleridge took Sara's hand 'for a long time behind my back, and then for the first time, Love pierced me with its dart, envenomed, and Alas! incurable!'[33] This description was written four years later; at the time, Coleridge recorded the evening in one enigmatic sentence: '[T]he long Entrancement of a True-Love's Kiss.'[34] We know that when Coleridge returned to Bristol, he carried in his pocket a love token: 'a little of Sara's hair',[35] a physical reminder of feelings that were to obsess him increasingly over the following years.

As the Wordsworths had done at Grasmere, Coleridge wrought this emotional connection into the Keswick landscape and immortalised it in verse. In August 1800 the friends made a seat at Windy Brow, 'by the Roadside Halfway up a Steep Hill Facing South'. On 10 October 1801, they sculpted what Coleridge termed 'the Sopha of Sods' at Greta Hall, but from the first its focus was Sara, for in her journal Dorothy simply called it 'Sara's seat'. The following April, Coleridge immortalised it further as 'the sod-built seat of Chamomile' in his 'Dejection: An Ode', wishing that Sara had been sitting there 'all this while'.

The seats were not the only dedication to Sara made by Coleridge and the Wordsworths. Under the shade of the trees at the back of the museum is a broad slab of rock, scored with familiar initials: S.H., W.W., D.W., S.T.C., M.H., J.W. This is what remains of the 'Rock of Names', a large boulder which once stood beside the road at Thirlmere, halfway between Keswick and Grasmere. This rock marked a spot chosen by them as a beacon and resting-place as they made regular pilgrimages between their houses. As they had done at Sara's gate and Mary's seat, they carved their ciphers here, engraving the presence of themselves and their friends into the landscape.

At first the rock was known as 'Sara's crag', named for Sara Hutchinson, and the first initials to be cut here were S.H., scored into the stone by Coleridge. The other initials were added later, but for some time this place was synonymous with Sara – and for Coleridge, it came to symbolise not just the person, but what he had come to feel for her, and the version of her he had created in his mind.

There is now nothing visible of the Rock of Names by Thirlmere, made into a reservoir in the 1890s, when much of the volcanic outcrop which had edged the old turnpike road was blasted away with dynamite, and the resulting stones used for building. However, under the auspices of

Canon Hardwicke Rawnsley, founder member of both the Wordsworth Trust and the National Trust, some small sections were salvaged and set into a small cairn some distance above the spot where they had originally stood. In 1984, Jonathan Wordsworth and Robert Woof oversaw an operation to move the pieces to a spot behind the museum, where they were set into a slab of slate. This is where they now live, growing a little more lichen with each passing year.

Midsummer's Eve approaches. The days before bring heavy deluges that soak the orchard, but the forecast promises that Saturday will be clear and dry. The omens are good. I decide to bring my violin to the party: I've been practising it almost every day since I arrived here, and sometimes find that a crowd of tourists have gathered below my window to listen. Emily, Polly, and Mark will bring their poems, and everyone else a platter or bottle, plates or glasses, or a few twists of weed.

Since our bouldering adventure I have felt an affection growing between Tom and me. Sitting outside the Old Dungeon Ghyll nursing pints and making promises of adventures yet to come felt to me like the beginning of a bond. Earlier that week we chanced upon each other in Keswick, and he gave me a lift back to Town End. On the way we stopped at Castlerigg, where a ring of leaning ancient stones rises from the earth in mimicry of the mountains that surround it. Shortly after we arrived it began to rain and, wearing nothing more waterproof than T-shirts and shorts, we sought shelter under a hawthorn hedge. The silliness of the situation made us giggly, and my heart leapt as I felt Tom squeeze between me and the hedge as the rain poured down.

On the morning of the party I don my favourite dress and, once work is over and the cottage and museum are closed for the night, make the short pilgrimage to the orchard. Trestle tables and as many chairs as the terrace can spare are grouped between the apple trees. Mark has mowed a broad circle in the middle, also cutting winding paths to link it with the gates. John has lugged his speakers and drums from across the road, and someone has liberated a few wooden boards – usually used for cheese and crackers at exhibition openings – from their cupboards in the museum.

The air is still, dry, and warm, stolen from a southern summer. Our neighbours' children thread the orchard as they search for raspberries and currants to supplement a dinner of crisps and half-cooked sausages. Mark's brother Jules has come up from Blackburn for the weekend, bringing his guitar, and his melodies filter through the air like smoke. I put my violin under my chin and begin to play, mixing the few tunes I know by heart with Jules's notes. Chatter and laughter are everywhere, and as the sun descends and its rays touch the top of Silver How, the air seems more golden than ever before.

As I lean on the gate to watch the sun setting across the valley, I find Tom standing next to me. We smile at each other, and he tells me how much he likes hearing me play my violin. I smile and redden, and he puts his arm across my shoulder. A thrill runs through me and I lean against his arm and long, strong body. We stand together, basking in the glow, before Mark shouts across to ask me if I'll come and

play some more. I walk back into the orchard and Tom follows, and I can feel mutual electricity crackling between us.

We are not the only ones to feel this kind of thrill. One of
the barmen at Tweedies, the one who curls his moustache
across his cheeks and wears women's stripey trousers, is
standing on the other side of the orchard next to Emily. I
have often seen him slipping the latch on the gate to House
Two, though no one admits that he has come to see them.
Mark reckons that on the top floor it could be any of three
doors that open for him. One night I saw him walking
quickly up the hill, hand in hand with someone whose back
I did not recognise; another night I thought I saw the face of
one of the barmaids against his shoulder in the far corner of
the pub garden.

Music and dancing fill the darkening air. Around eleven
o'clock the light slips from the sky, and Mark holds a match
to a pile of wood and broken chairs heaped at one side of the
orchard. The bonfire crackles into life, and John cranks up
the volume on his speakers. Standing beside the table I find
Tom at my shoulder, and I reach for his hand. Wordlessly we
make our way to the gate and across the road, and under the
streetlamp beside Dove Cottage exchange a kiss. 'Do you
want to come up to my room?' I ask Tom, and he kisses his
assent. I lift the latch upon the gate, and we slip inside the
house and shut the door.

9

A Fancy in the Heart

'I was no Prophet, nor had even a hope,
Scarcely a wish, but one bright
*   pleasing thought,*
A fancy in the heart of what might be
The lot of others, never could be mine.
The place from which I looked was soft
*   and green,*
Not giddy yet aerial, with a depth
Of Vale below, a height of Hills above.'

William Wordsworth, 'Home at Grasmere'
(draft manuscript, c.1806)[1]

July ushers in an excess of rain and thunderstorms, sunshine and heat. It is the kind of humid weather where skin stays damp throughout the day and night. Bodies stick together, and lightning rends the evenings with electric passion impossible to ignore. The air crackles with tension and we all feel its energy. High pressure has

Town End in its grip and rainy night follows hot day night after day.

Rain drumming on the roof is the soundtrack to this new courtship. At night Tom and I lie awake and watch lightning shock my bedroom into blue-bright relief. The air is heavy but our hearts are light, and when morning comes and the world is washed new again Tom takes the short walk back to his home to get ready for a day working in one of the village's many outdoor-equipment shops. The culverts sing and gurgle as the lake swells to the brim with this heavy summer rain.

At first our relationship is kind of secret – not from our friends, but from Tom's parents. Dating the boss's son adds a difficult dimension to one's working life, and I am far from sure about how to navigate this situation. However, Jeff himself is more accustomed to such an arrangement; Tom's eldest brother Joe went out with the Trust's exhibitions officer before I arrived in Grasmere. Though they broke up months ago, she still goes round for dinner with the family once or twice a month. Tom's parents are fond of her, keen to keep up their connection. What my own relationship with them will be is much less clear. I am not yet sure what they feel about me, or how I might fit in to a situation where work, love, and family life are so closely intertwined.

Work is now extremely busy, with as many as five hundred visitors in a day. The school holidays have begun, and we must share our paradise with thousands of people who want to enjoy the same things that we love about this place. Though the Trust is open almost year round, closing only for deep cleaning in January, high summer is the busiest time, bringing in money that will keep the organisation afloat through the winter. It is a bittersweet necessity: everyone grumbles about having so many extra people, but we also know that without them most of us wouldn't be here.

When we're not at work, Tom and I spend a lot of time planning adventures. I am eager to know the fells better, and Tom is a ready guide. We pore over maps and Tom shows me how the valleys link and flow together, helping me to thread routes around the crags. The rough volcanic rock of Scafell, the sharp slates of Skiddaw: to me they are little more than names, but to him they are physical realities, places where he can lose and find himself again. My ardour for the mountains is doubled by my feelings for him: everywhere is more exciting with the promise of exploring it together.

Exploring mountain landscapes for entertainment only became desirable – even fashionable – among western European society in the late eighteenth century. Before the 1790s, 'mountaineers' as we recognise them today did not exist: the noun referred solely those who lived among mountains, not those visiting for sport. These shepherd-farmers walked among the high peaks because they had to: their livestock lived and grazed there, the peat and trees that fed their fires had to be cut from the mountains' flanks, and the animals they hunted had their homes among the crags. Their paths and passes arose out of necessity, often tracing routes between farmsteads lower down the mountains and shepherds' huts higher up. When ice and snow made the high hills dangerous, they kept their distance, but as spring warmed the air they led their livestock towards rich summer grazing. The word *alp*, now applied to high mountains, was originally given to the land beyond the tree line and, like *fell*, it meant uncultivated hill pasture best suited to summer grazing.

Two things occasionally brought non-mountaineers into alpine realms: territory disputes, and extreme religious or spiritual fervour. In many cultures, mountains were – and are – believed to be home to the gods owing to their proximity to the heavens, so pilgrimages into the hills were sometimes made in quest of Paradise. In 1492, Charles VIII of France commanded military engineer Antoine de Ville to climb Mont Aiguille because he believed he had seen angels swarming around its summit. Supported by a team of ten, de Ville reached the top, but instead of seraphs he found meadows filled with flowers and chamois, a very different kind of heaven.

By the mid-seventeenth century, scientific curiosity rather than spiritual hunger was drawing a new kind of explorer to the hills. A growing number of scientists or 'natural philosophers' wanted to observe meteorological conditions at altitude, gather botanical specimens, and take geological samples. In 1639 London apothecary Thomas Johnson climbed Yr Wyddfa (Snowdon) in pursuit of plants for use in his remedies. A similar desire sparked the first known ascent of Ben Nevis in 1771 by Edinburgh botanist James Robertson, and the following year Astronomer Royal Nevil Maskelyne climbed Schiehallion in central Scotland. The mountain's unusually steep slopes, combined with its relative distance from other mountains, made it possible for Maskelyne and his colleagues to measure its gravitational pull, which they extrapolated to ascertain the world's mass.[2]

What has been called the first competitive or 'sport' climb – a mountain ascent purely for the sake of it – came in response to the financial prize first offered twenty years earlier by Swiss naturalist Horace Bénédict de Saussure for summiting Mont Blanc. Jacques Balmat, a Swiss chamois hunter, and Michel-Gabriel Paccard, a local doctor, set off from Chamonix, pitching camp high above the valley on the Grand Plateau. After spending the night there, they headed to the summit and reached it at half past six on the evening of 8 August 1786. Telescopes in Chamonix followed their ascent, and from the summit, Paccard took several scientific measurements. Curiosity had been his motivation; it was Balmat who collected Saussure's money and gloried in the nickname *Balmat de Mont Blanc*.

The appeal of the mountains was not limited to the continental Alps. In 1786, artist-schoolmaster William Gilpin published an illustrated guide to the Lake District, noting that these 'vast regions, whose parts are thus absorbed in the immensity of a whole, have the strongest effect on the imagination'. Seeing, rather than summiting, the mountains was enough for Gilpin, for '[t]hey distend the mind, and fix it in a kind of stupor'.[3] Other writers and artists followed his example: J. M. W. Turner made his first painting tour of the region in 1797, and the resulting pictures of Lodore Falls, Crummock Water, and Coniston Water were exhibited at the Royal Academy, popularising dramatic Lakeland views among London audiences. The search for sensation – sublimity in beauty which could simultaneously terrify, intoxicate, excite the viewer – was becoming part of the appeal of spending time in the Lake District.

As the appeal to people's imaginations of visiting mountains for their own sake grew, so did the desire to climb them. The term 'mountaineer' began to shift in meaning: Joseph Budworth, whose *A Fortnight's Ramble in the Lake District* was published in 1792, described his Lakeland guide Robin Partridge as 'so bold a mountaineer, he can go any where that a sheep can', thereby infusing the word with a sense of capacity for climbing. In 1810, when the third edition of the *Ramble* appeared, Budworth referred to himself and another guide, Paul Postlethwaite, as being 'like hardy mountaineers'[4] as they ascended Langdale's Pike o' Stickle in 1797.

Budworth acknowledged that, unlike Partridge and Postlethwaite, he was a 'stranger' on the mountain; the fells were already well known to those who lived and farmed upon their slopes. When Thomas Wilkinson, anti-slavery campaigner and sometime poet from Yanwath near Penrith, first climbed Helvellyn in 1805, he was surprised to be passed by a 'mountain-maid' with 'the bloom of health upon her countenance' driving a pony and sledge stacked with peats with 'as much agility and spirit down the mountain as the fair citizen does her curricle along the level streets of London'.[5] Wilkinson had been goaded into climbing the slopes by Elizabeth and Catherine Smith, sisters living at Patterdale. He had been wary of climbing in early spring when a 'wreath of snow and ice' hung on the mountain, but they 'ridiculed [his] effeminacy' and told him they had already reached the summit without a guide. Having thoroughly enjoyed it, the sisters repeated the ascent the following day.[6]

Coleridge was a lifelong devotee of sensation-seeking, and his appetite for thrill and novelty was awakened amid mountain landscapes. After arriving to live in Town End, the Wordsworths made their own explorations of the fells around Grasmere, beginning with a frosty walk towards Rydal in late December 1799, as well frequently walking to Ambleside and back in search of mail, but they did not aim for summits and the ensuing thrill. In May 1800 William and John walked through the mountains to the north-east of Dove Cottage on their long trek to visit the Hutchinsons at Sockburn, and all three siblings had become familiar with the valleys of Grasmere, Easedale, and Rydal, but it was Coleridge who initially sought to explore the upper reaches of the mountains for their own sake.

Coleridge's first adventure in the hills took place in Wales in 1794, when he and his friend and fellow writer Joseph Hucks were narrowly dissuaded by a young local guide from setting off to climb Snowdon an hour before midnight. He was also the first of the Wordsworth circle to reach the top of Helvellyn. Having set off to walk from Greta Hall to Dove Cottage one late-August afternoon in 1800, he eschewed the usual turnpike road along Thirlmere, taking a more easterly path and ending up on Helvellyn almost by accident. Finding himself on the summit as darkness fell, he walked down as the stars came out and arrived at Dove Cottage after eleven that night. Giddy with the success of this adventure, he spent most of the rest of the night discussing the possibility of building a house on Helvellyn with the Wordsworths, and four days later persuaded William, John, and a neighbour, Mr Sympson, to repeat the ascent with him in reverse.

Coleridge's escapades among the mountains were the latest in a long line of experiments into high-stakes self-medication. He wanted to 'see into the life of things' through extremity of experience, both psychological and physiological, and recognised in himself that climbing mountains was 'one sort of gambling, to which I am much addicted'.[7] Laudanum and other drugs, including nitrous oxide (laughing gas), provided other-worldly feelings of a different sort. His appetite for giddiness knew few bounds; it was part of what made him simultaneously stimulating and infuriating company.

In August 1802 he embarked on a solo nine-day 'circumcursion'[8] of the Lake District, which saw him explore some of the region's highest peaks – again more by accident than by design. The decision to summit mountains was almost incidental, for Coleridge initially envisaged the trip as a visit to the library in the west coast village of St Bees, which was reputedly very good. He walked west from Keswick to the coast, but unfortunately the library turned out to be, for his purposes, 'utterly worthless'.[9] As he headed back towards Keswick via Wasdale, the massive bulk of Scafell drew him like a lodestar, and he decided to climb to its top.

Walking up Wasdale, he raced thunderclouds to the summit, and once there had to urgently find 'an imperfect Shelter'[10] as a storm raged round him. The thunderclaps were amplified by the rocks, and as he heard them, Coleridge was exhilarated by their reach and power: 'the most heart exciting of all earthly things I have beheld'.[11] Instead of looking 'round about & wind about 'till I find a track or other symptom of safety', Coleridge wandered on. Having skirted Scafell Crag and finding himself 'cut off from a most Sublime Crag-summit', Coleridge lit upon the gap at Broad Stand and 'determined to go thither'.[12]

From Scafell, Coleridge observed that a stretch of rocks appeared to be linked to the neighbouring summit of Scafell Pike. There was no path to follow, and so his 'confident – or indolent' method was to make his way 'where it is first *possible* to descend, there I go – relying 'upon fortune for how far down this possibility will continue'.[13] A slabby set of rocks formed a kind of giant's staircase below him, which he 'slipped down, & went on for a while with tolerable ease', but soon came to 'a smooth perpendicular Rock about 7 feet high'.[14] Looking down, he saw 'a succession of these little Precipices', realising that this 'in a very hard Rain is, no doubt, the channel of a most splendid Waterfall'.[15] Grandly, he later claimed that 'this was nothing – I put my hands on the Ledge, & dropped down'.[16]

Soon, however, the gaps between these precipices lengthened beyond the compass of his legs, and before long he was having to drop down higher and higher ledges, which left 'my whole limbs in a *Tremble*'.[17] Having marooned himself halfway down the rock face, Coleridge recorded that, despite his shaking body, he did not panic. Instead, he lay down and began 'according to my custom, to laugh at myself for a Madman'.[18] Tension relieved, he relaxed and watched clouds scud by, and before long slipped into a kind of 'Trance and Delight'. He felt suffused with awe, and suddenly a solution to his predicament appeared: he noted a notch between the rocks (today called Fat Man's Agony), took off his rucksack, and slipped between them. Coleridge later wrote to Robert Southey to share his delight at having spent 'the greater part of the ... Day *mountaineering*',[19] and with this neologism began a cultural obsession with climbing for sheer exhilaration that endures to this day.

As a guide to rock climbing Coleridge's route is folly, though as a record of a climber's 'shaky leg' and dizzy elevation it is a fair account. That summer I have my first taste of such palsied panic on Middlefell Buttress, a stout crag on Langdale's eastern side. Though Tom promised me Scafell, he first brings me to Middle Fell to practise. The Buttress is not a difficult climb, but it is long, and plenty high enough that a slip or fall could be fatal. We step into harnesses, and Tom works a slender knot of rope between them, anchoring me to one end of the rope whilst tying himself to the other. With his body security against a fatal fall, this is a pact of trust as great as any I have made.

Tom goes up first to secure pitons, and from above encourages me to have a go. 'Don't rely on your hands to hold you,' he calls as I reach for a hefty hold, 'the muscles in your legs are stronger – they hold your full weight all the time.' I stop, push my foot down, and extend my leg so that I can rise up to meet my hands. Then reach out again, push up, extend. Breathe and reach again. The rope and tiny nuts and cams are some protection against disaster.

Climbing is an antidote to physical detachment. It requires concentration in every muscle, a measured tension in toes and tendons to keep you from falling. Feeling disconnected from the rest of the world had been a hallmark of my depression; at times it had been so acute that I had been unable to focus on simple tasks like hanging out the washing. I could only stand and gaze, my eyes unseeing, as the phantasmagoria in my head played out. At that time, climbing would not only have been dangerous, it would have been impossible. That I can now focus on the interplay between my body and the stone is a sure sign of being better.

Tom leads the dance, a kind of slow ballet on the rocks. I try to follow the confident sway of his body, finding the same safe spots on the rock, but he is a head taller than I am and his limbs have a compass that exceeds mine. Some of the holds we can share – a big jutting jug at the side of an overhang and a broad platform where trembling limbs can rest – but my hands need to search out their own small clefts and rocky nubs. My smaller, thinner fingers squeeze into cracks that will not hold his flat, wide hands. Where his body cannot bend, mine easily curls around to reach a crimp just big enough to hold. I am slow, slow, slow where he is quick, and at first I need his eyes as well as mine to help me navigate this world.

When you're climbing, you have to stay with reality. Fooling yourself is a matter of life and death on the crags; if you cannot make the hold that you promise your body you can, the results can be fatal. After a few easy pitches I suddenly realise I do not know where to put my hand next. My fingers skitter across the rock, searching for a lip of stone to grip, but nothing feels big enough to hold on to. My heart gallops, flooding my muscles with adrenaline. I have to calm it down before my legs begin shaking so much they will not keep me up. Panic palsies my limbs, but above me Tom is calm and reassuring. 'Trust your body, and if you do slip, my body and this rope will hold you.'

Eventually I reach the flat slat at the top of the Buttress and detach myself from the rope. Relief at reaching the top of the climb giddies through me. Sitting on the rock in the sunshine, we see farmers gathering hay in the fields below, and a red Mountain Rescue helicopter flies beneath us. We watch it skirt the crags with a sick flicker in our stomachs. Round and down it goes, getting as close to the rock as it dares, before eventually pulling back and flying off. The sight of it makes us shiver: we hope that whoever called them out isn't still lying stuck or injured on the fellside.

Climbing is about adrenaline as much as it is about control. The surging thrills of height and new perspectives, the triumph of one's body over the apparently impossible. As we walked into Langdale earlier that day, Tom told me about his relationship with climbing. It hadn't started young, as I'd assumed; though he'd grown up amid the fells, it was only in his late teens that he'd wanted to challenge himself by climbing rocks. After a course at Plas y Brenin in Wales, his skill and passion for the crags had developed further during his time at university. The rocks were a promise of distraction, a different and very physical reality from the grind of urban study.

When I first met Tom, I noticed that, though he was always friendly, there was sometimes a quality of sadness about him. In a few late-night moments at the pub, I had asked him to tell me why he occasionally seemed melancholic, but he hadn't wanted to explain. Now that we are in each other's confidence, he tells me that his wild day out on Helvellyn back in January had been more than a thrilling hike: it had been an attempt to shift the miasma of lonely self-doubt that had dogged him for months. Not long before I came to Grasmere, he had broken up with a long-term girlfriend, someone who had been an important constant in his life. Climbing helped him deal with the shock of being suddenly alone, providing an absorbing distraction from this seismic life shift.

As we talk, he opens up about walking the line between putting yourself in real danger and enjoying the sharp edge of your limitations. Dizzy, anxious masculinity is a common trope in mountain literature, found in, among others, Andy Kirkpatrick's *Psychovertical*, Jon Krakauer's *Into the Wild*, and Andy Cave's *Learning to Breathe*. For anything to be worth doing, it has to be dangerous; there has to be a risk, the chance for something to go badly wrong. There is no point playing safe, following a footpath or well-tested route. Climbing occupies and distracts, issuing a challenge, giving you the chance to prove to no one in particular – or perhaps yourself – that you are strong, able, adventurous. The alternative is scary. We fly from what we fear as much as we gravitate towards what we desire.

A couple of weeks after our ascent of Middlefell Buttress, Tom and I are standing at the top of Broad Stand. The day began in glorious warm sunshine as we set off from

Wha House Farm in Eskdale, but by the time we've skirted Hare Crag and walked four miles north to Scafell a cold wind is swirling mist around us. Cutting across the flank of Esk Fell, we're now almost 880 metres above sea level. Even as we make our way along the summit ridge, sole adventurers on this pinnacle, through gaps in the mist we can see knots of people gathering on Scafell Pike, unable to resist the magnetism of England's highest peak. The lure of extremity is strong in our culture: be the fastest, run the longest, climb the highest. For us, it doesn't matter that everyone else is climbing the adjacent mountain; we are on a different pilgrimage, retracing other footsteps across the Scafell massif.

We reach the top of Scafell, a summit fourteen metres lower than the top of its more famous neighbour, in the early afternoon. Below us is a deep gully, with the fang of Scafell Pinnacle pointing skywards to the north. From the summit we can see the tops of distant fells, and try to read weather omens, good or ill, in their relative clarity. These patterns are succinct and striking portents of what has been and might become: clouds build up in the west, and a grey smur of rain blankets the northern fells. Thin smudges of misty clouds race past below us, streaming down Eskdale like victory banners heading home.

Loosening the trademark asthmatic mucus from my throat, I feel warm pride in my body's achievement. Whilst I haven't enjoyed the slog and sweat of the walk, to be standing higher than the clouds is thrilling, relief with a tingle of triumph. As my breathing slows, it gives my blood a lift, flooding my limbs with oxygen. Joy made physical again: my heart delights at being here, grateful for the rest and challenge.

Reaching the shallow gully above Broad Stand, we prepare for the trickiest part of the descent. Though the summer has been warm, the slabs are greasy underfoot, slick with mossy slime. It is nothing like the dry, grippy tuff we climbed on in Langdale. Even compared with the rest of the Lake District, Scafell is an extremely wet place, receiving almost double the UK average rainfall. Staying upright is difficult, and I hope my £5 boots and novice limbs can meet the challenge of climbing down these rocks.

I soon realise that they might not, and so we decide to put on harnesses, rope up, and use the little hardware we have to help us get down. Tom puts the rope around a heavy boulder, and gestures to me to begin climbing downwards. When I get down to the first broad platform where I can rest securely, he takes the rope off the belay. Rope up, belay, repeat, repeat, repeat – all the way down to a sheer corner of overhanging rock. Below us is a drop of almost three metres with a large sloping ledge beneath. At the top is a metal piton: from here we will abseil across the abyss below.

When you're abseiling, you're trusting your life to the rope and whatever it is bound to. This rusty piton looks like it has been in place for some time; Tom is not certain it will hold our weight. Instead, he takes out a couple of climbing nuts and places them into crevices as backup, and anchors himself to the belay. Satisfied that they will hold us if required, he lowers me down the gap. I feel excitement, but no paralysing nervous tension. At the bottom is Fat Man's Agony, and I squeeze through it with only mild discomfort.

Having seen the piton hold firm, Tom then removes the backup anchors and abseils after me, pulling the rope down behind him. No gear lost or parties injured, we celebrate with a sweaty kiss before beginning the long walk out.

Love – or lovesickness – was also a factor in inspiring Coleridge's adventure among those fells; we are only familiar with his extraordinary day on Scafell because of a letter he sent to the object of his affections, Wordsworth's soon-to-be sister-in-law Sara Hutchinson, who copied his missive into her journal. The original no longer exists, as many of the letters between the two do not, for much of their correspondence has been purposefully destroyed. Someone – possibly Mary, William, or their grandson Gordon Graham Wordsworth – took a pair of scissors to the few letters which do survive, slicing off everything beyond the mundane and domestic. These snippets are preserved inside a volume of Coleridge's letters at the Wordsworth Trust, though the missing parts raise further questions about their relationship. The fact that someone on their behalf had a weather eye on the morality and judgement of the public, whether real or imagined, means that we can only glimpse at the truth of what happened between them.

We know from Sara's answering letters that much of Coleridge's correspondence contained poems written to and about her. In the winter of 1801–2, Coleridge had sent Sara a 'complaining Scroll' which caused her 'bodily Sickness'; apparently she was rendered 'weak & pale with Sickness, Grief and Pain', and Coleridge confesses: 'And I – I made thee so!'[20] This 'scroll' was sent from Coleridge during a trip to London, and around the same time, he wrote in his notebook: 'Miss Sara Hutcheson's [*sic*] new gospel – alias – Honesty.' He also noted that he was planning a poem which painted a lively picture of 'a man, disappointed in marriage, & endeavouring to make a compensation to himself by virtuous & tender & brotherly friendship with an amiable Woman – the obstacles – the jealousies – the impossibility of it'.[21]

In the draft version of this poem (titled 'A Letter to —' and dated 4 April 1802), Coleridge gives an explanation for the 'heartless mood' he sought to escape: trapped in an unhappy marriage, he imagined himself mad with love for Sara. Calling her his 'Heart within my Heart', in his mind's eye he returns to a cherished memory of himself cradled in the arms of the Hutchinson sisters:

> 'It was as calm as this, that happy night
> When Mary, thou, & I together were,
> The low decaying Fire our only Light,
> And listen'd to the Stillness of the Air!
> O that affectionate & blameless
> Maid, Dear Mary! on her
> Lap my head she lay'd—
> Her Hand was on my Brow,
> Even as my own is now;
> And on my Cheek I felt thy eye-lash play.
> Such Joy I had, that I may truly say,
> My Spirit was awe-stricken with the Excess
> And trance-like Depth of its brief Happiness.'[22]

This description of his embrace with his best friend's betrothed and her sister exposes Coleridge's quandary: he wants an emotional closeness that cannot be sustained.

The poem was inspired by a meeting that took place between Coleridge, Mary, and Sarah at the Hutchinson farm at Gallow Hill sometime between 2 and 13 March 1802. We do not know if Coleridge ever sent this poem to Sara; no record remains of him doing so, or of her response. We do, however, know that he read the poem to William and Dorothy on 21 April 1802 ('Coleridge came to us & repeated the verses he wrote to Sara') and that Dorothy 'was affected with them & was on the whole, not being well, in miserable spirits'.[23] The date on the top of the manuscript is 4 April, the day before William left Grasmere to propose marriage to Mary, the 'affectionate & blameless Maid' who appears to have placed Coleridge's head in her lap a few weeks earlier. Mary's acceptance of William's proposal sparked the chain of events necessary for the wedding to take place, including William travelling to France to formally end his relationship with Annette Vallon and meet his daughter Anne-Caroline. Coleridge supported William in his plans, urging him to do what *he* could not: finish one relationship so that he might realise another.

Coleridge's relationship with the Wordsworths and the Hutchinsons echoes the intensity of the involvement between him, Southey, Lovell, and the Fricker sisters in Bristol years before. The lure of multi-person attachment had been a strong impulse in the dream of Susquehanna, only partially realised in the resulting marriages. Coleridge sought intense friendship and emotional closeness, sexual excitement, and domestic comfort. Though he was still married and part of another multi-sibling household with the extended Southey–Coleridge family at Greta Hall (Sarah's sister Edith, her husband Robert Southey, and their children had moved there too), by 1802 he had pinned his hopes – romantic and creative – on the sibling commune of the Wordsworths and Hutchinsons at Dove Cottage, where Sara, Mary, and their sister Joanna regularly stayed.

For Coleridge, loving Sara was part of a web of complex emotions that involved not only romantic attachment but also creative stimulus and social support.[24] His passion for her was also contextualised within his relationship with her sister, and within the compass of his friendship with the Wordsworths: 'as I love thee, Mary, & William, & dear Dorothy'.[25] In his description to Sara of walking down from Broad Stand on that stormy August day, Coleridge wrote that he delighted in calling out the names of William, Mary, Sara, and Dorothy (followed by his children Hartley and Derwent, and finally Joanna Hutchinson, Mary and Sara's younger sister) and hearing them echo off the rocks: 'I shouted out all your names in the Sheep-fold-when Echo came upon Echo.'[26] In the vastness of the hills, Coleridge could test out the version of an idealised 'home', one which could not exist, but which he had come to desire most of all.

We follow Coleridge's route down into Eskdale. The clouds and mist have cleared again and the Esk winks at us as we traverse the remaining miles. Looking up, we see the gloomy bulk of Cam Spout Crag on Scafell's south-eastern face and the boulders known as Sampson's Stones clustered below it. A peregrine circles the air, keening its defensive screech across the sky. My feet start to ache long before we reach the road that leads back to Wha House Farm, but I hardly mind. We have walked, scrambled, slithered, and suspended ourselves into almost mythic places. Sore feet are a small price to pay.

Though the Romantics provide the pretext for our walk, Tom and I are not so much in pursuit of Coleridge as on a quest for something that might exist between us. Ours is a courtship of two quite different minds: he is methodical, calm, scientific, whilst I am impulsive, excitable, romantic. Our shared goal in conquering this mountain is a unity of selves and purpose. It is a space, real and imagined, where we can find something to please and excite us, a doorway to a new world offering a landscape and a love that multiplies delight for being shared.

In making this pilgrimage we are following not only Coleridge's footsteps, but also those of Pete Laver, the Wordsworth Trust's former librarian. Pete – together with his wife Mags and their two children – became a memorable and integral part of the Town End community during the 1970s and early '80s. The moniker 'librarian' belies the variety of Pete's social, intellectual, and creative interests: as well as being a meticulous administrator, Pete was also a political activist, a talented artist, and a published poet. He had studied with Robert Woof at Newcastle, and it was this connection that brought the Lavers to Town End.

Pete's politics were firmly on the left; during his time at university, he had been arrested, charged, and sentenced in connection with an anti-apartheid protest. Committed to anti-racism, environmental protection, and the right to peaceful protest, he frequently attended political demonstrations, marched against nuclear proliferation at Aldermaston, and was interested in anarchist theory: for a time, he was involved with Tyneside Free Press, lynchpin of the 1970s alternative zeitgeist in Newcastle. Pete's interest in progressive politics extended into the academic sphere – his doctoral studies had focused on the American naturalist, writer, and philosopher Henry David Thoreau. Shortly before his death, Pete had been planning to write a book with Michael Foot, then leader of Britain's Labour Party, on nineteenth-century socialist pamphleteers.

In addition to his political convictions and his intellectual interest in socialist philosophy, Pete loved art, music, and poetry, and was deftly skilful in pencil and ink. The Wordsworth Museum carries copies of his work – books written and illustrated by him, including *Guillotine*, *Pete Laver's Anarcho-Marxist Fun Book*, and *Water, Glass, The Toad of Guilt*. He was charming, vivacious, and a lover of a good party: Town End tales are still told of the gatherings he and Mags would host, where conversation and debate would go on late into the night, lubricated by red wine and idealism. He was attentive to almost everyone he encountered, and being around Pete made people feel special. He had a huge fan club, and many people – both men and women – regarded him as their closest confidant, with several professing to have been in love with him.

Each August Grasmere plays host to writers and academics attending the Wordsworth Summer Conference, an annual celebration of Romanticism at which Pete – alongside luminaries, including Seamus Heaney – would sometimes tutor. Many stayed on for holidays in the Lakes afterwards. After the 1983 conference had finished, a group planned a walk to the top of Scafell. Their aim was not only to recreate that famous Coleridgean walk, but also to get some photographs of the route, which would form the basis of an exhibition about Coleridge due to open at the Wordsworth Trust the following year.

It was a week after Pete's thirty-sixth birthday when the little group began to climb Scafell. On that hot August day, the air was close, almost oppressive. The walkers decided to approach the mountain from the Seathwaite side, but as they came up the steep path beside Grains Gill, Pete fell behind. The others turned and waited for him; he signalled, with a wave, that he was fine, and urged them on. They continued to the summit, but Pete did not – could not – follow. He died on the mountainside that summer afternoon.

Pete's body was found between Black Waugh and Hind Side, on the lower slopes of Seathwaite Fell. A post-mortem revealed that he had died of a heart attack, the consequence of advanced coronary artery disease probably caused by familial hypercholesterolemia – a genetic disorder which affects the liver's ability to process cholesterol. Four decades later, Pete's immediate family continue to feel the impact of his untimely death and the circumstances surrounding it, and for those who were on Scafell that day, the memory of what happened will never leave them.

After Pete's funeral, a crowd of mourners wept in Grasmere's cemetery, surrounded by the fells he came to love. They wished to further mark his life and passing, and several later climbed Grains Gill to build a stone cairn at the spot where he died. At the following year's Summer Conference, Seamus Heaney quoted Yeats as he mourned Pete's absence: 'all things the delighted eye now sees / Were loved by him'.[27] The following year *Coleridge's Imagination: Essays in Memory of Pete Laver* was published, dedicated to a man whose 'gift for friendship' was missed above all other qualities, 'for it was this that gave his talent a special life'.[28]

This was far from the only tribute. New Zealand poet (and fellow librarian) Fleur Adcock included a paean to Pete in her 1987 anthology *The Incident Book* in a poem drafted shortly after his death, which describes a Town End party held during a thunderstorm earlier that fateful summer. There, Fleur described how she and Pete had laughed over a nineteenth-century literary annual filled with drawing-room dramas, comic verses, and sentimental stories, which he then gave to her, writing 'on loan perpetual' on the flyleaf. That it was titled *The Keepsake* now seems particularly apposite. On the day after his death, Adcock turned her memories into a poem of the same name, dedicating it to Pete.

Pete's last – and lasting – creative legacy came in the form of a posthumous volume of poetry. Titled *Offcomers* and published by Pig Press in 1985 under the aegis of Richard (Rik) Caddel – another alumnus of Newcastle University involved with the Morden Tower readings – it features poems Pete had been writing and illustrating just before his death. The final verse in the collection, 'Rowing

Round Belle Isle', is dedicated to Pete's son and describes a boating adventure the two of them had on Windermere. Written only the day before that fateful walk on Scafell, the poem paints a vivid picture of a little rowing boat crossing the lake, its sailors roused by the rattle of the ferry's chain and metallic trembles from the ropes of empty yachts. William Wordsworth's description of stealing a rowing boat on nearby Ullswater in *The Prelude* haunts the poem – as do Stygian echoes of the boatman Charon transporting his other-worldly cargo. Its final lines are an evocative panegyric not only to Pete, but also to the power of poetry, shared experience, and the Lake District landscape:

> And all that mystery
> of waters tamed our words
> moving together amiable
> observant, not afraid
> of losing light
> among the islands
> and the deeper swells.

Tom and I get back in the car and head home, turning on the heating to take the ache out of our cold, tired legs. As we wind our way through Ambleside, listening to the crackly tape player belting out old rock songs, I feel a rush of warmth and happiness in my chest. It is a sensation I have had only twice before, a radiance that spreads outward from my heart to suffuse my body with a kind of glowing joy. It is a wellspring of delight that rises unawares, a feeling of contented bliss that arrives without warning.

The first time I experienced it was in the Cotswolds one June afternoon. With university examinations scheduled to start the next day, my friend Sally and I had decided to escape. We'd revised for weeks already, and nothing we did now could much improve our chances. Laying aside our notes and books, we took the first bus out of the city, and spent the day walking through the wolds. We found a pub in time for lunch, and by late afternoon were climbing a little hill beside fields full of ripening corn. As we reached the crest the sun appeared from behind a cloud, setting everything aglow. It lit something inside me; my heart lightened and a rush of revelation came upon me. These exams didn't matter, they weren't important: there would be other golden days like this, days of delight that were in no way dependent on a piece of paper. We whooped and ran along the field edge towards the river. No matter what came tomorrow, bliss was our birthright.

The next time I experienced this rush of joy was two years later. It was a bright day in late July, not long before I left for Japan, and I was making my way home after a liaison with a friend I'd fallen into sleeping with. Sitting in a train rattling slowly out of King's Cross station, the sun streaming through the window, I opened a newspaper someone had left on the seat beside me. Struggling to hold up the broadsheet, I propped it against the window, but as the train jolted it fell against my face. Warmed by the sun and translucent with its light, it felt like a benediction. Joy rose in my heart and bliss rushed through my body. Those words from 'Tintern Abbey' echoed in my head: 'felt in the blood, and felt along the heart'.

After a year of being depressed, feeling light again is intoxicating. As the tall conifers that cluster on Helvellyn's slopes rush past, this feeling floods me like the warmth from a hug. It feels like love. Being with friends amid the fells lifts my heart, and so does the possibility of being well, and the promise of the summer. This is a levity of spirit that a year earlier I would not have thought possible. I wriggle with the joy of it, and as Tom looks across he sees me beaming. We exchange a smile that seems to light up the whole valley.

10

Fretting the Land

'Holding tight here, fast by the wall, a small
rock cricks my neck, the ferns tickle my throat
and a welsh poppy leans by my knee. Wind
whips, but the wall holds against it, my head
shielded by the oh so ponderable
labour of time long past. It was slow work –
creating such firm boundaries and subtle
loops of stone, fretting the land.'

from 'Extempore Effusion: Wall /
Gerard Benson!', Sally Woodhead,
The Thorn Apple (2007)[1]

Late summer makes a rainbow of the valleys. Valiant flags of foxgloves wave above the ferns and spires of rosebay willow-herb straining for the lessening sun. The end of August brings one last bank holiday hurrah when the field across the main road from Town End hosts Grasmere Sports, a sweaty, muscu-lar celebration of local life and history. Westmorland wrestlers, clad in white overalls under black embroidered knickers, are squaring up to each other, and teams of villagers strain against a rope as a straw-hatted gentleman marks victory by waving a red handkerchief. High above the field a long line of runners snakes along the fellside, each of them competing to be the first to get home from the top of Butter Crags.

The origin of Grasmere Sports lies in the annual sheep fairs that, for centuries, have been an important part of the Lakeland calendar. Taking place at the end of summer, the fairs were where tups and ewes were traded, and where shepherds, farmhands, and domestic servants were hired for the winter season. Displays of physical strength indicated a capacity for hard work, and the competitions have their roots in the economic need to be noticed for one's skill, speed, or power. This too was the time for landowners to hire itinerant drystone wallers, whose practised hands and arms would make good the boundaries that keep sheep where they should be.

Drystone walls fret Cumbria like stitches in a quilt. The skill in their construction lies in placing stone upon stone so that each supports the other, their only cement being gravity combined with centuries of moss. In upland country, where the soil is thin and stones lie close to the surface, drystone walling turns impediment to useful purpose. Broad 'consumption walls' swallow stones like hungry beasts, their wide bulks becoming boundary and shelter. Rising above fields and outpacing grass, sedge, and heather, they march up the fells almost to the summits.

Lakeland's architecture, like all vernacular building, is a product of its locale. Most traditional Cumbrian structures are barns and cottages, hunkered down in a landscape scattered with a few stone-built inns and churches. Almost all are roofed in slate, the rough masonry of their walls drawn from the mix of volcanic and sedimentary stones that form the backbone of the fells. Many are 'laith houses', combining human and animal habitation under one roof in a style unchanged for centuries. Across the fellside, now as then, are scattered smaller, simpler buildings known as field barns, used to shelter livestock and store fodder. The dry-stone walls thread them together, barn to field and house to track, acting as a guide and providing shelter for shepherds and animals.

My introduction to the walls of the Lake District came early in my time at Grasmere, when we were invited to a talk by Laurence Harwood, a former regional director of the National Trust who saw his mission as the preservation of farming life in the north-west of England. He was also the godson of C. S. Lewis, and the two shared a genius for story-telling. One dark, rainy evening we sat for hours as Laurence introduced us to the built heritage of Cumbria. With each click of the slide projector carousel, another gem was laid before us. A Viking-era long-house farm, a barn whose wooden crucks had held up the roof for more than a thousand years. Walls covered with moss deep enough to sink your whole hand in and still not touch the stone. I was entranced.

As August turns to September, Tom and I head to Wray near Windermere to gap a stretch of drystone wall. Over the last six months we have continued to volunteer with the conservation charity with which we cleared land drains as we were first getting to know each other, also learning how to build paths and lay hedges. Today we'll be repairing a two-metre portion of an old wall which has collapsed. It's an odd sort of 'date', but we know that our time here together is short. There are just three months left of my internship, and in a couple of weeks Tom will leave the Lakes to begin his postgraduate course in Edinburgh. Now is our chance to do something to testify to our time here. We both want to leave evidence of ourselves, a useful legacy of purpose, within this landscape.

We start by sorting the stones. Gapping an old wall is a jigsaw puzzle in three dimensions: all the pieces lie before you, and the challenge is to slot them into their best place. First we set aside the caps or coping stones, angular pieces used to top the wall, and lay them furthest from what will be its edge. Then we earmark the flat, heavy footings for the foundations, before laying out the mossy edge stones that will make up the outer faces of the wall. Through stones are next: these will pierce the wall at right angles to the rest, giving it strength. Lastly it is the turn of the 'heartings', the smallest stones that fill the gaps.

The section of wall we need to replace has been marked out with string and sticks, forming an elongated 'A' that tapers from the broader base to the narrow top. Beginning at the bottom, we heave the footings into place with long-handled crowbars. These foundation stones will bear the weight of all the others, and once this lowest course is true, we can lay the rest on top. Working from large to small, we stack and lean the stones into parallel courses, then fill in the gaps between with heartings. It is slow, painstaking work, and several times I trap my clumsy gloved fingers between the stones.

*

Building this wall reminds me of the shepherd's fold in William's poem 'Michael'. Written in the closing months of 1800, 'Michael' is set about a mile from Dove Cottage, on the fells to the east of Grasmere. On 11 October 1800, Dorothy and William climbed Greenhead Ghyll to find the ruin of a stone sheep pen, one described to them by the Fishers as being 'built nearly in the form of a heart unequally divided'.[2] They felt a keen sense of interest in, and connection to, this place and its story, and over the following two months, William translated this ruin into the narrative heart of a poem. On 9 December Dorothy recorded in her journal that 'Wm finished his poem today', and in January 1801 'Michael' appeared as the valedictory poem in the second edition of *Lyrical Ballads*.

'Michael' explores the bond between Cumbrian shepherds and their land. All his life Michael has tended sheep on the fells that flank Grasmere. His household depends upon his skill and experience, and together the family not only tend the flock but also process its fleece and milk. Whilst his wife Isabel fills the house with the busy hum of spinning wheels, turning wool to yarn, Michael shepherds the flock and make sheep's cheese to supplement their diet of oat cakes, porridge, and milk. In the window of their fellside cottage hangs a lantern to illuminate their work – 'a public symbol of the life [t]hat thrifty Pair had lived'[3] – and from it comes the cottage's name, The Evening Star.

Michael feels such kinship with this spot that the fields and fells give him 'a pleasurable feeling of blind love'. His has been a tough and simple life, but this physical hardship has not hardened his soul. For all that Michael is 'of a stern unbending mind', he is tender to his only son; Luke is 'his heart, and his heart's joy!' As Michael introduces Luke to the land, these places 'which the Shepherd loved before' become 'dearer now', appearing like 'light to the sun and music to the wind', the effect being that 'the old Man's heart seemed born again'.

When Luke reaches adulthood, the family experiences a crisis when Michael's brother comes to ask them for money which he desperately needs. At first the only thing Michael thinks that he can do to help is to sell his land. However, discussion with Isabel reveals another option: Luke will go and earn instead, returning to farm the land once the debt is paid. Before Luke leaves, Michael makes a solemn pact with him. Taking his son to a spot not far from the Ghyll, the shepherd asks that Luke will 'do thou thy part; I will do mine'. Luke promises to work hard in the city, whilst Michael vows to continue his commitment to the land. With these words they place stones to begin the building of a sheepfold, and the next day Luke leaves Grasmere. Over the following months Michael returns to fulfil his promise to complete the fold. Letters from Luke arrive that tell of his success, but before long the young man begins to 'slacken in his duty', and after falling into 'evil courses' runs away to sea and is never seen again.

Michael and Isabel remain in Grasmere, and for seven more years the shepherd tends his flock. He returns many times to the site of the half-built sheepfold, but his heart is too heavy to let him lift any stone to finish it. At the age of ninety-one Michael dies, and after Isabel follows three years later the land is sold and their cottage knocked down.

The only remnant of their existence in this valley are 'the remains [o]f the unfinished sheepfold' that stand 'beside the boisterous brook of Greenhead Ghyll'. Pride and personal merit, wealth and worth – all lost with these lands.

'Michael' is not just a cautionary tale: it is a call to arms. Families like the Fishers and the Ashburners inspired its creation, and in exchange for their stories, William was implicitly charged with trying to protect their way of life. Once the poem was finished, William sent a copy of the second edition of *Lyrical Ballads* to the Whig politician Charles James Fox, along with a letter making clear his point that 'men who do not wear fine clothes can feel deeply':[4] these farming people and their way of life are culturally and socially significant, and should be protected.

The Wordsworths had a ready understanding of that heart-sore home-longing at a personal level, and now observed its effects in their neighbours. Dorothy's conversations with the Fishers, the Ashburners, and others showed the 'debt of grief' these yeomen farmers felt to the land; the Wordsworths could not return their farms to them, but William gave their experience immortality and prominence, writing them into history. He also shared a kinship – or perhaps a kithship – with their desire to be 'at home': it was the distance from home he had felt when in Goslar that showed him the depth and importance of his bond with the landscapes of his childhood.

'Michael' speaks eloquently for the humanity of ordinary people. It raises their experiences and sense of kith from the intimate and individual to the universal, as something intrinsically important and worthy of protection. Though

William never tills the land beyond his garden, he gives
voice and verse to those he wishes to protect: the Lakeland
farmers who have shaped this valley, now facing their own
loss of kith, and the *Heimweh* or *hiraeth* that follows. What
was a '*maladie du pays*' for mercenaries and travellers is now
threatening to become, in the words of the artist Svetlana
Boym, a '*mal du siècle*'⁵ – a sickness of the changing times.
People cannot be cured of their heartache because they
cannot be returned to bygone days, to how things were –
there is no repatriation to the past.

As the shadows shrink then lengthen with the sunlight, our
wall rises into the sky until it is too tall for me to place the
final course of capstones. Their position needs to be just
right to angle the rain away from the centre of the wall.
Tom lifts those into place, and once our section of the wall
is finished, someone takes a photograph. Tom and I stand
behind it, and, hidden by the stones, our bruised hands are
clasped. These are the hands that hold us to the fells. This
is a courtship measured in stone, stones that yoke us to the
landscape that brought us to each other.

  After a day of walling we are starving, and as we climb
back into Tom's car he suggests we head to Yew Tree
Farm near Coniston. They do the best scones in the
Lake District, and there's a nice bit of wall to see nearby.
Laughing, I say that sounds like a good idea, and soon we
are twisting westwards along the narrow Lakeland roads,
racing to make it there before they close.

  We are the day's last customers, and have just enough
money between us for a pot of tea and a single scone. When

our order arrives, it has multiplied. The waitress explains that as the two remaining scones were 'a bit on the small side', she couldn't sell them singly in good conscience. They spill over the side of the plates, jostling with a dish of homemade damson jam and a slab of golden butter, and we delight in the good fortune, for once, at having been late.

Once we've drained the pot of tea and mopped up every smudge of jam, we go to see this wall. Or rather these four walls, set at right angles to form a sheepfold in Tilberthwaite. Though it sits comfortably in the landscape, this is no ancient construction or ruin, but a recent addition by the artist Andy Goldsworthy. Twelve such stone artworks are threaded through Cumbria. Some are rebuildings of older enclosures that have fallen down, whilst others are entirely new. This is one of the latter, named 'A Touchstone Fold' by Goldsworthy.

Such folds are William's 'spots of time' made manifest. They connect us to the past using techniques that have survived for over a thousand years. Yet building a fold or wall is also an act of hope, a tacit promise of a future. From a distance they look ordinary, but up close they reveal the skilful balance and implicit beauty of drystone building. Each waller is an artist: these walls are lines drawn from the landscape and the whole valley is the gallery.

It is a good job that Tom knows exactly where Touchstone Fold is. The bracken has grown so high that I might have walked past it without a backward glance. Burnished fronds reach the top of its walls, smothering it in a late-summer bed of rusting green. At first I am not sure this is anything more than a normal sheepfold, but as we trace its edge, flattening a path through the bracken on each side, I see that each wall holds an opaque 'window', a circle of angled slate that runs at forty-five degrees to the rest of the stones.

As Tom and I leave the sheepfold he takes my hand and we follow the track that leads up Tilberthwaite, away from the trees and along the gill to where the valley is scarred by hundreds of years of mining. Old leats cut the hillside with angular purpose, and a deep wheel pit fills with water where once a ten-metre wheel powered a copper mill. There is a bittersweet quality to this walk, the last we will make together before Tom leaves. As we look at the past, our talk is of the future. How soon will I come and visit him, and when will he be back here? Over us hangs the immense, unspeakable question: will this new love survive the pressures of the coming separation?

With September come departures. Tom leaves first, off to Edinburgh to study Arctic glaciers, then Helen heads to Liverpool for a job with the university's archives. Towards the end of the month, Laurie leaves for Cambridge and Wendy returns to Blackpool and a new job with a local heritage organisation. Relief and celebration greet each new placement – getting experience for securing jobs was why we'd come here – yet something else taints the air. There is a tinge of sadness at knowing that our time together in this place is coming to an end.

These bittersweet departures and the attendant arrival of autumn bring back memories of my first months in Japan. There, the colour change of leaves is almost as much of a cultural event as *hanami*, the blossom-viewing parties that follow the flowering-cherry season as it sweeps the country. *Momijigari* ('hunting for red maple leaves') is so popular that the Japan Meteorological Agency produces an annual 'foliage forecast', indicating the dates leaves will start to change across the country. *Kōyōzensen* is the name for the 'red leaf front' that marches from north to south as the maples sugar from summer green to autumn crimson. I would have been content to admire the trees that were reddening on the hills around Kikugawa, but my neighbours had other ideas.

One weekend in early autumn the Fujinos took me to see the smouldering crater of a volcano on the island of Kyushu. It was a long drive and we were to stay overnight at a small *ryokan*, or country inn. As it was a traditional establishment, we were encouraged to bathe naked outside before dinner – men and women in separate areas – and after a banquet of small seasonal dishes eaten in *yukata*, the dark cotton kimonos of the bath-house, we slept on futons on the floor in the same tatami-covered room.

On the way home we stopped at a tiny mountain cafe. We ate our lunch from exquisite handmade bowls, slurping up buckwheat noodles and pale mushrooms from pools of sweet-savoury broth. Outside, maples rioted in red and gold, and I told my neighbours that this place was even more beautiful than I had dreamed. They were delighted, but I had already felt a thin mist of sadness rise behind my breastbone.

This year I register a tinge of melancholy too, but the greater feeling is one of triumph. My depression and anxiety have faded as the months have passed, and as the year winds on I have felt increasingly well and happy. I have held down a job, made friends, lived my own life. For the first time since beginning university, I feel confident that I have a future – if not yet a paying job – and that the future will be good. As my mid-October birthday draws near, I know I want to celebrate with a party.

I invite my old schoolfriend Michelle, who decides to make a week-long holiday of her visit. When I left Suffolk to come here in January, Judy had given me a poster from the UK Youth Hostel Association to put on my wall. It was a picture of their most remote youth hostel, Black Sail, a tiny stone building hunkered down in front of Red Pike, Haystacks, and High Crag, about twenty miles from Grasmere. As a tourist, the only way to reach it is on foot or by bike. There is no road through Ennerdale, and the closest you can get on a bus is Buttermere, the little village that lies on the other side of a tall and wooded ridge of hills.

Michelle and I have long been companions in adventure. In the days between university and me leaving for Japan, we embarked on a cycle tour of the West Country, crossing Exmoor and following the curve of Devon's northern coast from Bideford to Minehead. We stopped to buy cider from remote farms, and slept in hostels that teetered on the edge of cliffs. Now we would make a pilgrimage to Black Sail: no cycling or cider this time, but a walked adventure through the hills.

Michelle is also a fellow traveller in depression. In the year of my breakdown, she too had been unwell, lacerating her thighs as a distraction from despair. Being in your early twenties is a dangerous time: serious mental illness – depression, bipolar disorder, schizophrenia – is typically diagnosed for the first time between the ages of eighteen and twenty-five. The median age for onset is twenty-two, so at twenty-three we are still in the danger zone.[6] This knowledge haunts me: was my breakdown a one-off occurrence, or the start of an illness that will shape the rest of my life?

By chance I was given a book which offered the possibility of a happy future. Listening to the radio not long after I came back from Japan, my mother heard someone describing the same racing, critical thought patterns that had so beleaguered me. Gwyneth Lewis, the first National Poet of Wales, was reading from her recently published memoir, which charts her struggle with mental health from adolescence into middle age. Recognising similarities in our symptoms, Mum bought a copy for me. Perhaps this would give me a way out of the whirl inside my head?

Sunbathing in the Rain describes Lewis's experience of depression, which began during her studies at university. As she charts bouts of illness through her twenties and early thirties, she begins to see a pattern in her melancholy. Though there is a physiological, chemical element to her episodes, each has its own 'emotional logic'. It flares up when Lewis ignores, intentionally or otherwise, her needs, leading her to view it as a kind of 'psychic white stick' that she can trust to show the truths in her life.

For Lewis, writing poetry is part of her self-medication against depression. Far from the soft-edged, romantic image it has garnered, for Lewis poetry is a blood-red life force that she ignores at her cost. Writing is the way she makes sense of the world. As a method of divining truth in her life, poems are 'the ultimate lie-detector test'.[7] As a poet, her imagination needs to be strong, but the forgeries of a life it sometimes promises can be beguiling.

Helping people to separate fantasy from reality, differentiating between how things *are* and how we imagine them to be, is a hallmark of modern psychiatric treatment. In its most extreme form, the gap between what an individual perceives and the reality experienced by others is the grand delusion of psychosis, which becomes an almost unbridgeable divide. In its mildest form, the difference between an individually held belief and the shared reality of others can manifest in anxiety and depression. Each person has their own perception of the world, carefully crafted over a lifetime to reflect their experiences, and some are more closely tethered to our shared reality than others.

As a child, I lived only partly in the real world. An element of this was self-preservation: from the ages of five to twelve, life was shaped by the dissolution of my parents' home, business, and marriage. Those years were lived on shifting emotional sands, full of hidden sumps. Sometimes I felt I was the focus of my parents' sadness and anger, my childish worries an unbearable camel's straw. As time went on, I became convinced that some part of me was unendurable to them. I had a knack for asking questions that were hard to answer, and these were seen as proof of my being 'difficult'. I was, in the words of some friends and relations, 'too clever by half' and, frequently, 'sharp enough to cut myself'.

My mother taught me to read before I went to school, and therein I at least had an escape. By the time I reached double figures, books were everything to me. I would rather stay up late with *Jane Eyre* than go to a schoolgirl sleepover, and preferred whiling away a day tucked up on the storage heater with *Little Women* to go-karting with my cousins. As a ten-year-old I became convinced I was dying of tuberculosis: I had read so many accounts of the illness in Victorian novels that every phlegmy cough or painful chest infection signalled my imminent demise. As I had asthma, coughs and colds were an almost daily part of my life in the winter, but one night my mother found me hysterical over a snotty tissue, convinced that the small bloody gobs of mucus were a portent of my death. I could not bear to tell her why I was crying in case she laughed at me – or worse, in case she also thought that I was dying. My cold cleared up and I lived to, laughingly, tell the tale, but my love of reading continued to give me access to another time and space where this might not have been the case.

As I entered my teens, I feasted increasingly on biographies. This seemed a good response to the challenges of growing up as, with adulthood looming, I knew I had to choose my route through life, and I longed for others to show me what might lie ahead. I might never become a ballet dancer or a spy, a wartime stretcher-bearer or an actor, but I wanted the comfort of real-life happy endings, of triumph over disaster. I wanted evidence that this was possible, as my parents' situation made me worry that it wasn't. What Gwyneth Lewis offered was another version of the future, but one which addressed the barriers that seemed to have been built inside my head.

Lewis's book also explores the connection between writers, particularly poets, and depression. Her argument is that, in order to undertake the 'acutely observational' work that underpins good poetry, writers must put themselves in a kind of emotional danger. Like 'walking over broken glass on your eyeballs'[8] is the description she borrows from Dylan Thomas of the acuity of vision required to hold up poetry's mirror to the world and make something meaningful from the mess it shows. But she also insists on the importance of personal joy, on taking time to immerse yourself in the granular detail of life, however you find it. For Lewis, there is no shortcut to a life well lived, and poetry is a force in hers which is vital – to deny its power and refuse to write is so self-damaging that she realises that she cannot live without it.

From the 'mad genius' of Leonardo da Vinci to the manic virtuosity of Vincent van Gogh, the trope of the troubled artist has cultural heft, though the connection between creative work and mental illness has only recently been supported by epidemiological evidence. Between the 1960s and the 2010s, a team of researchers from the Institute of Psychiatry, Psychology & Neuroscience at King's College London conducted a long-term study of students in Sweden, comparing the mental health of arts students with that of the rest of the population. The results, published in the *British Journal of Psychiatry* in 2018, found that those who studied an arts subject – including everything from visual art to media studies – were 20% more likely to develop schizophrenia than the general population. This mirrored findings from other studies in the Netherlands and Iceland. Even once these studies were adjusted for other factors, including age, gender, educational attainment, and IQ, students of creative disciplines were statistically far more likely to develop severe mental illness.[9]

What was cause, and what was effect? The study demonstrated that certain cognitive styles seemed to correlate with both creativity and psychosis: that the ability to make inventive, intuitive, and original connections between ideas is both central to the creative process and a feature of disordered thinking and delusions. The boundary between the two can be whisper-thin, and the difficulty of making a living from this fragile seam extreme.

The Wordsworths and Coleridge knew what it was like to live on this line. Though from his late teens he believed himself to have a poet's calling, William found the process of writing poems physically painful. When he sat down to write, his head hurt, his side ached, and sometimes his eyes would become so dimmed he could hardly see. Dorothy, Mary, and Sara attempted to lessen these agonies by working as amanuenses, but even then William's physical symptoms could be overwhelming. Coleridge did not suffer the same bodily agonies of composition, but struggled to live with the internal schism between the realities of life and the preferred version provided by his vibrant imagination.

Coleridge was also intensely interested in the nascent science of psychology. 'Metaphysics and psychology have long been my hobby-horse,' he wrote in his autobiography *Biographia Literaria*, and some of his neologisms bear out this fascination. As well as 'mountaineering', his additions to the English language include 'psychoanalytical', 'psychosomatic', 'narcissism', 'pessimism', and 'soulmate'.

'Psycho-somatic'[10] and 'narcissism'[11] are two terms which only appear in Coleridge's notebooks and private letters, which were published (in 1995 and 1971 respectively) long after their unrelated invention by psychologists and doctors in the early twentieth century.

'Psycho-analytical',[12] penned by Coleridge almost a century before it became part of the lexicon of Freud, was a term he used in a notebook to explore similarities of belief and understanding across Greek myth, Renaissance verse, and Christianity – and as an attempt to recover faith through increased cultural understanding. Freud's development of the term, relating specifically to analysis of the individual, was an independent neologism; though coined in 1805, Coleridge's notebook containing the term was not published until 1962.

The notion of a 'Soul-Mate', appearing in a letter in 1822 that was published in 1836, was distinct from that of a spouse: 'You must have a Soul-mate as well as a House or a Yoke-mate,'[13] presumably borne out by Coleridge's experiences of love, attraction, and his marriage. 'Pessimism', used by Coleridge to describe the atmosphere at his brother-in-law Robert Lovell's house, was a borrowing from the Latin *pessimus*, meaning 'worst', whilst 'narcissism' derived from Coleridge's reading of the Greek myth of Narcissus.

Having read psychiatric case studies of the German doctor Karl Philipp Moritz, Coleridge became an early adherent of 'medical mentalism', the idea that most operations of the body are controlled by the mind. Dr Thomas Beddoes, an English doctor and author known to Coleridge and Wordsworth, popularised Moritz's idea that psychological analysis could help a person understand themselves and their body. Beddoes also believed that everyone suffered physically from 'suppressed passions', and that analysing these 'suppressions' could bring relief from a variety of psychological and physical symptoms.

In the early 1800s, Coleridge sought to follow Beddoes's theory, searching his notebooks for significant events or emotions which he may have unconsciously suppressed. This period coincides with his reignited passion for Sara Hutchinson, and we know that he revisited old diary entries and reinterpreted them through a Moritzian lens to try to understand – and hopefully relieve – his ills. Yet this kind of 'treatment' was experimental and a long way from the medical mainstream. Psychoanalysis as a therapeutic mainstay was still a hundred years in the future; in Coleridge's day, the realities of life with a recurrent psychiatric illness were very different.

Coleridge had observed severe mental illness at close quarters. As well as witnessing Charles Lloyd's derangement at Nether Stowey, in 1795 Coleridge had supported his friend and fellow author Charles Lamb, who spent six weeks living in what he termed 'a mad house, at Hoxton'.[14] Lamb and Coleridge had been friends since their shared schooldays at Christ's Hospital; now Lamb was experiencing a period of acute mental illness he described as both 'a tide of melancholy' and a 'strange turn [of] frenzy'.[15] Writing to Coleridge after being released from the 'mad house', he reassured his friend: 'I am got somewhat rational now, and don't bite anyone. But mad I was – and many a vagary my imagination played with me'.[16] Charles Lamb, then aged twenty, was lucky to regain his mind so quickly.

The following year, his sister Mary Lamb experienced her own episode of mental distress – but with fatal consequences. Following several days of worsening symptoms and an argument with a kitchen maid, on 22 September 1796 Mary took up a case knife and stabbed her mother, Elizabeth. Throwing a fork at her father's head, she also wounded him. Charles, who had been frantically worried about his sister for some time and had only left her side to try to find a doctor, came back to the kitchen to find his sister holding a bloody knife, his mother dead, and their father badly hurt.

As soon as Charles saw what had happened, he arranged for Mary to be confined in a private asylum in Islington. Had he not done so, she would almost certainly have been sent to Bethlehem Royal Hospital, known as Bedlam, the infamous madhouse-prison in East London. Then the only state-run institution in the capital, it was staffed by doctors who 'treated' their patients by chaining them to the wall and administering a series of interventions which included bloodletting and blistering. Providing neither care nor a cure, Bedlam was nothing short of a prison for those who were poor and deemed too dangerous to remain at home or be cared for by relations. Its legacy remains with us: the practice of detaining people under the Mental Health Act (also known as a Section) isolates the individual from their community and ordinary environment and is often used in combination with sedative drugs to calm the person's more florid symptoms.

Charles gave evidence at the coroner's enquiry into Elizabeth Lamb's death. He spoke eloquently not just about what had happened on that awful day, but also about Mary's character and their family history. There were three surviving Lamb siblings – Mary and Charles had an adult brother, John – but family life had been chequered by both a lack of money and a series of miscarriages, stillbirths, and neonatal deaths. John was Elizabeth's favourite, and both Mary and Charles keenly felt their mother's displeasure at their imaginative, questioning characters. They responded by banding together, and Mary, eleven years Charles's senior, taught her younger brother to read at an early age and encouraged his studies at Christ's Hospital.

Elizabeth and Mary were victims not just of illness, but of the medical and economic challenges of their lives. In the months preceding Mary's attack, Elizabeth had had a series of strokes which left her partially paralysed. Her husband John was also gravely ill, gripped by progressive dementia, and their elder son John had recently returned to the family home, delirious with infection after a serious accident. Charles, then aged twenty-one, was serving an accountancy apprenticeship for which he was barely paid, and so it fell to Mary to support the family by sewing mantilla veils and taking care of a clutch of ill relations. Charles noted that his sister was 'worn down to a state of extreme nervous misery by attention to needlework by day and to her mother at night', and he believed her descent into madness to be the result of a mind put under intolerable strain.

Both Charles and Mary understood the cause of her illness to be a direct response to the stress of her circum-stances, coupled with a childhood overshadowed by her parents' struggles. The pressure on Mary to earn money and physically care for her relations was acute: 'I saw to the hurting of her health, and most probably in great part to the derangement of her senses,' wrote Charles to Coleridge on 17 October 1796. The coroner agreed and Mary was not sent to prison or an asylum, but the condition of her release into what we might term 'care in the community' was that her brother had to take charge of her – which he did, until his own death in 1834.

This was not an easy solution, for Charles was often ill himself. He came to rely on alcohol to stimulate his creative imagination, as it relieved him of a stutter that had beset him since childhood and lent him an impressive verbal fluency. In the right company – frequently Coleridge's – drink would also alleviate the melancholia to which he remained prone. Nevertheless, Mary and Charles developed a system of mutual support. When she was well, they lived together and Mary not only ran the household, but also wrote and collaborated with him on books and essays. When Mary realised that she was becoming unwell, usually signified by mania and strange thoughts, the siblings walked to a nearby asylum, carrying a straitjacket between them and weeping as they went. After a few weeks or months, Mary's condition would improve, and she would return home.

Through Charles's friendship with Coleridge, the Lambs came to know the Wordsworths during their time at Racedown in the 1790s. William and Dorothy were aware of Mary's illness, but they knew her better as an intelligent, thoughtful woman, one who rewrote several of Shakespeare's stories for children (*Tales from Shakespeare*) with her brother, as well as authoring another book of children's tales (*Mrs Leicester's School*) and several essays, one of which specifically addressed the 'chaining' of women to domestic work.

When she was well, Mary's mental strength and capacity were remarked upon by almost all who knew her. Essayist William Hazlitt described her as 'as good as sensible, and in all respects as exemplary as the best of them could be for their lives'[17], and she is elsewhere described as 'the last woman in the world whom you could have suspected, under any circumstances, of becoming insane, so calm, so judicious, so rational was she'.[18] The Wordsworths were of a similar opinion, and both Mary and Charles themselves understood her illness as a direct, understandable response to the pressures of a life shadowed by poverty, familial illness, and a lack of support and opportunity.

Today, we are beginning to see this type of family-centred treatment becoming popular – and possible – on a population-wide scale. The Open Dialogue psychiatric service, pioneered in Finland, combines a philosophical approach to people experiencing a mental health crisis with a supporting system of family care. It is primarily community based, offering an integrated way of engaging with families, or a person's social network, from the very start of help being sought (usually within a day of the initial crisis). Instead of isolating the individual, the service aims to address the realities of their life in the context of their community. Open Dialogue was developed in the 1980s as a direct response to a crisis of schizophrenia in northern Finland, a region with one of the worst incidences of severe psychotic illness in Europe. This area now has the best documented outcomes in the western world: a 78% reduction in hospital in-patient bed days, a two-thirds reduction in the use of anti-psychotics, and more than a one-third reduction in relapse rates for the psychosis population. About 75% of those experiencing psychosis return to work or study within two years, with only around 20% still taking anti-psychotic medication two years after starting it. In 2015, the first Open Dialogue training programme for mental health professionals in the UK was trialled by the NHS near London, to great acclaim, with feedback from the families and communities involved being extremely positive.[19]

Michelle and I set off for Black Sail in the middle of a rainstorm. Water pelts the bus as it slugs up Dunmail Raise, drawing us into the clouds. The rain is so heavy that the reservoir at Thirlmere appears like a swirling blur. As the bus labours uphill towards Castlerigg we can see that the higher fells are smattered with snow. They look bleak, foreboding, difficult, and I begin to question our decision. Are we sufficiently prepared? I am wearing wellies instead of hiking boots, and Michelle has the pair of trainers she usually wears for walking along the streets of London. We have coats, rucksacks, some food and drink – but what if the weather worsens?

As the more experienced walker, I have the unspoken responsibility for our safety. After discussing our options, we decide to continue, and when we reach Keswick we transfer on to the tiny bus that battles its way down Borrowdale to Rosthwaite and on to Buttermere. This is the nearest village to Black Sail, and from the edge of Lake Buttermere we plan to climb up the side of Sour Milk Gill and cross the pass at Red Pike before descending into Ennerdale. The weather can change quickly, and we decide that if we reach Buttermere and the fells look treacherous, we will catch the last bus back to Keswick.

As we lurch and jolt over Honister Pass the clouds clear. The mine's slag heaps run with water and the road is axle-deep in puddles, but the bus ploughs on at speed. Descending from Honister, we swish past Gatesgarth and come in sight of Buttermere. I look towards the west. The sky is blueing in the late-afternoon light, and though Great Gable wears a diadem of ice, the Red Pike pass looks clear. I can see dots of bright red, purple, and yellow on the fellside, and the presence of other people reassures me in my decision.

We start our walk by crossing the thin, flat fan of land between Buttermere and Crummock Water. The lakes are full, and the wind makes waves that lap like tongues against the path. Leaves spin through the air and land upon the water, chestnut-brown against its pale grey-blue. With it being so wet and windy, we revise our route, eschewing the now roaring, foaming gill and instead taking the path on the south-west side of Buttermere. As we leave the edge of the lake the path turns up the hill, and soon we are out of the trees, away from their swish and rustle. Cutting between Low and High Wax Knott, we are blasted by the cold air funnelled through Scarth Gap Pass. This is our gateway to Ennerdale. Forebodingly regular fir plantations fill the valley, and from where we stand it is not apparent that there are any buildings here, much less a place for us to stay.

What is now Black Sail hostel was built as a shepherd's bothy in the nineteenth century. When Ennerdale was planted with rows of conifers after World War I, there was no more need for shepherding, and so the YHA acquired the building. Teams of young people worked to convert the place from bothy to hostel. All materials had to be brought on a two-wheeled farm cart. Beds were carried in kit form and assembled on site, pieces of canvas strung between simple wooden frames. The hostel opened its doors in April 1933, and has been in use ever since.

We duck through the low wooden door into a cosy white-washed room. Chairs and tables are grouped at one end, and a pan of something that smells delicious bubbles on the stove top at the other. There are a handful of people in the room, all lone male walkers with their heads bowed over tomorrow's maps like monks at prayer. Some look up and smile as we come in, but there is a tacit understanding that quietness is the right mode of being here.

Before dinner we sit on a bench outside the hostel and marvel at our luck and daring. The clouds have cleared and the air is so cold my teeth are chattering, but still we sit and talk about poems, writing, our surroundings. As stars appear and the sky darkens, I feel another heart-swell of contented joy. These last weeks of this year of adventure in the Lake District don't feel like an ending. They feel like the beginning of the rest of my life.

II

Enough Within Ourselves

'[W]e have enough within ourselves,
Enough to fill the present day with joy
And overspread the future years with hope'

William Wordsworth,
'Home at Grasmere', ll. 860–2 (1805)[1]

November comes, and with it the end of Grasmere's poetry season. There will be no more readings in the church until the spring, for the cold and wet of a Lakeland winter seem to make all but the most dedicated lovers of poetry loath to leave their houses. Time is also called on this year's poetry residency. Tweedies will host a celebratory reading from the outgoing poet, providing a few bottles of on-the-house wine to bid farewell to someone who is often one of their best customers. This will also be the launch of a new poetry pamphlet, written by the poet over the course of their year in Town End and inspired by their experiences of living there. Trust staff and Grasmere neighbours make up most

of the audience, and these pamphlets, beautifully designed
and small enough to be carried in a deep coat pocket, are a
tacit gift to us: a distillation of the time that we have shared,
and a talisman to carry with us in the future.

Over the last two decades, the Trust has published several
booklets of poems written by its official Poets in Residence,
as well as by other writers resident in Town End. The pamphlets, usually printed in limited editions of four hundred,
are something of a collector's item, even a connoisseur's
item: the paper they are printed on is thick and pleasingly
textured, with the poet's name, the book title, and a carefully chosen motif embossed on the cover. One of these, a
pale green chapbook we've seen many times on the shelves
of the Dove Cottage shop, was written by Sally Woodhead,
and one quiet, cold November day, as we wait for the next
group to tour Dove Cottage, one of our colleagues tells us
Sally's story.

In the early 1990s, there were no interns at Dove Cottage
and there was no structured training programme. Instead,
the Trust relied on volunteers looking for short-term placements. At that time it was possible to claim unemployment
benefit if you were volunteering for a charity, and housing
benefit could be used to cover rent for a room in a shared
house. Hundreds of young people came to Town End in this
way; most stayed for a few months, but some lasted years,
and several of those who still work for the Trust arrived as
volunteers in the weeks and months following their gradu-
ation from university. In those days, when volunteers came
and went throughout the year, it was not Mark Ward who
held court in House Two, but Sally Woodhead.

Sally had studied English with Robert Woof at Newcastle, where she stood out as a brilliant scholar with an acute ear for the nuances of poetry. After graduating, Sally started to work for Robert, first at the university and then in Grasmere. Letters written, reports compiled, funds raised – if something needed doing efficiently and thoroughly, Sally was the one to do it. She helped both Robert and Pamela prepare publications, working on what remains the definitive edition of Dorothy Wordsworth's *Grasmere and Alfoxden Journals*.[2] More than a colleague, she was a friend to the Woofs, and to their children, who, like her, split their life between Town End and Newcastle. Echoing Molly Fisher's patient vigil before the arrival of the Wordsworths in 1799, Sally would light a warming fire at Sykeside if she knew the Woofs were due in Grasmere. She also sent papers, letters, and books to Newcastle if, as sometimes happened, they were left in one house but needed urgently in the other.

From the stories we are told by some of those who knew her, it seems that, in contrast to this image of domestic dependability, Sally's personal life could be chaotic. Though she had a loving partner in the daughter of George Kirkby, the former chief guide, alcohol was often Sally's steady companion. She could be irascible and short-tempered, her whims governing what daily life was like in the terraces. A small domestic matter could become something of great significance. One of Sally's firmly held beliefs was that kindling was a waste of money. Instead, her housemates should scour the ground for sticks any time they went outside. This legacy lives on: one former housemate tells us she still cannot go for a walk without her fingers twitching when she spies a likely looking stick.

Sally's other legacy, more enduring and endearing, was her poems. As well as supporting the Trust generally and the Woofs particularly in their work, for much of the time she lived in Grasmere Sally was 'a secret writer'.[3] For years she kept her poetry private, but in 1996 she won the Scottish International Poetry Prize for her sonnet 'The Thorn Apple'. After her early death from cancer, her friends discovered a cache of further poems, finished and in chronological order. The resulting pale green volume, *The Thorn Apple*, was published by the Trust in 2007. The poems are precisely dated, beginning on 27 May 1975 and ending on 1 April 2001, and show not just sides of Sally but vignettes of life in Town End. Each page contains a glimpse of places we see every day, snapshots of then-in-now, of a time in Grasmere just before our own. Sally's was a too-short life – she died in her early fifties – but through her poems and the stories told about her, Sally has achieved a measure of immortality.

Town End mythology is almost a literary genre of its own, and we know that the poems written during this year's residency are good. A few days ago, boxes of the slim black pamphlets, silhouettes of candles picked out in silver on their covers, arrived at the shop for us to unpack. Their words are luminous, mirroring the stars that twinkle against Grasmere's dark skies, where they appear 'like powder on a psalter'. When the poet intones them from the little stage placed semi-irreverently by the bar, the words fill the quiet air like bells. Towards the end of the reading, Jane and I stifle giggles as the poet begins one poem with the statement 'Life isn't all hookers and blow, you know.' We never thought it was.

The reading ends with the arrival of a thunderstorm and, after finishing the wine, we head back to Town End in a raucous mood. The windows of the shared houses are dark, so the poet invites us to continue the party at his cottage, and somehow it is almost two o'clock before I realise that I've drunk far too much. Emboldened by the wine, I pick up a pen and add my own words to the page of a book left lying open on the poet's sofa. The next morning I can't remember what I wrote, but when I look in the bathroom mirror there are a few letters printed in reverse across my cheek. I pick up my notebook and suddenly out spills half a poem. After I run out of words, I take it to Emily, and the keenness of her ear helps me make it whole:

> I defaced your book last night,
> took your good black pen and danced my words
>   across its flyleaf.
>
> You'd already torn the covers off so
> Hugo Williams lay there naked, splayed
>
> I stole words to make my marks with
> strung them together and scalpelled them
>   to the page.
>
> Part-remembered part-forgot.
> We were writing on top of one another.
>   Me, you, him.

It's my hands that won't be hidden, today. Won't
    scrub off.
Stained with last night's ink and shreeved in sweat
where I creased my face against the sheets and left
a black transferring mark across my cheek.

Since coming to Grasmere, I have fallen in love with the poetry of now. I have always adored reading and listening to poems – Mum taught me Roger McGough's rhymes and Spike Milligan's silly sentences before I could read. School introduced me to Shakespeare, Sylvia Plath, John Donne; university opened the world of Gerard Manley Hopkins, Beowulf, Geoffrey Hill. In Grasmere, I have learned that verse is a living entity. Poetry takes the stuff of lives like ours and shines light through it until it gleams like jewels. Fascination and horror, meaning and purpose – they are already there, and beautiful if we can but see it.

By the time we're halfway through November it is our turn to help out at the interviews for next year's interns. Another group of young people, eager-nervous for a future here, will soon arrive, and it is our responsibility to help them sound out Town End. Rooms have to be cleaned and spare sheets stretched across mattresses, and everyone offers to join in with the evening meals where the wine and talk flow more freely. These off-the-record conversations are important. Madness and sadness are no barrier to coming here, but if you don't like the close proximity of other people, it would be hard to live and work in Grasmere.

It starts to rain heavily on the morning before the

interviews are due to start, and for days it does not stop. By the following day rivers are spilling their banks, and nearby towns are in a state of emergency. Bridges are washed away and people evacuated from their homes. We worry that the same will happen in Grasmere, and every hour Mark and Jeff go out in wellies to keep an eye on the water level in Stock Lane. If the rising tide breaches the roundabout, Town End might be imperilled.

In Dove Cottage, Mark and Jeff are busy building a wall of sandbags on the edge of the buttery, where the stream that keeps it cool threatens to overspill into the houseplace. Outside the garden door the Trust's director is busy building another barricade in case water from the garden finds a way under the door and comes flooding down the stairs. The back steps of the museum are similarly blocked, and we watch as a new waterfall is formed along their course.

The museum and cottage are closed to the public, and we are instructed to place sandbags around the doors to all the houses. Armed with sticks, we check the drains along the roads; leaves shed in the autumn can easily block them. Tom has come to stay for the weekend, and together we walk up the hill with our eyes trained on the road. We are gratified at being able to clear one channel; after pushing aside mud and debris, the drain gives a satisfying greedy gulp and water swirls away under the road.

As we watch the waters on the security camera screens from the safety of the staffroom, Jeff tells us the story of the day that his eldest son Joe was born. A summer storm raged across Cumbria, turning the roads to rivers. Driving the baby and his mother home from the hospital, Jeff came into Town End to be greeted by the sight of George Kirkby, naked except for waders and a minute pair of shorts, battling to save Dove Cottage from the rising waters. As the storm lashed around them, Jeff ran to help pile up sandbags, leaving his new-made family in the single room they were sharing in the terrace. It was a day of elemental battles, a Town End drama that rages to this day whenever rain threatens to overwhelm the hamlet's ancient drains.

Since getting to know Tom I have discovered how Town End drew his parents together almost thirty years before. Like us, they were in their twenties when they came here. Jeff came from Alnwick in Northumberland, where his mother had died from early-onset Alzheimer's disease just after he finished university. Tom's mother came from Liverpool, where she had left a volatile marriage to train as a teacher at Ambleside's Charlotte Mason College. To both of them, Grasmere represented safety, a chance for new and better lives. Like Town Enders before and since, they tumbled into each other's path at Tweedies (which at the time ran a regular disco night), and after a year together found themselves parents to Joe. Tom followed three years later, and Laurie three and half years after that.

My relationship with Tom seems to be surviving our necessary separation. At first we wrote to each other, rather than calling on the phone. We both knew that those early weeks at university can be full of impromptu gatherings, and that a yoke to somewhere else can take away from the joy of working out how to live in this new life. Letters, on the other hand, can be read at any time, squeezed around meetings and parties, work, and hungover mornings. A few weeks after the start of term, I took the train north to visit, and was glad to find that our affection for each other was as at home surrounded by Edinburgh sandstone as it had been amid the Lakeland slates.

Nevertheless, Tom's absence, combined with other friends leaving Grasmere and the threat of imminent unemployment, has caused a few remaining embers of depression to reignite. Panicked, I go to see my doctor, but she reassures me that feeling low for a few days, or even a week, in response to a change in one's life is normal. If the low mood persists beyond two weeks, then I am to call her, but she is hopeful that things will resolve themselves without further treatment. In the meantime I am to keep doing the things that have helped to keep me well: a daily walk, early bedtimes, three good meals a day. Alone they cannot cure me if these feelings deepen into illness, but they are relatively effective ways of reducing the likelihood. She also reminds me to keep writing: my jottings will bear witness to any shift in mood, making long-term changes observable no matter what I'm feeling day to day.

I have kept a diary since I was seven. My grandmother encouraged me to do so, giving me a soft-covered journal for my birthday and recommending that I write in it every day. I never manage that, but over the years I have filled notebooks with my thoughts and feelings. I write poems too, and my mum has kept a copy of my earliest effort, a rhyming epic about three witches. I wrote it in a classroom lull, a small window of time that opened once when I'd finished my work before the rest of the class. Written in vivid blue, green, and yellow pencil, it made my primary school teacher laugh, and she pinned it on the wall. At middle school I branched out into fiction: I became so utterly absorbed when writing my own Viking fairy tale, set in Asgard, that I had sleepless nights. When my teacher told me she thought it good, my heart almost burst with pride.

Since writing my poem 'Inked', I have continued to share some of my poems with Emily, eager for her keen-eared feedback, but whilst I might fluke the odd good verse, Emily has poetry in her veins. Her poems are silver-quick, driven by a rhythm that seems to come as easily to her as breathing. She already has a clutch of beautiful poems inspired by the last eleven months here, where bright bird feathers are likened to nail polish, '[b]rilliant gold and green', and a woodpecker's nest appears as a 'raucous bunch of ventricles'.[4] Earlier in the autumn she announced that she'd come second in the prestigious Edwin Morgan Poetry Award, and we realise that she is already one of the poets who has immortalised the experience of living and working here. I have my own dreams: I want to be a proper writer too, though of prose, not poetry. I am not sure how I will make this happen, but after a year in Grasmere it feels like anything is possible.

By the end of the month my mood is good again, and I have secured an interview for a job which would carry me through the coming year. Wordsworth House, the large Georgian building in Cockermouth which was the Wordsworths' natal home and is now run by the National Trust, is looking for people to work as costumed interpreters. There are three vacancies, and though the jobs are not perfect – the pay is meagre and the work part-time – if I get one, I will be able to stay in the Lakes a little longer. My friend and fellow intern Catherine is also called for interview, and together we take the bus north to what we hope will be our future.

When Catherine and I arrive in Cockermouth we are greeted with scenes from an apocalypse. The November flooding had been bad in Grasmere, but in Cockermouth it was catastrophic. Thirty-one centimetres of water poured from the clouds in less than twenty-four hours, and the two rivers that edge the town – the Cocker and the Derwent – became so full of rain that they burst their banks. Shops swam in over two metres of water that carried their stock out to sea, and the whole town is still caked in stinking, drying mud. At nearby Workington, a policeman was drowned as the bridge he was standing on was washed away by flood-water. The Wordsworths' birthplace suffered too, its cellars filled with water to the ceiling and the plants in its garden drowned or carried downstream by the water.

The staff at Wordsworth House assure us that the building will open again in the new year, but although they want us to work for them there won't be anything for us to do until February. I gratefully accept the job, and Tom asks his parents if I can stay with them in the gap between my internship ending at Christmas and this new job starting. They say yes – and Jeff does even more, putting me in touch with the man who will become my landlord. Since the floods displaced so many people, the town's rented accommodation has been taken up by people whose ordinary homes are uninhabitable. Every spare house is already needed, but the director of a local charity has a room available, and agrees that Catherine and I can share it until we find somewhere else to live. There is only one bed, so we agree to take turns in it, alternating with sleeping on a mat on the floor.

As we prepare to leave Grasmere, we want to take a souvenir of this time with us. We need the talismanic energy of this place as we continue to navigate our adult lives, and for me it comes from 'Home at Grasmere'. Whilst 'Michael' was William's paean to the long-term residents of the village, 'Home at Grasmere', begun in the spring of 1800, bore witness to the Wordsworths' view of themselves within this place. The poem opens with a recollection of the vision of Grasmere that appeared in 'The Vale of Esthwaite' in 1787: 'Once on the brow of yonder Hill I stopped, / While I was yet a School-boy ... and sighing said, "What happy fortune were it here to live!"'[5] Looking down from Loughrigg, a 'soft and green' spot 'not giddy yet aerial', there appears 'a perfect place; / All that luxurious nature could desire'. The wind billows through the grass and corn, butterflies and birds dance in sunshine and shadows, and the poet feels that he and they share one soul: 'stirred in Spirit as I looked, / I seemed to feel such liberty was mine'.[6]

This memory was revisited and treasured in the intervening years. 'From that time forward was the place to me / As beautiful in thought as it had been / When present to my bodily eyes'. Memory burnished it to a glowing 'spot of time', accompanying William like a friendly sprite: 'a haunt / Of my affections, oftentimes in joy / A brighter joy'. Though the poet admitted that of sorrow 'I have known little', he has still felt 'the Realities of Life – so Cold, / So cowardly, so ready to betray. / So stinted the measure of their grace' with the death of his parents and subsequent separation from his sister as a child.

At the age of thirty, William returned to this dream: 'Dear Vale, Beloved Grasmere (let the Wandering streams / Take up, the cloud-capped hills repeat the name), / One of thy lowly dwellings is my home!'[7] This was (and remains) a worked and peopled valley – William hymned 'Thy Church and Cottages of mountain stone – Clustered like stars', and saw evidence of 'flocks and herds' of animals. The ecology of this place depended – and still depends – upon the farmers and the farms, whose small cottages and carefully tended fields of corn provide a striking domestic contrast to the wildness of the framing mountains.

William's call to the mountains is like that of a child to a parent: 'Embrace me then, ye Hills, and close me in; / Now in the clear and open day I feel / Your guardianship; I take it to my heart; / 'Tis like the solemn shelter of the night.' Though Dorothy's company was an important part of this delight ('The thought of her was like a flash of light / Or an unseen companionship'), William's chief joy was in the particular nature of Grasmere:

> The one sensation that is here; 'tis here,
> Here as it found its way into my heart
> In childhood, here as it abides by day,
> By night, here only; Or in chosen minds
> That take it with them hence, where'er they go,
> 'Tis (but I cannot name it), 'tis the sense
> Of majesty and beauty and repose,
> A blended holiness of earth and sky,

> Something that makes this individual Spot,
> This small abiding-place of many men,
> A termination and a last retreat,
> A Centre, come from wheresoe'er you will,
> A whole without dependence or defect,
> Made for itself, and happy in itself
> Perfect Contentment, Unity entire.[8]

We need writers to lyricise landscapes for the same reason that we need them to lend their pen to love – to give voice to the things we feel but fear might not be shared. Their words can rekindle our instincts and amplify their force. Without them, dulled as we can be by the hammer blows of living, we may gradually forget that love is strength, not weakness, a force that moves us beyond ourselves. Love is the antithesis of vacuum, an antidote to nothingness, and we can apply its power to place as much as we can to people.

Our need for connection with the natural environment and our desire to better understand the world represent a kind of search for home. The word 'ecology' comes from the Greek οἶκος (*oikos*), meaning house or home.[9] *Oikos* can also mean family: the Ancient Greeks understood it as the smallest unit of society. Ecology is the study of that nexus between place and purpose, an investigation and knowledge of living things and their environment. Economics is another linguistic descendant of *oikos*, originally meaning 'the art or science of household management'. 'Home at Grasmere' was envisaged as the first part of *The Recluse*, the poem which William thought would follow *The Prelude*. As William had drafted two books of *The Prelude* in Goslar, he, Dorothy, and Coleridge hoped that upon returning to England he would begin writing his magnum opus. In September 1799 Coleridge wrote, 'I am anxiously eager to have you steadily employed on "The Recluse",' and a month later, 'I long to see what you have been doing. O let it be the tail-piece of "The Recluse"!, for nothing but "The Recluse" can I hear patiently.'[10] Months pass, and the Wordsworths move to Grasmere, but nothing more is written until spring 1800. We can reckon the date almost exactly: William tells us it was when 'thrice hath the winter Moon been filled with light / Since that dear day when Grasmere, our dear Vale, Received us'. The first three full moons of 1800 were on 11 January, 9 February, and 11 March, and the poem was begun when 'the gates of Spring / Are opened [and] churlish Winter hath given leave'.[11]

William spent the rest of his life failing to finish this poem. He returned to the lines begun that spring many times, occasionally filleting them for other projects. Some appear in his *Guide to the Lakes*, which included perhaps the earliest published call for a national park ('a sort of national property, in which every man has a right and interest who has an eye to perceive and a heart to enjoy'[12]), and which was instrumental in popularising the Lake District, attracting tourists from across the world. Yet the grand dream of finishing *The Recluse* remained unrealised, though in 1814 William did complete 'The Excursion', the poem's envisaged second section. Extracts from drafts of 'Home at Grasmere' were eventually published by his descendants in 1888, but it was only in 1977 that it was published in its entirety, with the

1800 manuscript put alongside later revisions to give the most complete picture possible of how the poem came to be written but failed to be finished.

'Home at Grasmere' remains, even among Wordsworth scholars, a niche work. It is an orphan with no complete parent text, proportionally neglected because William considered it unfinished, but for me it captures all the joy of living in this place in that giddy time of early adulthood. Its beauty is its fleetingness, ephemeral as the joys of life – William's clearest statement on what making a home meant to him. It shows an idyll, albeit edged by life's difficulties, when heart and home elide and where one's imaginative and domestic pleasures can be drawn from the same well. This elision rarely lasts a lifetime. Our lives shift and merge, and hearts and hopes rarely swell or shrink in tandem over decades. Though other dwellers in the valley experience hardship (a widower struggling to look after his 'many helpless Children'; a 'Cripple in the Quarry maimed'), heartache (another resident becomes a 'lawless Suitor' of his family's maid), and distress (a widow is described as 'withering in her loneliness'), these difficulties serve to remind the poet that 'the silent mind / Has its own treasures' and make him aware, 'Newcomer though I be', of the powerful humanity shared with those around him.

In 1804 Coleridge was given a copy of what was then the five-book *Prelude* (known then as 'The Poem to Coleridge'), and took it with him to Malta, where he lived until 1806. In the meantime, William continued to work on the poem with the assistance of Dorothy and Mary, expanding it to thirteen books by 1806. But by 1810 the 'poem to Coleridge' had lost its intended audience. After a series of slights and spats following their move to the Lakes, the friendship between William, Dorothy, and Coleridge soured. Coleridge's marriage also broke down, to the extent that he never returned to live at Greta Hall. His family remained there with Sarah and, following the deaths of Robert and Edith Southey's little daughter, the former Fricker sisters united their households. Keswick became home to both the Southey and the Coleridge families, but not to the man who had been so insistent that they live there.

Though the Wordsworths continued to live in Dove Cottage until 1808, from 1803 the cottage became something different: the home of a young and growing family. William and Mary married in October 1802, and their first child, John, was born in June 1803. That too was a happy time – in early 1804 Coleridge wrote of the family, 'It does a man's heart good, I will not say, to know such a Family, but even to know, that there is such a Family ... [Wordsworth's] is the happiest Family, I ever saw.'[13] Dorothy continued to live with William and Mary after their marriage, retaining her roles as amanuensis, creative collaborator, and practical domestic worker. For long periods Mary's sisters Sara and Joanna lived with the family too, supporting the Wordsworths through the arrivals and childhoods of their five children and their attendant joys and heartbreaks.

The latter began in 1805, when the Wordsworths experienced what William later termed 'the first great grief of [their] adult lives'[14] when John was drowned at sea. Between 1804 and 1810 four more children were born to William and Mary (Dora, Thomas, Catherine, and Willy), necessitating a move to larger houses, first the Rectory and later Allan Bank in Grasmere. Tragically, in 1812 two of the children, six-year-old Thomas and three-year-old Catherine, died within months of each other. Catherine died from complications of a then-unrecognised condition which caused her to have seizures, heart problems, and difficulties swallowing,[15] and Thomas died from measles. Remaining in the house where the children had died was unendurable for the remaining family, and in 1813 the Wordsworths left their 'happy valley' for Rydal Mount, a large house in nearby Rydal. They remained there for the rest of their lives, but those early years in Grasmere provided much of the raw material from which William built a legacy of poetry that continues to this day.

Dorothy did not keep up her Grasmere journal after 1803. However, she continued to write, producing travelogues, letters, poems, and other jottings, as well as drafting and redrafting her brother's poetry. Some of Dorothy's work was published, including her description of the first recorded ascent of Scafell Pike which she made with her friend, painter and poet Mary Barker, and a mountain guide in 1818, though it appeared under her brother's name. She became ill in the 1820s with what may have been an autoimmune disease, which made her intermittently bedridden, though she continued – sporadically – to write, and remained an important part of Wordsworth family life.

After William's death in 1850 at the age of 80, Dorothy and her sister-in-law continued to live together at Rydal Mount. Mary, her task set by William before his death, ensured that *The Prelude* eventually reached its audience, and the 8,000-line poem was published in 1850. That same year, Tennyson's *In Memoriam* appeared, and the two great poems, with their themes of life, love, and loss, bookend the close of the Romantic era and the beginning of the Victorian era.

Dorothy died in 1855 aged 83, but her words outlive her. Though she did not envisage that her journals would be published – indeed, she declared on beginning them that she wrote only 'to give W[illia]m pleasure by it' – she had, as Pamela Woof has noted, 'approached her readership'[16] in other ways. In 1803 she produced a compelling travelogue of a tour of Scotland made that year with William, and in 1805–6 four copies of that manuscript were shared with her friends. Dorothy revised a further copy in 1822–3, this time actively considering publication, though in the event, *Recollections of a Tour Made in Scotland* only appeared in 1874. In her lifetime, Dorothy's widest readership was for her poems, several of which were published alongside her brother's but not (then) acknowledged as hers. Regarding writing published under her own name, her 1808 'Narrative Concerning George and Sarah Green' reached a broader audience, as it was distributed by subscription to raise money for the orphaned Grasmere children of the Green family whose plight it described. It was not published formally until Ernest de Sélincourt took the decision to do so under the title *George and Sarah Green: A Narrative* in 1936.[17]

The first time part of Dorothy's journal appeared in print was in 1889, when William Knight selected extracts from the diary kept at Alfoxden and published them in his *Life of William Wordsworth*. In 1897 he produced a two-volume edition titled *Journals of Dorothy Wordsworth*, though he deliberately excluded entries which he believed were too 'domestic' and so not of sufficient interest to the public – or in some cases, perhaps too interesting. No complete manuscript survives of the Alfoxden journal, though a few sentences survive in a notebook the Wordsworths used there, and the surviving four volumes of Dorothy's Grasmere journal have been 'corrected', though it is not known by whom. Famously, the section describing Dorothy's reaction to William and Mary's wedding has been heavily inked over, and some pages seem to have been cut from the diary. We cannot know exactly what was lost, but the challenge to represent and reinterpret the experience of the Wordsworths as young people continues to beguile.

December dawns, and with the new month comes bitterly cold weather. The lake is stilled with ice, and instead of rain, snow falls, burying the village under a deadening white cover. Back home for the Christmas holidays, Tom and his brother dig out their childhood sledges from the shed, and Emily and I go with them to walk across the gentle slopes by Allan Bank in the weird light-darkness of a snowy evening. In the shadows of the chestnut trees it feels like we are looking at an old black-and-white film of the village, where the snow has obscured the real colours of the world.

There are hardly any visitors to Dove Cottage in this cold, dark month, and on quieter days I go upstairs into the little room above the porch and thumb my way through old visitors' books. After the Wordsworths moved out in 1808, the cottage was extended, and in one of these 'outjuttings' there is now a small staffroom. On shelves bowed under their weight, row upon row of visitors' books record more than a century of poetic pilgrimages to this house. The pilgrims started to come long before Dove Cottage was opened to the public; over two thousand visited the Wordsworths at Rydal during their lifetime. I thrill to know that perhaps a million more have sat close to where I am now, and maybe felt something of the magic of this place.

I am also working on my own project to become a writer. On a visit to Edinburgh to see Tom a few weeks earlier, I came across a leaflet advertising a short-story competition on the theme of 'The Book that Changed My Life'. The best entries will be printed in an anthology by the Scottish Book Trust, and I know instantly what I will write about: *Sunbathing in the Rain*. I want to pass on the gift that meant so much to me, in the hope that someone else, struggling as I was, might find their own way to a better future. I put together a thousand words and send it off. A few weeks later, I receive an email telling me that my essay will be published. My dream of writing has started to become reality, though it takes me another decade to see my first full book in print.

December passes with all its usual busy, jolly rhythm. We go to the Trust's staff Christmas party at a pub on the village's northern edge, walking there along roads so thickly covered with snow and ice that we need hiking boots and walking poles to arrive with dry feet and intact ankles. Having reached the safety of the Traveller's Rest, everybody drinks too much, and before we know it, people are kissing in the half-dark, and someone is having a panic attack in the toilets. In the middle of what has suddenly become a dance floor, the Trust's estates team – who stopped work for the

Christmas holiday at midday and have been liquefying their Christmas bonus ever since – are making strange shapes as they dance, draped in tinsel and with flimsy paper crowns from crackers wedged drunkenly on their heads.

Five days before Christmas, Jane, John, and I stand in Dove Cottage, trying to dodge each other's shadows as we crowd round a candle to throw light on our carol sheets. Every year on 20 December, the anniversary of the Wordsworths' arrival in Grasmere, the Trust invites those who live in the village to join its midwinter celebrations. The guides have decked the place in greenery, and the education staff have been helping the village school children to stuff oranges with cloves and tie them with ribbons. For the past week our makeshift choir has been practising Christmas carols, and now it is time to perform. With 'The Boar's Head', 'Silent Night', and 'Adeste Fideles', we'll lead our community in this year's last act of celebration.

The cottage glows in the candlelight, and the smell of mulled wine warming on the fire drifts through the house. The stairs are garlanded with green branches, and the mantelpieces proffer the children's pomanders. For most villagers, this is the one day in the year when they visit the cottage. By four o'clock they have filled the houseplace, and it becomes hard to move for all the bodies well wrapped in cosy coats.

Before we sing, the Trust's current director – titled the Robert Woof Director after his inspirational predecessor – signals that he wishes to make a speech. This is the time of year for thanksgiving, and it is also the end of us interns' time in Grasmere. As he says every year, the Trust could not run the place without us. All the tours, exhibitions, poetry readings, events – our support has underpinned them and made them a success. He also announces that Jane will be staying at Dove Cottage as the new assistant curator, and we exchange grins as everyone applauds.

In the bustling glow of the fire, I feel that strange-familiar heart-swell in my chest. The joy of living has been returned to me during this year. I feel at home again: not just in Grasmere, but in myself. I am anchored to life once more, and though the thought of leaving Town End carries sadness, it also promises a good future. For this singular year in Grasmere the elements of life that I hold dear – love, language, landscape, stories, people, and purpose – have cohered. It is not just my life that has been enriched; I am surrounded by people whose experiences at the Wordsworth Trust have given them something valuable to take with them through life. As the last plate of mince pies is passed round, Jeff stands up to read a final poem. It is a valedictory sonnet to the river Duddon, written by William long after leaving Grasmere, and as he reads its closing lines, I know that every one of us feels tasked with carrying the torch of hope and love it proffers into the future:

> Enough, if something from our hands have power
> To live, and act, and serve the future hour;
> And if, toward the silent tomb we go,
> Through love, through hope, and faith's
>   transcendent dower,
> We feel that we are greater than we know.[18]

*

I moved away from the Lakes in 2015 and now live in Scotland, but I still dream about that year in Grasmere. About Mark Ward, standing in the kitchen, rolling a joint, his voice booming through the house. About Helen and Jane on those mornings-after-the-night-befores, when we crawled into work and hoped that no one would come in wanting a tour until after that first reviving coffee. Of those darkening winter afternoons spent in companionable stupor-silence by the fire, listening to gossip and old stories as we twisted last week's newspapers into makeshift firelighters to feed into the grate.

I dream too about the coffin path, following it up the road and past the pond to the Badger Bar and, unsteadily, back again. About wet weather that wouldn't lift for weeks, when the whole world seemed to be made of clouds and dripping slate. Occasionally I dream of John, of Carrie, of Jeff; of the ghosts of George Kirkby, Sally Woodhead, Robert Woof. Many of those I knew well during my time working for the Trust have since moved away; the constant scrabbling for pennies sadly common to most small arts organisations takes its toll, as does the insecurity of relying on poetry – and government funding – for your bread and butter. Some became disillusioned with the impermanence that they first had loved: the shifting nature of the place and its people. And yet they all continued to know the value of the vulnerable yet essential vitality of this little hamlet and the creative community it continues to draw around it.

Five years after that golden, transformational year, Tom and I married in the Lakes, in the tiny Quaker Meeting House at Colthouse visited by William in his Hawkshead schooldays. We return to Grasmere regularly, bringing our children to visit their grandparents and to let them get to know the place which feels like their creative inheritance. We often meet up with our close friends from our time in Town End, continuing to share our lives, remaking the bond we built in Grasmere, and sharing our affection for the place with each other's children. Most of these friends have continued to work in the arts, in education, and in helping young people to find their place in the world. At Grasmere, we shared a sense of *kith* and closeness, when all life's meaning and promise crystallised in the early-morning air beside the lake. When the world felt more beautiful than it had ever been, and anything was possible. Freedom, love, and hope. The spirit of the place that made me love it then, that makes me love it still, endures. The legacy of the Wordsworths, their writing, and their home lives on.

Acknowledgements

First and foremost, thank you to the Wordsworth Trust, who took a gamble on employing me as an intern fifteen years ago and in doing so changed my life in ways I (and no doubt they) could never have imagined. My biggest debt is to Jeff Cowton MBE, who interviewed me one chilly December morning as snow blanketed Grasmere and didn't mind that I cried. His continued support is much appreciated, initially as my boss, and then as my father-in-law, and also as one of the first readers of the manuscript that has become this book. Thank you too to my mother-in-law, Gill Cowton, who kept the family fed, watered, and cared for both during the process of writing this book and in the years before, and for sharing her memories of living and bringing up a family in Grasmere over the last forty years. And thank you Joe and Laurence, for being part of this adventure and my wider famly.

The Wordsworth Trust's president Dr Pamela Woof gave generously of her time, expertise, and experience of more than fifty years of living and working in Grasmere, and I am especially indebted to her for sharing her memories of her late husband, Dr Robert Woof CBE FRSL, and their life together. Thanks are also due to Catherine Kay, with whom I worked closely throughout my time in Grasmere, and who is one of Town End's finest tradition bearers, for sharing her memories and for correcting sections of this manuscript in its draft stages. I would also like to thank Emeritus Professor Stephen Gill for talking to me about his memories of Grasmere as a young scholar in the 1960s and '70s, and sharing his own childhood experience of Wordsworthian connection with the natural world.

To the Town End poets, particularly Mark Ward, Neil Rollinson, Adam O'Riordan, and Polly Atkin: thank you for making the written word come alive for me again in Grasmere – and for the chats in the houses, out on the fells, and down at Tweedies. To Josephine Dickinson, whose poetry first held me spellbound in 2009, and to the other writers who have been inspired by their time in Grasmere and whose work I have read and reread whilst researching this book: thank you for writing poems that continue to bring me a sense of comfort and connection. In particular, I want to record my gratitude to Anna Fleming, Emma Smith, Kim Moore, Carola Luther, Helen Mort, Judy Brown, and Zaffar Kunial for writing so well about the physical and creative legacy of living and working in Town End. Grateful thanks are also due to Paul Farley, who generously shared his experiences of life as Poet in Residence in Town End during the early 2000s.

The 'Terns '09 Cohort – Jane Sparkes, Catherine Foster, Helen Donald, Wendy Woodhead, Emily Hasler, Matty O'Neill, Heather Anderson, Vicky Weaver, and Molly

Heal – without you there would have been no book! Thank you for friendship, good humour, adventures, and inspiration. Thank you too to the many other friends who came into my life through working in Grasmere, in particular Naomi Garnett, Sophie Miller Wallace, Stephen Miller, Rob Sparkes, Kate Hollier, and their families, who have been invaluable sounding boards at various stages in writing this book. Thank you to Amy Concannon, who accompanied me on my first Wainwright (the Old Man), and to Jules Ward for the music that night at the Great Feast. Thanks too to colleagues, housemates, and friends from Grasmere: John Coombe, Beccy Turner, Michael Mitchell, Peter Foster, Michael McGregor, Stephen Sharp, Melissa Mitchell, Lucy Clarke, and Victoria Mitchell, all of whom contributed to this book in a variety of ways. Heartfelt thanks are also due to Mags Laver for generously sharing her memories of her husband Pete Laver and allowing me to reproduce lines from his poem 'Rowing Round Belle Isle'.

To the Dove Cottage guides of 2009 – the late Barbara Crossley, Peter and Sue Coward, Anne Duffield, Marion Veevers – and senior guide Sally Hall, thank you for teaching me the classic Dove Cottage tour, and for sharing stories whilst we sat round the houseplace fire. To Dove Cottage custodian Angela Kenny – I'm sorry there wasn't enough space to include the pole dancing in the final manuscript. To the Tweedies team, particularly Alex and Laura Goodall, Stevie Down South, and John Shedwick, thank you for the pints, the laughs, and the good craic on many a wet and windy Lake District night. And many thanks to Andy Beeforth, who provided me with a new home in

Cockermouth once I'd left Town End; to Helen and Robert Goodsell, who gave me a room to hide in whilst I avoided studying journalism; to Judy Chisman for letting me share her house in Thetford; and to Sally Gall, who welcomed me to the Highlands when I was at my lowest, and who read an early manuscript of this book.

The team at Granta and my agent, the inimitable Jenny Brown: thank you for seeing the potential in this book and supporting me whilst I worked on writing it. To Bella Lacey, a kind and thoughtful editor whose feedback is always on the money, and who supported me through difficult decisions regarding what to include in – and leave out of – this book; to Christine Lo, a fastidious and thorough managing editor who shepherded *All Before Me* into becoming a physical thing; and to Pru Rowlandson, a press and publicity wizard who delights in finding a book its audience: heartfelt thanks for getting the book out into the world whilst I was busy looking after one small child, and latterly whilst I was growing, birthing, and caring for another. Thanks are also due to Jack Alexander, who did a terrific job of copyediting the manuscript from Japan at short notice after a hiccup in the publication schedule, and to proofreader Mandy Woods. Your feedback was not only prescient, timely, and thorough, it also made me laugh.

My own parents, Michael and Gabrielle Rutter, have played a huge role in the writing of this story and I have a great debt of gratitude to them both, not only for giving me a childhood with plenty to write about but also for being generously spirited about me writing about our family. To my brothers, Theo and Derek, who appear as footnotes in this particular narrative but who have been and continue to be central supports in my life: thank you, and never stop taking the piss. And to my school and university friends, both those who appear in this book and those whose presence in these pages is faint but whose place in my life is tremendous – Michelle Brookes, Emma Mathers, Pip Parmenter, Kirsty Wright, Jenny Willett, Sally Gall, Hannah Morphet, Thea Goodsell, Martha Gill, Alexandra Scott, and Hannah Bulmer – you have been there all along (whether I've needed a shoulder to cry on or a bed to sleep in – or frequently both) and your support for me has never wavered.

To Pauline Krawehl and the rest of the Radical Care team at Moniack Mhor: thank you for providing the time, space, and childcare necessary to complete this manuscript. To my fellow Moniack Maws – Amy Liptrot, Kirstin Innes, Rachelle Atalla, Catherine Munro, Alice Clark, Skye Loneragan, and Cailean Steed – thank you for friendship, solidarity, and feedback during the latter stages of writing this book. Thanks are also due to the School of Geography and Sustainable Development at the University of St Andrews, who awarded me an Honorary Research Fellowship during the period of researching and writing this book.

And to my own dear little family, Tom, Rose, and Kit, who do their level best to stop me from becoming that lonely writer in the garret: thank you for the love, time, and space to write this book (each and every naptime was appreciated).

Permissions

Extract from 'Regret vii', *Thunder Alley* (Aussteiger Publications, 2008) by Mark Ward is reproduced here with the kind permission of the author.

Extract from 'The Keepsake', *Collected Poems* (Bloodaxe Books, 2024) by Fleur Adcock is reproduced here with permission of the publisher.

Extract from 'Remains', *Selected Poems* (Faber and Faber, 2013) by Tony Harrison is reproduced here with permission of the publisher.

Extracts from 'To a Woodpecker' and 'Belle Isle', *Natural Histories* (Salt, 2011) by Emily Hasler are reproduced here with the kind permission of the author.

Extract from 'Extempore Effusion: Wall / Gerard Benson!', *The Thorn Apple* (The Wordsworth Trust, 2007) by Sally Woodhead is reproduced here with permission of the publisher.

Extract from 'Rowing Round Belle Isle', *Offcomers* (Pig Press, 1985) by Pete Laver is reproduced here with the kind permission of Mags Laver.

Notes

Prologue

1 W. Wordsworth: *The Prelude* (1805), MS B (hand of Dorothy Wordsworth); Book 1, ll. 14–18, published in *The Thirteen-Book Prelude* (Cornell University Press, 1991), p. 51

2 Description from Thomas Gray's 1769 travel journal, published in William Mason's 1775 edition of *Poems of Thomas Gray*, from introduction to *William Wordsworth's Guide to the Lakes*, ed. S. Yoshikawa (Oxford World's Classics, 2022), p. x

3 Stopford Augustus Brooke annotates his copy of *The Prelude* with this term, crossing out 'Autobiographical' and replacing it with 'autolalestical', a neologism that combines the Greek 'auto-', meaning self, with the present-tense 'laleis' (transliterated λᾰ́λει), meaning speaking, singing, or crowing (to make the sound of a rooster).

4 W. Wordsworth: 'Tintern Abbey', l. 35, *Lyrical Ballads* (1798), published in *Lyrical Ballads and Other Poems, 1797–1800*, ed. J. Butler (Cornell University Press, 1993)

5 B. Darlington: Introduction to *Home at Grasmere*, published in *Home at Grasmere: Part First, Book First, of The Recluse* (Cornell University Press, 1977), p. 32

6 W. Wordsworth: 'Michael', ll. 37–9, *Lyrical Ballads* (1800), published in *Lyrical Ballads and Other Poems, 1797–1800*, ed. J. Butler (Cornell University Press, 1993)

1 Calls Home the Heart

1   D. Wordsworth: 16 May 1800, published in *The Grasmere and Alfoxden Journals* (Oxford World's Classics, 2008), p. 2

2   D. Wordsworth: letter to Catherine Clarkson, 23 December 1815, *The Letters of William and Dorothy Wordsworth: III. The Middle Years* (Clarendon, 2000), letter 378, p. 259

3   Elizabeth Threlkeld's obituary, quoted in J. Barker: *Wordsworth: A Life* (Harper, 2006), p. 14

4   W. Wordsworth: *The Prelude* (1805), Book V, l. 277, published in *The Thirteen-Book Prelude* (Cornell University Press, 1991), p. 169

5   Ibid., l. 258, p. 168

6   W. Wordsworth: *The Prelude* (1805), Book I, l. 528, published in *The Thirteen-Book Prelude* (Cornell University Press, 1991), p. 121

7   Ibid., ll. 477–8, p. 119

8   D. Wordsworth: 7 December 1801, published in *The Grasmere and Alfoxden Journals* (Oxford World's Classics, 2008), pp. 45–6

9   W. Wordsworth: 'Composed Upon Westminster Bridge, September 3, 1802', published in *Poems, in Two Volumes, and Other Poems 1800–1807* (Cornell University Press, 1983), p. 147

2 This Little Unsuspected Paradise

1   T. Gray: *The Poems of Mr Gray, to which are Prefixed Memoirs of his Life and Writings*, ed. W. Mason (1775)

2   S. A. Brooke: *Dove Cottage*, 1892, p. 14, quoted in R. Woof: *Treasures of the Wordsworth Trust* (The Wordsworth Trust, 2004), p. 2

3   Edmund Lee wrote *Dorothy Wordsworth: The Story of a Sister's Love*, first published in 1886

4   S. A. Brooke: *Dove Cottage*, 1892, quoted in S. Hebron: *Dove Cottage* (The Wordsworth Trust, 2009), p. 109

5   In this case, D.W. most likely refers to Dora Wordsworth, William's daughter, named after her aunt Dorothy

6   From the notes of Eleanor Rawnsley, quoted in S. Hebron: *Dove Cottage* (The Wordsworth Trust, 2009)., p. 120

7   S. A. Brooke: quoted in S. Hebron: *Dove Cottage* (The Wordsworth Trust, 2009), p. 88

8   This was not the only death that winter. By the time the boys returned to school, Hugh Tyson was also gravely ill. He died weeks later, and was buried at Hawkshead churchyard on 3 March 1784. In just two months, the Wordsworth boys lost both father and foster father.

9   Source: Currency Calculator, National Archives, https://www. nationalarchives.gov.uk/currency-converter/# (last accessed 16 June 2022)

10   D. Wordsworth to Jane Pollard, Penrith, November 1787, *The Letters of William and Dorothy Wordsworth: I. The Early Years (1787–1805)* (Clarendon, 2000), p. 9 (hereafter referred to as *EY*)

11   Equivalent to more than £307,000 in today's money. https://www. nationalarchives.gov.uk/currency-converter/#

12   Jack (born 1768), Henry (1769), Mary (1770), Margaret (1772), Thomas (1773), Sara (1775), Betsy (1776), George (1778), Joanna (1780), and William (1783)

13   D. Wordsworth to Jane Pollard, Sockburn, April 1795, *EY 49*, p. 141

14   Ibid.

15   D. Wordsworth to Jane Pollard, Penrith, August 1787, *EY 2*, p. 8

16   The poem appeared in 1787 under the moniker 'Axiologus', a Greek translation of his surname. The subject of this ode, Miss Helen Maria Williams, was a popular novelist and poet of the period, and William Wordsworth and Robert Taylor, a fellow schoolboy lodger at Ann Tyson's, had written poems waxing lyrical on the delicate nature of her sensibility. Only William's was deemed fit for publication – though later he sought to distance himself from this early poem, and it was never reprinted during his lifetime.

17   All quotations from 'The Vale of Esthwaite' are taken from Text 1 in W. Wordsworth: *Early Poems and Fragments 1785–1797*, ed. C. Landon and J. Curtis (Cornell University Press, 1997)

3 These Living Mountains

1   D. Wordsworth: *Alfoxden Journal*, 15 April 1798, published in *The Grasmere and Alfoxden Journals* (Oxford World's Classics, 2008), p. 152

2   D. Wordsworth to Jane Pollard, 27 January 1788, 'How we are squandered abroad!' (repeated in D. Wordsworth to Jane Pollard, 25–6 January 1790), *EY 5*, p. 16

3   D. Wordsworth to Jane Pollard, 16 June 1793, *EY 30*, p. 96

4   W. Wordsworth: 'An Evening Walk' (1793), l. 10: *An Evening Walk*, ed. J. Averill (Cornell University Press, 1984), p. 30

5   Ibid., l. 419, p. 78

6   W. Wordsworth to Dorothy Wordsworth, 1793, quote by D. Wordsworth in a letter to Jane Pollard, *EY 30*, p. 96

7   W. Wordsworth to Dorothy Wordsworth, 6 and 16 September 1790, *EY 10*, p. 35

8   A phrase borrowed from Horace's eleventh Epistle; W. Wordsworth to William Mathews, June 1791, *EY 15*, p. 44

9   W. Wordsworth to William Mathews, 17 February 1794, *EY 36*, p. 111

10 D. Wordsworth to Jane Pollard, 16 February 1793, *EY 28*, p. 89

11 D. Wordsworth to Jane Pollard, Forncett, 8 May 1792, *EY 22*, p. 72

12 D. Wordsworth to Jane Pollard, 16 February 1793, *EY 28*, p. 86

13 D. Wordsworth to Jane Pollard, Forncett, 10 July 1793, *EY 31*, p. 97

14 D. Wordsworth to ?, unsent letter, Windy Brow, April 1794, *EY 37*, p. 112

15 Ibid., p. 113

16 W. Wordsworth: 'An Evening Walk' (1794), ll. 125–32: *An Evening Walk*, ed. J. Averill (Cornell University Press, 1984), p. 135

4 Flawed Coleridgeans

1   M. Ward: 'Regret vii', *Thunder Alley* (Aussteiger Publications, 2008), p. 24

2   S. T. Coleridge: 'Kubla Khan', ll. 53–4, first published in 1816 with the subheading 'Or, a Vision in a Dream. A Fragment' alongside 'Christabel' and 'The Pains of Sleep'

3   W. Wordsworth: 'Michael', l. 20, from *Lyrical Ballads* (1800), published in *Lyrical Ballads and Other Poems, 1797–1800*, ed. J. Butler (Cornell University Press, 1993)

4   E. Lee: Dorothy Wordsworth: *The Story of a Sister's Love*, pp. 28–9

5   Ferguson Letters, 11 March 1795, New York Public Library. https://archives.nypl.org/mss/18092

6   W. Wordsworth to Richard Wordsworth, Keswick, 10 October 1794, *EY 44*, p. 133

7   W. Wordsworth to William Mathews, Penrith, 7 January 1795, *EY 47*, p. 141

8   Codicil to the will of Raisley Calvert, quoted by W. Wordsworth in a letter to R. Wordsworth, c.17 October 1794, *EY 41*, p. 134

9   DW letter to Jane Pollard, 26 June 1791, *EY 16*, p. 46

10 Elizabeth Rawson to Samuel Ferguson, March 1795, in Ferguson Family Papers 1727–1943 in the New York Public Library Archives and Manuscripts, https://archives.nypl.org/mss/18092

11 WW to William Mathews, 23 May 1794; *EY 34*, p. 105

12 Ibid.

13 D. Wordsworth to Mrs John Marshall (formerly Jane Pollard), 2–3 September 1795, *EY 50*, p. 145

14 Ibid., p. 146

15 D. Wordsworth to Mrs John Marshall (formerly Jane Pollard), 2–3 September 1795, *EY 50*, p. 145

16 Ibid., p. 149

17 D. Wordsworth to Mrs John Marshall (formerly Jane Pollard), Racedown, 30 November 1795, *EY 55*, p. 160

18 D. Wordsworth to Mrs John Marshall (formerly Jane Pollard), Racedown, 30 November 1795, *EY 55*, p. 160

19 D. Wordsworth to unknown recipient, winter 1795–6, *EY 56*, p. 164

20 D. Wordsworth to Mrs John Marshall (formerly Jane Pollard), Racedown, 30 November 1795, *EY 55*, p. 162

21 W. Wordsworth to Francis Wrangham, 7 March 1796, *EY 59*, p. 168

22 W. Wordsworth to Francis Wrangham, 20 November 1795, *EY 54*, p. 159

23 W. Wordsworth to Francis Wrangham, 20 November 1795, *EY 54*, p. 159

24 W. Wordsworth to Joseph Cottle, Racedown, January 1796, *EY 57*, p. 163

25 W. Wordsworth to William Mathews, 21 March 1796, *EY 60*, p.166

26 D. Wordsworth to Mrs John Marshall (formerly Jane Pollard), Racedown, 7 March 1796, *EY 58*, p. 162

27 D. Wordsworth to Mrs John Marshall (formerly Jane Pollard), Racedown, 30 November 1795, *EY 55*, p. 160

28 W. Wordsworth to William Mathews, 21 March 1796, *EY 60*, p.166

29 W. Wordsworth to Francis Wrangham, March 1795, *EY 59*, p. 164

30 Ibid, p.165

31 D. Wordsworth to Jane Pollard, Sockburn, April 1795, *EY 49*, pp. 141–2

32 D. Wordsworth to Jane Marshall, 19 March 1797, *EY 65*, p. 178

33 W. Wordsworth to Mary Wordsworth, 11 August 1810, reprinted in *The Love Letters of William and Mary Wordsworth*, ed. B. Darlington (Cornell University Press, 1981), pp. 61–2

5 Romance and Terror

1 Reprinted as 'The Keepsake', F. Adcock: *Collected Poems* (Bloodaxe Books, 2024)

2 Written on the back of Dove Cottage shutter by W. Martin, paperhanger, on 7 July 1891.

3   D. Wordsworth to Jane Pollard, 16 February 1793, *EY 28*, p. 87

4   https://www.theguardian.com/theguardian/2003/may/17/week-end7.weekend2

5   U. M. Marcinkowska et al.: An experimental test of the Westermarck effect: sex differences in inbreeding avoidance. *Behavioural Ecology* 24(4), pp. 842–5, 2013. https://academic.oup.com/beheco/article/24/4/842/220309

6   W. Wordsworth to William Mathews, Racedown, late October–early November 1795, *EY 53*, p. 156

7   Ibid.

8   Charles Lamb to S.T.C, 15 April 1797, *Letters of Charles and Mary Lamb VI–VII*, Number 103

9   M. Wordsworth and W. Wordsworth to Sarah Coleridge, 7 November 1845, *The Letters of William and Dorothy Wordsworth: VII. The Later Years Part 4 (1840–1853)* (Clarendon, 2000), p. 9

10 D. Wordsworth to Mary Hutchinson, June 1797, *EY 70*, pp. 188–9

11 S. T. Coleridge to Joseph Cottle, c.3 July 1797, *Letters of S. T. Coleridge*, Vol. 1, pp. 330–1. https://www.gutenberg.org/ebooks/44553

12 S. T. Coleridge to Joseph Cottle, c.8 July 1797, *Letters of S. T. Coleridge*, p. 195

13 S. T. Coleridge to Joseph Cottle, 8 June 1797, *Letters of S. T. Coleridge*, p. 190

14 D. Wordsworth, Grasmere Journal, Tuesday 27 April 1802, in *Dorothy Wordsworth, The Grasmere and Alfoxden Journals* (Oxford World Classics, 2008), p. 92

15 D. Wordsworth, Grasmere Journal, Friday 12 February 1802, in *Dorothy Wordsworth, The Grasmere and Alfoxden Journals* (Oxford World Classics, 2008), p. 67

6 Second Selves

1   William Wordsworth, 'Michael', *Lyrical Ballads, with Other Poems*, 2nd ed. (Longman and Rees, 1800), 2 vols

2   Poetry Foundation. https://www.poetryfoundation.org/poetrymagazine/articles/150913/morden-tower

3   Allen Ginsberg, as quoted in *N. Vall: Cultural Region: North East England 1945–2000* (Manchester University Press, 2011), p. 107

4   E. Mottram: *Primary Sources*, quoted by the Poetry Foundation. https://www.poetryfoundation.org/poets/tom-pickard

5   B. Bunting: 'The Poet's Point of View' (1966), included in B. Bunting: *Briggflatts* (Bloodaxe Books, 2009)

6   N. Vall: *Cultural Region: North East England 1945–2000* (Manchester University Press, 2011), pp. 106–8

7   S. Heaney: in *Writers' Houses: William Wordsworth Lived Here* (BBC 2, 1974). https://www.youtube.com/watch?v=5wFnBAWyp0c

8   It is now thought that Dorothy Wordsworth became addicted to opium as her health worsened in later life. For a fuller discussion of Dorothy's health, see P. Atkin: *Recovering Dorothy: The Hidden Life of Dorothy Wordsworth* (Saraband, 2021)

9   S. T. Coleridge, *The Night – A Dramatic Fragment*, published in *Sibylline Leaves – A Collection of Poems* (1817), p. 139

10   W. Wordsworth: Preface to *Lyrical Ballads* (1800), published in *Lyrical Ballads and Other Poems, 1797–1800*, ed. J. Butler (Cornell University Press, 1993)

11   W. Wordsworth: *The Prelude* (1805), Conclusion, Book IV, published in *The Thirteen-Book Prelude* (Cornell University Press, 1991), p. 370

12   W. Wordsworth: *The Prelude* (1805), Book VI, l. 263, published in *The Thirteen-Book Prelude* (Cornell University Press, 1991), pp. 267–8

13   W. Wordsworth to James Losh, 11 March 1798, *EY 85*, p. 213

14   W. Wordsworth to James Losh, 11 March 1798; *EY 85*, p. 213

15   J. Dickinson: quoted in J. L. Luck: *Sound Mind: Josephine Dickinson's Deaf Poetics* (University of Manitoba, 2009). https://www.jstor.org/stable/44030658

16   S. Merchel and M. Altinsoy: Music-induced vibrations in a concert hall and a church. *Archives of Acoustics* 38(1), pp. 13–18, 2003. https://journals.pan.pl/dlibra/publication/116766/edition/101497/content

17   Y. Yamazaki and S. Hasegawa: Department of Information and Communications Engineering, School of Engineering, Tokyo Institute of Technology, Japan, quoted in S. Merchel and M. Altinsoy: ibid.

18   B. Gick and D. Derrick: Aero-tactile integration in speech perception. *Nature* 462, pp. 502–4, 2009. https://doi.org/10.1038/nature08572

19   W. Wordsworth: 'Tintern Abbey', ll. 107–8, first published in *Lyrical Ballads* (1798); published in *Lyrical Ballads and Other Poems, 1797–1800*, ed. J. Butler (Cornell University Press, 1993)

20   W. Wordsworth: *The Old Cumberland Beggar*, l. 154, first published in *Lyrical Ballads* (1800); published in *Lyrical Ballads and Other Poems, 1797–1800*, ed. J. Butler (Cornell University Press, 1993)

21 Notes written by Pamela Woof to aid the preparation of this manuscript, November 2022

22 W. Wordsworth, 'Home at Grasmere', l. 144, from *Part First, Book First, of The Recluse*, ed. B. Darlington (Cornell University Press, 1977), p. 41

23 W. Wordsworth, Book Two of *The Prelude* (1805), l. 471

24 W. Wordsworth, 'Lines Composed a Few Miles above Tintern Abbey, On Revisiting the Banks of the Wye during a Tour. July 13, 1798', l. 50, from *Lyrical Ballads, with Other Poems* (Cottle, 1798)

25 Ibid., l. 72–4,

26 Ibid, l. 50.

7 Spots of Time

1 W. Wordsworth: *The Prelude* (1805), Book XI, ll. 258–64, published in *The Thirteen-Book Prelude* (Cornell University Press, 1991), p. 301

2 Translated into English in G. Rosen: Nostalgia: a 'forgotten psychological disorder', *Clio Medica* 10(1), pp. 28–51, 1975. https://pubmed.ncbi.nlm.nih.gov/1105625/

3 J. Scheuchzer: Von der nostalgia, oder dem so genandten Heimwehe, *Sammlung von Natur und Medicin wie auch hierzu gehörigen Kunst- und Literatur-Geschichten* 2 (Sommer-Quartal), pp. 832–7, 1717

4 T. Zwinger: *De Pothopatridalgia, vom Heimwehe* (1710); as translated by P. Bojanić in At home, at mine (*chez moi*): return to oneself, *Colloquium: New Philologies* 6(1), 2021. https://colloquium.aau.at/index.php/Colloquium/article/view/155

5 G. Rosen: Nostalgia: a 'forgotten psychological disorder', *Clio Medica* 10 (1), p. 29, 1975

6 Hofer uses terms in Latin, German, and French. For more detail on his translation of terms relating to homesickness, see P. Bojanić: At home, at mine (*chez moi*). Return to oneself. *Colloquium: New Philologies* 6(1), 2021. https://colloquium.aau.at/index.php/Colloquium/article/view/155

7 J. Hofer, 1688, 8, English translation, pp. 376–91, 1934

8 The earliest recorded usage of 'homesick' in English dates from the 1740s, when it appears as part of 'homesick-feelingly' in a translation of the German *seiten-heimweh-fühlerlich* from a Moravian Brethren hymnbook, Oxford English Dictionary

9 K. Goodman: 'Uncertain disease': nostalgia, pathologies of motion, practices of reading, *Studies in Romanticism* 49(2), pp. 197–227, 2010. https://muse.jhu.edu/article/741916

10   D. Wordsworth to Samuel Taylor Coleridge, Goslar, 14 or 21 December 1798, *EY 105*, p. 242

11   S. T. Coleridge, 21 July 1832, *Specimens of the Table Talk of the late Samuel Taylor Coleridge* (2 vols; John Murray, 1835), II, pp. 70–1

12   W. Wordsworth: *The Prelude* (1805), Book X, l. 108, published in *The Thirteen-Book Prelude* (Cornell University Press, 1991), p. 278

13   W. Wordsworth to Samuel Taylor Coleridge, June 1799, *EY 110*, p. 252

14   J. Worthen: *The Life of William Wordsworth: A Critical Biography* (Wiley-Blackwell, 2014), p. 389

15   *Notebooks of Samuel Taylor Coleridge Volume I: 1794–1804, Text and Notes*, ed. K. Coburn (Bollingen, 1950), entry 1588

16   W. Wordsworth to Dorothy Wordsworth, 8 November 1799, *EY 124*, p. 271

17   *Notebooks of Samuel Taylor Coleridge, Volume I: 1794–1804, Text and Notes*, ed. K. Coburn (Bollingen, 1950), entry 1799

18   W. Wordsworth to Dorothy Wordsworth, 8 November 1799, *EY 124*, p.271

19   William names himself and Dorothy thus in 'Home at Grasmere', l. 233 (MS B, DCMS 59)

20   W. Wordsworth to S. T. Coleridge, 24 and 27 December 1799, *EY 126*, p. 275

21   D. Wordsworth, letter to Sara Coleridge, 1818, *Letters of The Wordsworth Family From 1787 to 1855: Collected and Edited by William Knight In Three Volumes: Volume III* (Haskell House, 1969), letter 34, p. 401

22   W. Wordsworth and D. Wordsworth to Samuel Taylor Coleridge, 24 and 27 December 1799, *EY 126*, p. 275

23   Ibid., p. 280

24   D. Wordsworth: unsent letter to unknown recipient, winter 1799, *EY 127*, p. 281

25   Ibid.

26   W. Wordsworth: *The Two-Book Prelude* (1798–9), ll. 133–5 and l. 141, published in *The Thirteen-Book Prelude* (Cornell University Press, 1991), p. 26

8 A Heart to Enjoy

1   First published anonymously in a large folio volume in 1810. Wordsworth's text went through several iterations before becoming known as *Wordsworth's Guide to the Lakes*. This quotation is from *Guide to the Lakes* (Oxford World's Classics, 2022), p. 68

2   W. Wordsworth to Samuel Taylor Coleridge, 24 and 27 December 1799, *EY 126*, p. 273

3   D. Wordsworth to ?, letter drafted in the winter of 1795–6 (likely December 1795), *EY 56*, p. 163

4   W. Wordsworth to Francis Wrangham, 7 March 1796, *EY 59*, p. 167

5   W. Wordsworth to Francis Wrangham, 25 February 1797, *EY 63*, p. 178

6   W. Wordsworth and D. Wordsworth to S. T. Coleridge, 24 and 27 December 1799, *EY 126*, p. 276

7   W. Wordsworth: Poem later titled 'A Farewell', composed May 1802, with a fair copy made by Sara Hutchinson, published in *Poems by William Wordsworth* (1815), l. 1

8   D. Wordsworth: *Grasmere Journal*, Tuesday 24 November 1801 (Oxford World's Classics, 2002), p. 41

9   Northern dialect word for bird cherry or *Prunus padus*, sometimes pronounced 'hagberry'

10 D. Wordsworth: *Grasmere Journal*, 14 May 1800 (Oxford World Classics, 2002), p. 1

11 D. Wordsworth: *Grasmere Journal*, 16 May 1800 (Oxford World Classics, 2002), p. 2

12 D. Wordsworth, Grasmere Journal, 28 May 1800; in *Dorothy Wordsworth, The Grasmere and Alfoxden Journals* (Oxford World Classics, 2008), p. 5

13 D. Wordsworth, Grasmere Journal, 31 May 1800; in *Dorothy Wordsworth, The Grasmere and Alfoxden Journals* (Oxford World Classics, 2008), p. 6

14 Episode described by S. Gill in *Wordsworth and the Victorians* (Oxford Academic, 1998) and repeated in interviews with Dove Cottage staff

15 George Kirkby interview, quoted in *Wordsworth's Gardens*, Carol Buchanan, Richard Buchanan & Peter Elkington (Texas Tech University Press, 2001), p. 83

16 C. Buchanan: in introduction to *Wordsworth's Gardens* (Texas Tech University Press, 2001)

17 Email from M. Ward, sent 16 June 2009. Reproduced here with kind permission of M. Ward.

18 E. Partanen et al.: Prenatal music exposure induces long-term neural effects, PLoS One 8(10): e78946, 2003. https://www.ncbi.nlm.nih.gov/pmc/articlcolles/PMC3813619/

19 S. T. Coleridge, letter to Tom Poole, 21 March 1800, *Letters of Samuel Taylor Coleridge*, Vol. I (of 2), ed. E. H. Coleridge (Heinemann, 1895), letter 328, p. 581

20 S. T. Coleridge to Humphry Davy, 25 July 1800, *Letters of S. T. Coleridge*, Vol. 1, p. 342. https://www.gutenberg.org/ebooks/44553

21 Sea-Captain John Wordsworth (1754–1819) was a nephew of the Wordsworths' father, John, and the son of his brother Richard Wordsworth of Whitehaven.

22 D. Wordsworth to Jane Marshall, March 1805, *EY 255*, p.467

23 S. T. Coleridge to Dorothy Wordsworth, c.10 November 1799, *Letters of S. T. Coleridge*, Vol.1, p. 543

24 J. Wordsworth to Mary Hutchinson, 9 and 10 March 1801, *The Letters of John Wordsworth* (Cornell University Press, 1969), p. 104

25 W. and D. Wordsworth to Mary Hutchinson, April 1801, *EY 160*, p. 275

26 W. Wordsworth, Advertisement for 'Poems on the Naming of Places, *Lyrical Ballads, with Other Poems*, 2nd ed. (Longman and Rees, 1800), Vol. 2

27 D. Wordsworth, letter to Jane Marshall, 16 March 1805, *EY 160*, p. 468

28 W. Wordsworth to Richard Wordsworth (brother), 19 March 1805, *EY 259*, p. 571

29 J. Wordsworth to Mary Hutchinson, 25 and 26 February 1801, *The Letters of John Wordsworth* (Cornell University Press, 1969), p. 96

30 J. Wordsworth to Mary Hutchinson, 12 September 1802, ibid., pp. 125–6. Angular brackets indicate crossings-out in the original manuscript.

31 C. Clarkson to Priscilla Lloyd, 12 January 1800 (quoted by M. Reed, I, *Wordsworth: The Chronology of the Middle Years*, 280n.24)

32 *Notebooks of Samuel Taylor Coleridge, Volume 1: 1794–1804, Text and Notes*, ed. K. Coburn (Bollingen, 1950), p. 555

33 S. T. Coleridge, *The Notebooks of Samuel Taylor Coleridge*, ed. K. Coburn, Volume 1 (1794–1804) (Routledge & Kegan Paul, 1957), October 1803, CN 1575

34 S. T. Coleridge, *The Notebooks of Samuel Taylor Coleridge*, ed. K. Coburn, Volume 1 (1794–1804) (Routledge & Kegan Paul, 1957), November 1799, CN 578

35 S. T. Coleridge, *The Notebooks of Samuel Taylor Coleridge*, ed. K. Coburn, Volume 1 (1794–1804) (Routledge & Kegan Paul, 1957), March–April 1800, CN 718

9 A Fancy in the Heart

1 In the hand of Mary, William, and Dorothy Wordsworth. This is the first fair copy of the poem. The exact date is unclear but is likely to be c.1806. ll. 14–17 (MS B; DCMS 59). *Home at Grasmere: Part First, Book First, of The Recluse*, ed. B. Darlington (Cornell University Press, 1981), p. 38

2 'Account of Observations made on the Mountain Schehallien for finding its attraction' (published by the Royal Society in 1775)

3 W. Gilpin: *Observations, Relative Chiefly to Picturesque Beauty ... [in] Cumberland, and Westmoreland*, 1786

4 S. Bainbridge: Romantic writers and mountaineering. *Romanticism* 18(1), pp. 1–15, 2012. https://www.euppublishing.com/doi/10.3366/rom.2012.0060

5 T. Wilkinson: *Tours to the British Mountains*, 1824

6 G. Lindop: *A Literary Tour of the Lake District* (Sigma Press, 2005), p. 84

7 S. T. Coleridge, letter of August 1802, recopied by S. Hutchinson in her journal, available online at https://lancaster.ac.uk/mappingthelakes/STC.HTML

8 One of Coleridge's many neologisms, it combines 'excursion' with 'circumscribe' to create a noun that embodies both an adventure but also a circularity of travel. Coleridge coined the term 'Circumcursion' in a letter to Sara Hutchinson on 10 August 1802

9 S. T. Coleridge, letter to Sara Hutchinson, 1–5 August 1802, *Letters of Samuel Taylor Coleridge*, Vol. I (of 2), ed. E. H. Coleridge (Heinemann, 1895), letter 450, p. 836

10 S. T. Coleridge, letter to Sara Hutchinson, 1–5 August 1802, *Letters of Samuel Taylor Coleridge*, Vol. I (of 2), ed. E. H. Coleridge (Heinemann, 1895), letter 451, p. 844

11 S. T. Coleridge, letter to Robert Southey, 9 August 1802, *Letters of Samuel Taylor Coleridge*, Vol. I (of 2), ed. E. H. Coleridge (Heinemann, 1895), letter 452, p. 846

12 S. T. Coleridge, letter to Sara Hutchinson, 6 August 1802, *Letters of Samuel Taylor Coleridge*, Vol. I (of 2), ed. E. H. Coleridge (Heinemann, 1895), letter 451, p. 842

13 S. T. Coleridge, letter of August 1802, recopied by S. Hutchinson in her journal, available online at https://lancaster.ac.uk/mappingthelakes/STC.HTML

14 S. T. Coleridge, letter to Sara Hutchinson, 6 August 1802, *Letters of Samuel Taylor Coleridge*, Vol. I (of 2), ed. E. H. Coleridge (Heinemann, 1895), letter 451, p. 841

15   S. T. Coleridge, letter of August 1802, recopied by S. Hutchinson in her journal, available online at https://lancaster.ac.uk/map-pingthelakes/STC.HTML

16   S. T. Coleridge, letter to Sara Hutchinson, 6 August 1802, *Letters of Samuel Taylor Coleridge*, Vol. I (of 2), ed. E. H. Coleridge (Heinemann, 1895), letter 451, p.841

17   Ibid.

18   Ibid.

19   S. T. Coleridge to Robert Southey, *Collected Letters of Samuel Taylor Coleridge*, Volume II (1800–1806), p. 846

20   S. T. Coleridge: 'A Letter to —', 4 April 1802, ll. 99–110, in *Poetical Works I: 289* (Princeton University Press, 2001) vol. 2, p. 682

21   S. T. Coleridge: *Notebooks* 1064, dated December 1801,. p. 290

22   S. T. Coleridge: 'A Letter to —', 4 April 1802, ll. 99–110, in *Poetical Works I: 289* (Princeton University Press, 2001) vol. 2, p. 682

23   D. Wordsworth: *Grasmere Journal*, 21 April 1802, (Oxford World Classics, 2002), p. 89

24   In a letter written a few months before the poem, he wrote to a friend that, having seen Sara at Bishop Middleham on his way home from Durham, he considered her to be 'so very good a woman, that I have seldom seen the like of her'. Though he clearly admires her, these do not seem like the words of someone in love.

25   S. T. Coleridge, letter to Sara Hutchinson, 4 April 1802, *Letters of Samuel Taylor Coleridge*, Vol. I (of 2), ed. E. H. Coleridge (Heinemann, 1895), letter 438, p. 794

26   S. T. Coleridge, letter to Sara Hutchinson, 6 August 1802, *Letters of Samuel Taylor Coleridge*, Vol. I (of 2), ed. E. H. Coleridge (Heinemann, 1895), letter 451, p. 841

27   From Yeats' elegy 'In Memory of Major Robert Gregory', Vol. VII, ll. 1–2, as quoted by Seamus Heaney in 'The Pete Laver Memorial Lecture – Place and Displacement: Recent Poetry from Northern Ireland', reprinted in *The Wordsworth Circle*, Vol. 16, Number 2 (Spring 1985): Special Issue: Papers Delivered at the Annual Wordsworth Conference in Grasmere, 1984

28   *Coleridge's Imagination: Essays in memory of Pete Laver*, ed. R. Gravil, L. Newlyn, and N. Roe (Cambridge, 1985), Introduction

10 Fretting the Land

1   S. Woodhead: 'Extempore Effusion: Wall / Gerard Benson!' *The Thorn Apple* (Wordsworth Trust, 2007)

2   D. Wordsworth, Grasmere Journal, Saturday 11 October 1800, in *Dorothy Wordsworth, The Grasmere and Alfoxden Journals* (Oxford World Classics, 2008), p. 26

3   All quotations from 'Michael' are taken from William Wordsworth, *Lyrical Ballads, with Other Poems*, 2nd edn. (Longman and Rees, 1800), 2 vols

4   W. Wordsworth to Charles James Fox, 14 January 1801, *EY 152*, p. 301

5   S. Boym: entry in *Atlas of Transformation*. http://monument-totransformation.org/atlas-of-transformation/html/n/nostalgia/nostalgia-svetlana-boym.html

6   R. C. Kessler et al.: Age of onset of mental disorders: a review of recent literature, *Current Opinion in Psychiatry* 20(4), pp. 359–64, 2007. https://www.ncbi.nlm.nih.gov/pmc/articles/PMC1925038/

7   G. Lewis: *Sunbathing in the Rain* (Harper Perennial, 2002), p. 144

8   G. Lewis interview by The Poetry Foundation, 1 April 2013, https://www.poetryfoundation.org/poetrymagazine/articles/69961/three-books-an-exchange

9   J. H. MacCabe et al.: Artistic creativity and risk for schizophrenia, bipolar disorder and unipolar depression: a Swedish population-based case – control study and sib-pair analysis. *British Journal of Psychiatry* 212(6), pp. 370–6, 2018

10   1834: S. T. Coleridge: *Shorter Works & Fragments* (1995) Vol. II. ii. 1444: 'Hope and Fear ... have slipt out their collars, and no longer run in couples from the Kennel of my Psycho-somatic *Ology*.'

11   1822: S. T. Coleridge: *Letters* 15 January (1971) Vol. V. 196: 'Of course, I am glad to be able to correct my fears as far as public Balls, Concerts, and Time-murder in Narcissism.'

12   S. T. Coleridge: *Notebooks* (1962) Vol. II. 2670: 'It requires a strong imagination as well as an accurate psycho-analytical understanding in order to be able to conceive the *possibility*, & to picture out the reality, of the *passion* at those Times for Jupiter, Apollo, &c/& the nature of the *Faith*.'

13   1822: S. T. Coleridge: *Let. to Young Lady* in *Lett., Conversations, & Recollections* (1836) Vol. II. letter 89: 'You must have a Soul-mate as well as a House or a Yoke-mate.'

14   C. Lamb to Samuel Taylor Coleridge, 27 May 1796, *The Letters of Charles Lamb*, Volume I (1911), p. 2

15   C. Lamb to Samuel Taylor Coleridge, 10 June 1796, *The Letters of Charles Lamb*, Volume I (1911), p. 16

16   C. Lamb to Samuel Taylor Coleridge, 27 May 1796, *The Letters of Charles Lamb*, Volume I (1911), p. 2

17   W. Hazlitt, referring to Mary Lamb in 'Essay II: Of Persons One Would Wish to Have Seen', published in *Winterslow – Essays and Characters Written There* (1839), reprinted in *The World's Classics XXV: The Works of William Hazlitt —III* (1902), p. 38

18   Unsourced quotation from L. Appignanesi: *Mad, Bad and Sad: Women and the Mind Doctors* (W. W. Norton, 2007), p. 45

19   Kent and Medway NHS Trust. https://www.kmpt.nhs.uk/information-and-advice/open-dialogue/ (last accessed 26 February 2023)

11 Enough Within Ourselves

1   *Home at Grasmere: Part First, Book First, of The Recluse*, ed. B. Darlington (Cornell University Press, 1977), MS B, ll. 860–2, p. 188. MS B (DCMS 59) refers to the earliest full text of the poem, a fair copy made around 1800–01 in the hands of Dorothy, Mary, and William Wordsworth. MS D (DCMS 76) is a hybrid manuscript produced a few years later.

2   *The Grasmere and Alfoxden Journals* (Oxford World's Classics, 2002), edited and with an introduction by Pamela Woof

3   P. Woof, Introduction to *The Thorn Apple* (The Wordsworth Trust, 2007), p. iv

4   E. Hasler: 'Belle Isle' and 'To a Woodpecker', *Natural Histories* (Salt, 2011)

5   W. Wordsworth: ll. 1–10 MS B, published in *Home at Grasmere: Part First, Book First, of The Recluse*, ed. B. Darlington (Cornell University Press, 1977), p. 38

6   Ibid., ll. 34–5, p. 40

7   Ibid., MS D, ll. 52–5, p. 42

8   Ibid., MS B, ll. 156–70, pp. 46–8

9   The word comes to English via German: zoologist Ernest Haeckel first coined it as *Ökologie* in 1866, and it was soon transliterated into English

10   S. T. Coleridge to William Wordsworth, 11–12 October 1799, *Collected Letters of S. T. Coleridge*, Volume I, p. 538

11   W. Wordsworth: ll. 278–9 MS B, published in *Home at Grasmere: Part First, Book First, of The Recluse*, ed. B. Darlington (Cornell University Press, 1977), p. 52

12   W. Wordsworth: *Guide to the Lakes* (Oxford World's Classics, 2022), p. 68

13   S. T. Coleridge to Richard Sharp, 15 January 1804, *Collected Letters of S. T. Coleridge*, Volume II, p. 1032

14   S. Gill: *Wordsworth: A Life* (Oxford University Press, 2020)

15   It has since been suggested that she had Down's Syndrome; for further discussion, see K. Waldegrave: *The Poets' Daughters: Dora Wordsworth and Sara Coleridge* (Penguin Random House, 2014)

16   P. Woof: in introduction to *The Grasmere and Alfoxden Journals* (Oxford World's Classics, 2008)

17   The manuscript of Dorothy's Narrative is kept at Dove Cottage in the form of a notebook bound in blue cloth. Written in her hand, the manuscript is titled 'Narrative: The Greens 1808' and begins 'A narrative concerning George and Sarah Green of the Parish of Grasmere addressed to a friend.'

18   W. Wordsworth: 'Sonnet from The River Duddon: After-Thought' (1820), ll. 10–14, published in *The River Duddon, A Series of Sonnets; Vaudracour and Julia: and Other Poems* (Longman, Hurst, Rees, Orme, and Brown, 1820)

Keep in touch with
Granta Books:

Visit granta.com to discover more.

GRANTA

THIS GOLDEN FLEECE

A Journey Through Britain's Knitted History

'Wondrous'
BBC *Countryfile*

'A yarn well told'
Irish Times

'Inspiring ... Rutter captures the magic of making in literary
lyricism that entices you to read on and on. I loved it'
Clare Hunter

For millennia Britain's people have farmed sheep and used
their wool, developing unique skills and beautiful crafts that
bound many communities together. Esther Rutter travels the
length of the British Isles to tell the story of wool's long history
here and its influence on our landscape and culture. From
Shetland to the Channel Islands, she unearths fascinating
histories of communities whose lives were shaped by knitting,
weaving and spinning, among them the mill workers of the
Border counties and the stocking knitters of Wales, reminding
us of the value of craft and our intimate relationship with wool.

'A great yarn ... illuminating'
Mail on Sunday

'[Rutter] is a likable guide with a good eye for a story ...
[She] gives us material culture combined with social history,
memoir, oral testimony and travel writing'
Guardian

'Joyous ... A compendious, intelligent book on all things woolly'
Country Life